# CHILD VICTIMS
# OF HOMICIDE

CHRISTINE ALDER

*University of Melbourne*

KEN POLK

*University of Melbourne*

CAMBRIDGE
UNIVERSITY PRESS

PUBLISHED BY THE PRESS SYNDICATE OF THE UNIVERSITY OF CAMBRIDGE
The Pitt Building, Trumpington Street, Cambridge, United Kingdom

CAMBRIDGE UNIVERSITY PRESS
The Edinburgh Building, Cambridge CB2 2RU, UK
40 West 20th Street, New York, NY 10011–4211, USA
10 Stamford Road, Oakleigh, VIC 3166, Australia
Ruiz de Alarcón 13, 28014 Madrid, Spain
Dock House, The Waterfront, Cape Town 8001, South Africa

http://www.cambridge.org

First published 2001

Printed in Singapore by Green Giant Press

*Typeface* New Baskerville (*Adobe*) 10/12 pt.   *System* QuarkXPress®   [BC]

*A catalogue record for this book is available from the British Library*

*National Library of Australia Cataloguing in Publication data*
Alder, Christine, 1950–   .
Child victims of homicide.
Bibliography.
Includes index.
ISBN 0 521 80221 0.
ISBN 0 521 00251 6 (pbk.).
1. Children – Mortality. 2. Children – Crimes against.
3. Homicide. I. Polk, Kenneth. II. Title.
364.152083

ISBN 0 521 80221 0 hardback
ISBN 0 521 00251 6 paperback

# Contents

# Figures and Tables

# Acknowledgements

This research was supported by grants from the Australian Criminology Research Council. Throughout, the work depended upon the close collaboration of Associate Professor David Ranson, a forensic pathologist with the Victorian Institute of Forensic Medicine. The cooperation of the Victorian Institute of Forensic Medicine has been especially helpful in providing access to the documents necessary for the carrying out of this research.

There were many research assistants who helped collect data and prepare the final manuscript, including June Baker, Nicole Hunter, Caroline Lambert and Damon Muller. The exchange of ideas with the staff at the Institute for the Study of Social Change at the University of California, Berkeley has been most helpful, and appreciation is due to its former director, Professor Troy Duster. We would also like to acknowledge the financial and intellectual support of Corpus Christi College, Cambridge University, during the formative stages of this research; and of the Department of Criminology at Keele University, Staffordshire, England, including Professor Tony Jefferson, during the final stages of manuscript preparation.

# CHAPTER 1

# *Overview*

Homicide generally is a horrific crime, but we are especially moved by the tragedy of children being killed. In general, communities do their best to protect children, surrounding them with the supports of family and other caring adults. At the same time, we have become increasingly aware of the significant numbers of children in our communities who are victims of physical and sexual abuse. In extreme cases a child's life is taken.

> Shirl Bennett* was 6 years old when she rode her bike to the local store on an errand for her mother. Her body was found three months later in a storm water drain. A 57-year-old Sunday school teacher was later found guilty of her kidnapping and murder. [Case No. 91-3189]

Such events are every parent's nightmare. The fear of the unknown stranger taking their young child is familiar to all parents and may come to form a backdrop to everyday decisions about family activities.

However, as with many forms of violence, the threat to young children's lives is most often found in the home.

> Doug Versaci was 2 years old when he died of severe abdominal trauma resulting from a number of blows to his stomach by his mother's de facto husband. The Coroner likened the injuries to those found in victims of serious road accidents. [Case No. 90-3384]

Doug's death provoked community outrage and a call for the introduction of mandatory reporting of child abuse. When the person

---

* Pseudonyms are used throughout the book to protect the privacy of family.

1

responsible for their protection murders a dependent child, many of our fundamental expectations about the relationship between adults and children are violated.

Community outrage can be even greater when a mother kills her own child.

> Charles Gunsten was 10 years old when his mother used a belt to strangle him to death in the family home. In the same incident the mother also hit her 12-year-old son repeatedly with a rolling pin and dragged her 7-year-old daughter by a belt around her neck through the house. [Case No. 93-2465]

On the face of it, such an action by a mother is a violation not only of broadly maintained understandings of women as non-violent, but also, perhaps even more powerfully, of dominant ideologies about the nature and role of motherhood.

Each of these cases was the subject of intense media coverage. In recent years newspapers across the Western world have carried stories of other homicides involving children. Such cases include: the killing of her two sons by Susan Smith in South Carolina in the United States; the killing of Jamie Bulger by two young boys in England; and the cases of 'nannies', or child-carers, in both the United States and the United Kingdom, who have been convicted of the homicides of infants in their care. Although such incidents became international media events, most child victims of homicide are not killed in these ways. In this book we attempt a detailed exploration of the actual circumstances and contexts of homicides involving child victims, that is, child homicides.

Research on violence highlights the extent of child homicide, and its importance to the study of violence. Children account for a significant proportion of all homicide victims in such countries as Australia, Canada, the United Kingdom and the United States. In Australia in 1991–92, children under the age of 18 accounted for 11 per cent of all homicide victims (Strang 1994), a figure equal to that found in 1991 in Canada (Statistics Canada 1992). In England and Wales children under the age of 16 make up a slightly larger proportion (16 per cent) of homicide victims (Home Office 1993). From 1985 to 1992, nearly 17,000 persons under the age of 18 were victims of homicide in the United States (Snyder and Sickmund 1995). This age group accounted for 9 per cent of all homicide victims in the United States in the years since the 1980s (Snyder, Sickmund and Poe-Yamagata 1996). The actual rate of child homicide in the United States is among the highest in the developed world (Unnithan 1996; Dowdy and Unnithan 1997).

Such overall statistical figures may not capture the significance of child homicides. In Australia, for example, a persistent finding has been that individuals under the age of one year are more at risk of homicide than any other age group (Strang 1993). In the United States, similarly, the risk of homicide has been found to be greater during the first day of life than at any other equivalent age span (Crittenden and Craig 1990: 202), a finding replicated in data from England and Wales (Marks and Kumar 1993). Other data suggest that the commonest age for fatal child abuse is the first year of life (Rose 1986; de Silva and Oates 1993). Also, in the United States, homicide is the leading cause of injury-related death for children below age 1 (Unnithan 1991a; Overpeck et al. 1998) and is the only cause of death of those under the age of 15 to have increased in the last thirty years (Christoffel 1984). In sum, there are significant risks of lethal violence in the early months and years of life, and if nothing else, the level of these in the total pattern of homicide merits closer inspection.

Child homicides present a number of distinctive features in relation to other forms of lethal violence. One of the most striking is the fact that they are committed by both men and women. In general, men are the perpetrators of homicide. Most investigations find that the proportion of male offenders in the total range of homicides falls somewhere between 85 and 90 per cent (Wolfgang 1958; Strang 1992; Silverman and Kennedy 1993; Polk 1994; Mouzos 2000). Child homicide, however, stands in sharp contrast. It is the one form of homicide where the offender is frequently a woman. In fact, some investigations have found women to be as likely as men to be the perpetrators. Of thirty-six parents who killed their children in Detroit between 1982 and 1986, 53 per cent were female and 47 per cent male (Goetting 1988: 341), with similar proportions reported in more recent studies in Quebec (Hodgins and Dube 1996) and Los Angeles (Sorensen, Petersen and Richardson 1997). Of the 395 parents suspected of the murder of their child in the United Kingdom between 1982 and 1989, 44 per cent were mothers (Wilczynski and Morris 1993). Among those cases where the victim was under the age of 1, the proportion accounted for by mothers was slightly higher, 47 per cent. Even more striking was the earlier study of filicide (that is, the killing of a child by a parent or parents) in the United States conducted by Resnick (1969), in which 67 per cent of the offenders were mothers of the victims.

The exploration of child homicide therefore provides a unique opportunity to consider the violent actions of both men and women. Across time and across cultures, predominantly men have committed violent crimes, in particular homicide, but until recently the maleness of violent crime was rarely considered as 'a variable, an analytic dimension, a causal factor, a discursive condition' (Allen 1988: 16; Miedzian 1991). More recently, in part as a development out of the substantial body of feminist research on male violence against women, the maleness and the masculinity of violence have become a focus of inquiry and theoretical debate (Messerschmidt 1993; Archer 1994; Newburn and Stanko 1994; Collier 1998).

Female violence has been less extensively investigated than male violence. The exception has been feminist analyses of the situations of women who kill their husbands who have abused them (e.g. Browne 1987; Walker 1989; Jurik and Winn 1990; Mann 1996). The mid-1990s witnessed a growing number of works on women's violence more generally (Kirsta 1994; Lloyd 1995; Pearson 1998). However, the issue of women's violence against their children has been 'virtually ignored' (Dougherty 1993: 92). Dougherty convincingly argues that in not addressing this issue, feminists have left a 'critical void in a field dominated if not defined by a perspective that provides fertile ground for misogynist assumptions to thrive' (Dougherty 1993: 94).

A general finding of existing research is that women kill for different reasons, and in different circumstances, than men. We are therefore not searching for a singular explanation or understanding of child homicide, but rather through an examination of instances of child homicide we hope to explore the complexity of these events and the varied contexts and circumstances of both men's and women's violence. It is our contention that an understanding of child homicide requires elaboration of the meaning and experience of being a man or a woman in everyday life and the structural situation of both the victims and perpetrators. Before presenting our analysis of case narratives, we turn first to an outline of the related literature.

## Women Who Kill Children

Until the 1990s women's violence had not been subject to the same degree of analysis as male violence. The form of women's violence that had been most extensively examined was 'infanticide'. The term 'infanticide' is used in a variety of ways, but in British law it refers to the killing of a child by its mother within the first twelve months of life. Most of the analyses of this phenomenon have been historical studies (e.g. Piers 1978) that note an inverse relationship between the availability of safe and effective contraception, especially abortion techniques, and infanticide, particularly the killing of newborn babies (neonaticide) (Wallace 1986: 25; Allen 1990: 38, 98, 110, 164). Filicide has been a method of eliminating devalued or unwanted children such as those lacking a socially acceptable father, deformed infants, infants possessing an undesirable physical characteristic such as the wrong skin colour or sex, and those conceived by rape (Jones 1980: 51; Rose 1986; Lomis 1986: 503; Backhouse 1985: 450).

In criminological theorising, criminal justice practice and in popular culture, explanations and understandings of female violence more broadly have traditionally focused on the mental state of the offender: she is either 'mad' or 'sick', or, at the other end of the pathological spectrum, extremely 'bad' (Wilczynski 1991: 78; 1997). We see this evidenced in criminal justice decision-making. In her examination of judicial decisions regarding female felons in England, Allen (1987) documented the significance given to psychiatric explanations of the behaviour. In terms of popular understandings of women's violence, in the United States Wilbanks (1982: 173) found that college students considered female killers to be more deranged than equivalent males.

Understandings of the violent woman as necessarily 'mad' or exceptionally 'bad' are embedded in dominant understandings of what it is to be a woman. Violence and femininity are understood as inconsistent; therefore 'normal' women are not violent. The killing of a child by a woman is even more incongruent with dominant understandings of femininity and motherhood. Consequently, the killing of a child by a woman may in itself be understood as evidence of psychiatric problems (Wilbanks 1982; Wilczynski 1997). It is not surprising therefore that much of the consideration of this issue has been in the psychiatric literature (Wilbanks 1982: 152; see as examples of the psychiatric literature Husain and Daniel 1984 and Resnick 1969).

Such conceptions of women who kill children also dominate 'common-sense' understandings. Silverman and Kennedy (1988) found that police were significantly more likely to classify women who kill their children as 'mentally ill' than they were the women who killed their spouses. Women who kill their children have been found to themselves believe that they should have been placed in a mental health facility rather than a prison (Totman 1978 noted in Weisheit 1986: 442).

This understanding of the situation of women who kill young children has been enshrined in British and Commonwealth law in the offence of infanticide. This law applies in circumstances where a mother kills a child, generally under the age of twelve months, while the balance of her mind is believed to be disturbed due to the effects of lactation or giving birth (Silverman and Kennedy 1993: 27). However, the medical assumption and its legal affirmation that some mothers may be pathologically predisposed to filicide faces increasing scepticism (Wilczynski 1991: 5; Silverman and Kennedy 1993: 155). As Wilczynski (1991: 7) notes, 'it is fallacious to equate the undeniable emotional and physical upheaval of the birth with mental illness, or even temporary insanity. Further, there is usually no evidence of psychosis or mental illness either before or after the birth.'

In the 1990s the continuing psychological focus of explanations of female violence is apparent in representations of these acts as emotional outbursts in response to situations of 'stress'. An image emerges of a woman extremely 'stressed', whose frustration and anger build to the point where she explodes in a highly emotional, uncontrolled moment of violence against her children. Speaking more generally of male and female aggression, Campbell (1993: 40) argues that, whereas men's aggression is instrumental, women's is expressive and represents a loss of control: aggressive behaviour for women is a consequence of a mounting anger that develops to a fury that 'can erupt into physical aggression'.

A similar representation of women's violence is found in the theory of Ogle, Maier-Katkin and Bernard (1995) about 'homicidal behaviour among women'. They argue that women have 'overcontrolled' personalities and that at 'somewhat random intervals' they erupt 'in a display of uncontrolled aggression that is very extreme and violent' (p. 181). Silverman and Kennedy (1988) also invoke the notion of loss of control over anger and frustration when postulating explanations for non-infanticide child-killing by mothers. Such explanations for female violence are essentially founded in dominant understandings of femininity, in particular its equation with emotionality and irrationality.

A further explanation for female violence draws attention to the violent experiences of the women themselves. Certainly feminist research on women who kill their husbands exposed the extent to which such events had to be understood in the context of the histories of extensive abuse that the women had suffered at the hands of the men they eventually killed (e.g. Jones 1980; Browne 1987). However, this issue has not been as extensively explored in the limited research on women's violence towards their children. Some of the literature on child abuse poses a notion of the 'cycle of violence' (Gordon 1988: 172), which suggests that those who are abused as children are more likely to abuse as adults. In interviews with mothers who killed their children Smithey (1997: 261) notes that physical and emotional abuse by their parents was a consistent theme. However, the notion of the cycle of violence remains a contentious proposition. Silverman and Kennedy (1988: 124) cite evidence that 'the child from a violent home is more at risk to be violent in his own home', while Goetting (1994: 187) concludes from a review of the literature that 'The evidence on this connection is contradictory and therefore inconclusive.'

Others have argued that women's aggression and violence entail a process of reproducing the physical and emotional harm they have suffered as adults at the hands of violent men (Daly 1994: 59). The women in Smithey's study of women who killed their children reported 'abusive, unsupported or antagonistic relations with the infant's father' (Smithey 1997: 263). Observing that non-infanticide child-killings by mothers may be best understood in terms of 'child abuse gone awry',

Silverman and Kennedy (1988: 124) suggest that, the more a woman is assaulted by her male partner, the more likely she is to be violent toward her children. They postulate that such women transfer their feelings of frustration, anger and hurt to the child as a 'convenient and perhaps frustrating target'. Some support for this general proposition is found in studies of maternal filicides: between 19 and 56 per cent of suicidal women in cases of maternal filicide have been found to have a history of being subjected to violence perpetrated by their partners (Cheung 1986: 188; d'Orban 1979: 5; Korbin 1986: 333).

However, the existence and nature of this proposed relationship also remains contentious. Gordon (1988: 173) observes that, although 'Many female child abusers are themselves victims, ... most wife beating victims did not beat their children.' Dougherty (1993: 104) also points out that some women who have never experienced violence do abuse their children, and she thereby challenges explanations for child abuse by women in terms of a 'mechanical modelling of violent behaviour'. Taking a similar position, Gordon (1988: 175) concludes from her historical study of child abuse that we cannot simply 'explain women's violence against their children with an analogy to referred pain or deflected anger'.

Their economic context is infrequently the focus of theories about women's violence. Nevertheless, poverty and unemployment have been consistently noted as features of the lives of women who come to official attention for child abuse and women who kill their children (Gordon 1988; Weisheit 1986; Kaplun and Reich 1976; Mann 1993; McKee and Shea 1998). While Baron (1993: 210) observed that 'A substantial amount of evidence suggests that poverty increases the likelihood of child homicide', the findings of his own macro-level research are inconsistent with this observation.

In the United States Smithey (1997: 267) observed 'economic deprivation and a lack of interpersonal support' in the lives of women who killed their children (see also Oberman 1996: 38). Similarly, a cross-national (United Kingdom and Canada) study of maternal filicide (McKee and Shea 1998) indicated that most often the women in the study were experiencing high levels of stress and a lack of resources (see also d'Orban 1979). Most of the women were caring for two or more children and were trying to cope with the demands of a new child, with the majority having given birth within the previous two years. They also had limited education and were unemployed, resulting in stressful economic dependence on others. Most of the women were raising children alone and many, though not most, were involved in ongoing abusive adult relationships. The authors conclude, 'These women lacked adequate resources with which to cope with the stressors preceding the children's death' (McKee and Shea 1998: 684).

A growing body of research indicates that economic marginalisation is a factor to be considered in efforts to understand female crime and delinquency generally (Jurik 1983; Carlen 1988; Alder 1986). Research based on women's own accounts of their lives provides the strongest evidence of the importance of their economic circumstances to their life decision-making (Miller 1986; Carlen 1988; Alder 1986). At the same time, feminist research also reveals that there is no necessary, simple, direct causal relationship between economic factors and female crime (Alder 1986; Daly 1994), nor with women's violence towards their children. Clearly not all women living in poverty physically abuse their children (Gordon 1988; O'Donnell and Craney 1982).

Relevant to consideration of the ways in which economic circumstances may play a part in some women's violence against their children is the observation that poverty is more than simply not having sufficient money to survive. Carlen (1988: 71) speaks of the 'multifarious ways in which women saw the relationship between poverty and law-breaking'. Poverty means not only limited access to financial resources, but also limited options and opportunities for dealing with the range of problems that confront women. Women's stories reveal the reality of the everyday life of poverty, the feeling of powerlessness, the boredom, the futility, and the dependence (Carlen 1988). All of these have consequences for the individual woman's sense of self, of future, of worth, her relationship to others, and the choices she makes in terms of dealing with the problems that confront her.

A woman's economic circumstances limit the options available to her to resolve her situation. Further, it has been suggested that in some circumstances the options that are available may aggravate her situation. Women with limited resources are more likely to seek out public social welfare agencies to help them find solutions to their problems with their children, while other women may have available to them more independent solutions (Gordon 1988; O'Donnell and Craney 1982). In turn, poverty influences the ways in which women are dealt with by professionals and government agencies, and the ways in which women relate to them, and in so doing can affect the form of coercive intervention to which they are subject (Carlen 1988; Worrall 1990). In the case of child welfare, it is often the same agencies from which they seek help that have the power to invoke coercive responses to the situation such as removing the child from the mother. Gordon (1988: 175) observes that 'the threat of losing one's children was an extremely anxiety-provoking stress in an already stressful life'. Intervention by government agencies not only caused embarrassment and humiliation, but the anonymity of informants also provoked distrust of friends, neighbours and relatives and thereby further isolated the mother. Gordon concludes, 'some women's violence was intensified, possibly even pro-voked, by intervening social agencies'(p. 175).

In conclusion, as we look to the literature for an understanding of women who kill their children, we find that it is sparse, and that pathological explanations predominate. In the criminological literature maternal filicide is most often represented as taking one of two forms: a psychologically disturbed young woman who kills her newborn or young infant; or a stressed mother who regularly loses control and physically abuses her children. Looking to the more extensive child abuse literature, explanations tend to be offered in gender-neutral terms (Dougherty 1993; O'Donnell and Craney 1982). Consequently there is a failure to elaborate on the broader social and economic context and the ways in which this is manifested and reproduced in the everyday experiences of mothers within the family.

More recently, these gaps in the existing literature are beginning to be identified and efforts are being made to develop more explicitly gender-based analyses that entail broader structural considerations (e.g. Dougherty 1993). In proposing a theory of female homicide generally, Ogle, Maier-Katkin and Bernard (1995) call for recognition of the par-ticular structural situations of women and an analysis of the implications of these for women. Their particular effort however, with very little refer-ence to data regarding the circumstances in which women kill, supposes a unitary phenomenon of female violence and ultimately represents these acts as emotional losses of control.

In part our understanding of the circumstances in which women kill their children is limited by a paucity of information and the tendency to seek to frame their actions as either evil or mad. It is hoped that the following analysis of case studies of mothers who kill their children will elaborate the complexities of the events, the women's circumstances and their actions.

### When Men Kill Children

Although men commit significant numbers of child homicides, studies of child homicide have tended to focus on those offences predominantly committed by women, in particular infanticide (Unnithan 1991a). This is consistent with the more general child abuse literature, which as several feminist writers have demonstrated either focuses attention on the mother's direct or indirect responsibility, or speaks in gender-neutral terms (Parton 1990: 43). 'Feminist work has drawn attention to the failure of mainstream child abuse literature, policy and practice to acknowledge and analyze the high level of men's abuse of children' (Parton 1990: 42; see also Archer 1994; Andrews 1994; Hearn 1990).

Consequently we need to turn to the more general literature on male-ness, masculinity and homicide to inform our analysis of child homicide.

That men predominantly commit homicide has been noted in most homicide studies. However, while noting the maleness of this offence, it is striking that until recently, few authors made this a key component of their analysis or theory. For example, Wolfgang and Ferracuti (1967: 258) noted that with respect to violent crime, 'almost universally … Males predominate everywhere.' They concluded from this observation:

> In general, a review of the statistical and clinical literature from many societies indicates that the age–sex category of youthful males exhibits the highest association with violent crime and that physically aggressive behavior for this group converges with notions about the masculine ideal. [Wolfgang and Ferracuti 1967: 260]

Despite this observation, their theory centred on the class and 'sub-culture' dimensions of violent behaviour. These became the focus of attention in research that followed, rather than their observation regard-ing the maleness of the behaviour, or the 'masculine ideal'.

Some of the most detailed investigations of homicide in more recent times which focus on the maleness of violent crime are those conducted by Daly and Wilson (1988, 1989). They note that there is no evidence that the women in any society have ever approached the level of violent conflict prevailing among men in the same society (Daly and Wilson 1988: 149). Working from a perspective based in evolutionary psy-chology, Daly and Wilson argue that male violence has to be understood in the context of the human reproductive process. They maintain that man's psyche is 'obsessed with social comparison, with the need for achievement and with the desire to gain control over the reproductive capacities of women' (p. 136). The most common type of homicide, according to Daly and Wilson (1988: 125) involves two acquainted, unrelated males, in a dispute over status or face.

One of the more influential criminological works in recent years is *The Seductions of Crime* by Jack Katz (1988). While Katz acknowledges at some points that men are more likely to engage in violent acts than women are, masculinity is not one of the 'contours of crime' that for him warrants direct attention in his conclusion to the book. Nevertheless most of the 'lived experiences' of crime considered by Katz are those of men. Katz's thesis is of interest to us because, in contrast to much recent homicide research, it is not derived from aggregate statistical data. Katz calls for us to 'track the lived experience of criminality' (p. 311). From this per-spective, he concludes in regard to homicide that 'In committing a righteous slaughter, the impassioned assailant takes humiliation and turns it into rage; through laying claim to a moral status of transcendent significance, he tries to burn humiliation up' (p. 312).

In a similar vein to Katz's interest in 'foreground', Campbell (1993: 84) is concerned with 'factors that are relevant *at the moment* when the action takes place'. However, for Campbell, gender is a key issue in an analysis of aggression. Campbell acknowledges the emotionality of men's aggressive acts: 'it is an almost automatic and well-practiced response to challenge, and it is accompanied by righteous fury' (p. 56). But the main thrust of her argument is that men's aggression is instrumental while women's is expressive. According to Campbell, men report that the trigger to their aggression and anger is a 'perceived threat to the man's sense of personal integrity, his pride, and his mastery of the social environment' (p. 56). In the face of such threats, men's use of aggression is strategic; it is a 'means of instilling fear and gaining power' (p. 72).

From the work of both Campbell and Katz emerges the notion of a generic aggressive experience, a universality of the moment of attack. Katz (1988: 18) details notable features of the 'typical' homicide. Campbell's aggressive scenarios involve men in a rage but nevertheless instrumental in their efforts to maintain or establish power. While there are clear differences between the works, basic to both are universalistic assumptions about men and violence.

In contrast, Messerschmidt (1993: 80) calls for us to begin with the notion that: 'Behaviour in men is considerably more complex than that suggested by the idea of a universal masculinity that is performed and embedded in the individual prior to social action' (see also Jefferson 1994: 13). He argues that gender is something that is accomplished in social interaction and thus 'diverse forms of masculinity arise, depending upon prevalent structural potentials and constraints' (p. 83). For Messerschmidt, 'crime by men is a form of social practice invoked as a resource, when other resources are unavailable, for accomplishing masculinity' (p. 85). Thus he argues that the home is an important site of authority for working-class men, and violence in the home is a means of affirming masculinity. Similarly, he argues, corporate crime is a 'means of accomplishing profit and gender'(p. 136). Since gender is situationally accomplished and crime is a means of accomplishing it, we can expect variability in masculinity, and diversity in the way men do or do not use violence to 'do masculinity'.

In his work, Polk (1994) has taken a slightly different approach, acknowledging that there are important ways in which patterns of masculine violence can be differentiated one from another. In his research Polk identified four scenarios of masculine violence that account for a majority of homicides. These included: violence arising out of men's attempt to control the sexuality of their female partner; male 'honour contests' (see also Polk 1999); male risk-taking behaviour in relation to such dangerous crimes as armed robbery; and attempts to settle simmering disputes through the use of violence (Polk 1995). Polk concluded that more than a unitary understanding of masculinity was required to explain the variety of homicide scenarios.

By the late 1990s criminologists were arguing for further exploration of the complexity and diversity of masculinities and their place in understandings of violence (Alder and Polk 1996). Newburn and Stanko (1994) pointed to the dangers of 'reification and essentialism' in simply referring to masculinity. They argued: 'It is crucial therefore to think about the power and variety of masculine values, the processes by which they become internalised, the processes of identification, the ways in which certain core values become associated with specific social groups, together with an historical analysis of masculinities and masculine practices' (p. 2).

However, with the growing acknowledgement of the maleness of violent crime and an increasing invocation of masculinity as an explanatory factor, a number of concerns and questions have been raised about the concept of 'masculinity' and the uses to which it is put (Collier 1998). An issue acknowledged by most authors in this area is the difficulty posed by the different understandings and uses of the concept in the academic literature: 'meanings stretch from essential self to deep center, gender identity, sex stereotypes, attitudes, institutional practices and so on' (Hearn 1996: 213).

Collier (1998: 16) critiques the notion of masculinity as being both politically ambiguous ('it is used in different ways within different discourses and perspectives'), and conceptually imprecise: 'Masculinity thus appears both as a specific form of culture and as something which varies within and between broader cultures.'

Concern is also expressed about the assumed dichotomy between sex and gender that underpins many discussions of masculinity (Cornwall and Lindisfarne 1994: 9; Collier 1998: 13). This dichotomy most often poses 'sex' as biologically determined, while 'gender' is socially constructed and ascribed. However anthropological evidence indicates that both sex and gender are culturally constructed and that there is significant, culturally dependent variability in related understandings. Collier (1998) argues the sex/gender duality is premised around other recurring binaries such as body/mind and nature/nurture. He rejects the assumption of the sex/gender binary of a 'neutral, pre-social, pre-discursive body', a body which is 'a passive recipient of certain gender "roles" or "messages"' which 'float free' of the body (pp. 24–6). Rather, drawing particularly on the 'sexed bodies' approach of Daly (1997), Collier (1998: 179) calls for us to focus on 'sexual difference and sex-specific corporeality'. He asserts that 'the materiality of the body and the lived experience of (sexed) subjectivity, the "lived-in"-ness of a psychical and libidinally mapped body, must itself be central to addressing the sexed specificity of crime' (p. 162). The promise of this approach is that it will allow 'recognition of the complexity and contradictory nature of men's subjectivity and lived experience itself' (p. 162).

The 1990s began with a call for further analyses of the maleness of crime, of the relationship between masculinity and violence. We have now a number of different perspectives and philosophical positions on the best approach to the general observation of the maleness of crime. Emerging across this breadth of empirical and theoretical works is a recognition of the diverse, complex, and contradictory understandings and experiences of men. While some theorists have rejected analyses in terms of 'gender', when the concept is utilised, the notion of a unitary set of understandings or expectations in relation to men has been rejected. It is now recognised that masculinity cannot be construed as independent from other social processes, or as necessarily an independent, isolated causal factor in social problems (Hearn 1996; Messerschmidt 1993). As Carrington (1993: 6) argues, a unitary masculinity cannot be 'isolated and described independently of race, class, sexual orientation, and the other realities of experience'.

While the general matter of relationship between masculinity/ies and violence has been the subject of increasing interest; the issues of men's violence in relation to children remains in need of further analysis. An exception is found in the work of Daly and Wilson (1988), who note that children are less likely to be killed by their biological fathers, and that fathers who do kill older children are likely to also kill themselves. Often the suicide is part of familicide, that is, where the man kills his wife and children. Familicide, they note, 'is a peculiarly male crime', which, they suggest, 'must be understood in terms of men's proprietary attitude toward women and their reproductive capacity' (pp. 82–3).

Katz (1988) also considers a case of a father who kills a child. It is a case in which the child dies as the result of a battering by the father, following the child's persistent crying. Katz suggests as an interpretation that 'the father defined the crying as defiant and enacted his violence to honor parental authority' (p. 13). For Katz, child homicides committed by men, like all other homicides, are characterised as self-righteous, unpremeditated acts that 'emerge quickly, are fiercely impassioned, and are conducted with an indifference to the legal consequences' (p. 18).

As we attempt to understand the phenomenon of men killing children, we will consider the range of circumstances in which such events occur. Children are killed by men both within and outside the family network, and across a range of ages. Across the circumstances and contexts in which men kill children, of particular interest to the present study is the examination of the commonalities and diversities of men's experiences, behaviours and understandings.

## Conclusion

Child homicide is a significant aspect of the general problem of violence in contemporary society, yet it has not been subject to the same close scrutiny as other forms of homicide. Here we have argued that, whether viewed from the outpouring of concern over the dramatic forms of child-killing that are found in the media, or the stark statistics that show the exceptional risk of lethal violence in some of the childhood years, homicide of children is a significant problem which merits investigation. As we proceed to this task, we have identified some of the distinctive contours that can be anticipated in such research.

Child homicide is a relatively unique form of violence in terms of the proportion of women who commit this offence. The fact that it is a form of violence committed by both men and women was one of the factors that drew us to this research. On the one hand, women's violence has not been extensively analysed; on the other, while men's violence has been the subject of a good deal of research, we are only beginning to critically consider the complexity and diversity of the maleness of violence. On the basis of the evidence and argumentation at hand we expected that the diversity of child homicides would allow us to explore a range of scenarios of male and female violence. In the qualitative analysis of the case narratives of children as victims of homicide which follow, we intend to explore the complexity of these events and the varied contexts and circumstances of both men's and women's violence.

# CHAPTER 2

# *Approaching Child Homicide*

When reading the term 'child homicide', the reader's mind may conjure up images of notorious cases extensively reported in both the fictional and non-fictional media. But what do we mean by the term in this research? This chapter attempts to respond to this question by addressing a number of issues. First, although they initially appear self-evident, both of the words in the expression 'child homicide' require clarification. We then turn to a description of the data gathered for this research, which further delineates the meaning of the term for the present investigation.

## Defining the Term 'Child'

A first definitional issue concerns the meaning of the word 'child'. This might seem a simple matter, and in one sense it is. This research deals with individuals who, under the laws of the State of Victoria, Australia, are legally below the age of adulthood, that is, victims of homicide who are age 17 and under. However, the diversity of definitions in the child homicide literature complicates the issue. Some writers have been concerned with the problem of 'infanticide', which in much of current law means a focus on deaths of children under the age of twelve months. Beyond these studies, there is an exceptional diversity in the age range of victims in child homicide research. Some studies have focused on the deaths of young children, including restricting the investigation to those deaths involving children under age 4 (de Silva and Oates 1993), under 5 years of age (Scott 1973b: 197; Wilkey et al. 1982; Christoffel and Liu 1983), or under the age of 8 (Hoffer and Hull 1981). For others, the net has been spread broader to include homicides of children under age 13 (Copeland 1985; Crittenden and Craig 1990), under age 14 (Myers 1967;

Silverman, Reidel and Kennedy 1990; Silverman and Kennedy 1993) under age 15 (Kaplun and Reich 1976; Strang 1993), under age 18 (Jason and Andereck 1983), and even up to the age of 20 (Resnick 1969).

The form of child homicide is related to the age of the victim: the younger the child, the more likely it is that it will occur within the family and that the mother is the perpetrator (Silverman and Kennedy 1993; Finkelhor 1997). Therefore the age range of the victims included in a study has important consequences in terms of the conclusions that are likely to be drawn about the nature of child homicide. Research restricted to events involving children under the age of 5 or 6 will be limited almost exclusively to homicides within the family (e.g. Wallace 1986).

In the present study, a wider age range than is found in most child homicide studies has been chosen that both is consistent with an appropriate legal definition and allows an examination of a broad range of forms of child homicide, including those with teenage victims. As will be seen, an immediate consequence of this decision is to alter the distribution in terms of the context of the homicide. There will be more non-family homicides in the present study than in investigations restricted to younger victims. The sex distribution of offenders, as will be seen in the chapters that follow, will also reflect the age distribution of the victims: although women offenders are common where the child victim is under 6, as victims approach the teenage years there are almost no female offenders.

## Defining Homicide

There is often confusion about the meanings of such terms as 'homicide', 'murder' and 'manslaughter'. In the present study, we are concerned primarily with 'homicide', which can be defined simply as the killing of one person by another; in this case the killing of a child by another person. The terms 'murder' and 'manslaughter' in general will be avoided, since these have both a technical legal definition and are tied to a complicated chain of decisions at various points in the criminal justice system. Criminal law texts typically devote several pages to the many features that must be present to define an act as murder. For example, the concept of 'intent' refers in murder not only to the intent to kill, but also to the intent to do grievous bodily harm when a death results from the intentional action. In addition, a death is not considered a murder in a strict sense unless several legal steps (a police charge, a committal process, and a legal hearing on the charge) have been completed, resulting in a court determination that the offender is guilty of the charge of murder (as opposed to a finding of either not guilty, or guilty to the lesser charges of manslaughter or infanticide). As a consequence, in a typical jurisdiction only a small number of homicides prosecuted in a year will result in a criminal conviction on the specific charge of murder. There may be many homicides worthy of study, but only a few of these can properly be called 'murders'.

Of course, not all forms of the killing of one person by another are regulated under criminal law, and this includes forms of the killing of children (accidental deaths, for example). Not only are such cases not necessarily dealt with by the criminal justice system, but also the killing of children by adults does not always engender the horror and outrage expressed frequently in media representations of contemporary child murders. At different times and across a number of cultures, including our own, the killing of children has under some circumstances been directly or indirectly tolerated. Infants and newborn babies in particular have been killed because they are devalued or unwanted. Reasons for this have included: a socially unacceptable father, the baby was deformed or possessed an undesirable physical characteristic such as the wrong skin colour or sex, the baby may have been conceived by rape, or may be considered an economic burden (Jones 1980: 51; Rose 1986).

Other adult practices and policies result in the deaths of large numbers of children that are rarely dealt with in the criminal justice system. In Australia, deaths of Aboriginal children are many times higher than for non-Aboriginal children, and the rate of such deaths is among the highest in the world. Many hundreds of children died as a result of the Bhopal disaster (Mokhiber 1989: 86–96). Unknown numbers of children die as the result of the continued distribution and pro- motion of infant health formula in Third World and war-torn countries, or as the result of the living and working conditions supported by multinational companies in the less developed countries. We might well ask ourselves why child deaths resulting from the actions of organi- sations in the pursuit of profit, or from the inadequate provision of public health services to some communities, do not engender the same level and extent of media coverage or general community outrage that is given to specific incidents of child homicide that find their way into the criminal courts. It is evident that our understandings of the killing of children and our responses to it are not fixed in time or place and are ultimately only understood in the context of much broader social and cultural processes.

Nevertheless, in contemporary Western societies, certain forms of child killing do excite feelings of moral outrage and come under the purview of the criminal law. Such events challenge understandings of human relations that are considered cornerstones of our society. How could a parent, a mother, kill her own child? How could a grown man kill a young child? Assumptions about what it is to be a mother, a father, a responsible adult, a child, assumptions about parental relations and human relations, are challenged by such events. These events remain a mystery to us, a source of fear for all parents, and are the subject of this research.

For the present purposes, child homicide is operationally defined as the death of a child under the age of 18, where the case has been referred to the Coroner's Court as a suspected homicide and where the subsequent investigation by either police or the Coroner concludes that the child's death was caused by another person. By law in Victoria, all cases of 'unnatural death' (including traffic accidents, suicides, deaths in the course of work, and deaths in custody, as well as suspected homicides) must be referred to the Coroner for initial investigation. Suspected homicides in particular will lead to a coroner's inquest. The advantage of the definition used in this research is that it is close to the origin point of data on homicides: there will be few homicides known to the police which do not get into these files. Such files are considerably better for research purposes than, for example, homicides derived from either court files of prosecutions or prison files of convictions for criminal homicide, since there are a great number of factors which contribute to the attrition of cases as one moves deeper into the criminal justice system. Specifically with reference to homicide, this attrition occurs when the offender commits suicide, where either at the police charging or committal stage a decision is made to charge for an offence other than criminal homicide, or where it is determined that the killing is justifiable. The loss of such cases can seriously distort the picture of child homicide that results.

### The Case Studies

The case study data for this investigation were drawn from files of the Office of the Coroner for the State of Victoria. Information on all cases of child homicide that were reported to the Coroner in the years 1985–95 formed the basis for the research. The files are those prepared for the inquest that is required in cases of suspected homicide. There are a number of steps that lead to this inquest. The likely sequence of a homicide investigation will begin with a report of the death to the police, followed by the police investigation, the analysis by forensic specialists, including the forensic pathologists, an autopsy, with the results of all of these brought together in the inquest conducted by the Coroner. Each of these steps contributes material that ultimately makes up the files employed in this investigation.

For each case defined as a homicide, a case study was prepared drawing upon the material in the coronial files. These case studies ranged anywhere from a few sentences where little information was available, to several pages of rich qualitative material where a large number of witnesses were available for accounts of the events surrounding the death. Wherever possible, material in the actual words of the main participants in the homicide was recorded. From these files for this 1985–95 period in Victoria, we were able to identify ninety cases of homicides involving individuals under the age of 18.

### The Problem of the 'Dark Figure of Crime'

The child homicides reviewed here do not represent all killings of children in Victoria for this time period. Official statistics in general are bedevilled by the problem of the 'dark figure' of crime, that is, the extent to which some criminal acts do not find their way into the records. With child homicide, there are a number of specific factors that aggravate this problem (Wilczynski 1997).

*Undiscovered Abandoned Infants*

First, it is clear from the available records that some perpetrators have attempted unsuccessfully to conceal the death of a child, especially a newborn infant. The accidental nature of the discovery of some of these small bodies found in dumpsters or sewerage screens suggests that there may be many other cases where the concealment was successful. Among the present case studies of neonaticide, for example, there is one mother who had successfully hidden a previous neonaticide, that death only coming to light when a second child homicide was reported some five years later. Further, once the parent (perhaps with the collusion of the family) has been successful in the concealment, there is no potential array of other relatives, friends or officials who might report the person as missing, as happens in some cases of homicides involving adults.

*Neglect Ignored*

Child deaths that are the consequence of parental neglect may be defined either as a natural death or an accident. An example is where the child dies as a result of systematic neglect or starvation by its parents, but the ultimate death is from an illness that is treated as a 'natural' cause of death. Thus, such deaths, while resulting from behaviour of the parents, may not fall within the boundaries of what is considered homicide

(Emery 1978; Christoffel, Zieserl and Chiaramonte 1985), as illustrated in the following case:

> In 1993, the Melbourne community was horrified to read of the case of a five-month-old infant who died of the complications of starvation. The child died after weeks of attempts by authorities to try to induce the child's mother (who had a drug addiction problem) to provide for proper medical and nutritional care for the child. There were several visits by both drug and child protection workers, even in the hours before the child's death. Workers on a number of occasions were close to removing the child from the home, but were unable to avert the final tragedy. After this event, a Victorian judge prepared a report for the Victorian Department of Health and Community Services which described five such deaths in recent years. [*Age*, 3 September 1993, p. 13]

In a similar 1996 case, a child died despite repeated calls to the Victorian Health and Community Services Department expressing concern for the child's welfare. In fact, the death was discovered by child-care workers entering the premises with a child apprehension warrant. In this instance, it appeared that the neglect took the form of denying the child proper medical care, since it was an illness rather than complications from starvation that caused the death (*Age*, 7 February 1998, p. 4). Although in this case, and the one above, the negligence of the mother was a significant contributing factor in the death, neither case was treated as a homicide by medical or criminal justice authorities.

Wilczynski (1997: 26) draws attention to other child deaths that are viewed as 'accidents' but may also be understood as the consequence of forms of parental neglect. Examples are deaths in fires caused by the negligence of parents or other child-carers, or in baths or when swimming where prudent parents might have exercised closer supervision. On rare occasions convictions have been obtained in these sorts of cases; for example, Wilczynski provides a summary of the 1988 *Burcher* case:

> A father went out leaving his two children (age 10 and 5) alone in the house, knowing that they would probably have a bath. The children took a hairdryer with a defective plug into the bath with them, and were subsequently electrocuted. The father was convicted of child cruelty. [Wilczynski 1997: 26]

Such actions by the criminal justice system are uncommon, however, and it is clear that Wilczynski is correct in her observation that authorities are not quick to define the results of such neglect as a form of criminal homicide. The point here is not to argue that such cases ought to be considered as homicide. Rather the point is to indicate the complexity of the understandings of what events do or do not constitute homicide. Clearly not all forms of child death that are the consequence of adult actions, or inactions, are dealt with as criminal homicides by the medical or the criminal justice systems.

### *Mistaking Homicide for Sudden Infant Death Syndrome*

Children sometimes die of what is diagnosed as sudden infant death syndrome (SIDS) when in fact the death may have been deliberate. In an Australian study, Armstrong and Wood (1991) examined a number of infant deaths where the initial diagnosis had been SIDS. They reported that in many instances the autopsy findings suggested that the death was not accidental. In the United Kingdom, one researcher described eighty-one children who had been found by the courts to have been killed, and among these forty-two had been certified initially as having died from SIDS (Meadow, 1999).

Among the case studies of the present research, there is one instance in which the detection of a later child homicide resulted in the confession by a mother of an earlier child homicide which previously had been classified as SIDS (Case No. 89-2009, described in Chapter 4). Wilczynski provides a description of a similar case:

Ruth confessed to smothering her six-week-old son. She also admitted having smothered another son of the same age two years earlier. At the time this death had been subject to a very brief police investigation and diagnosed as SIDS. The post-mortem revealed no external or internal signs of violence. [Wilczynski 1997: 27]

Public attention was drawn to this issue in the United States in the notable conviction of Waneta Hoyt in a New York court for the murders of her five children between 1965 and 1971 (Pinholster 1994; Bergman 1997). Not only had these deaths previously been classified as SIDS, but the clinician responsible for that diagnosis had extracted data from these cases for a remarkable, but now largely discredited, theory about the causes of SIDS (Steinschneider 1972).

It needs to be emphasised, of course, that the overwhelming majority of SIDS cases are not homicides. Authorities in the United Kingdom were quick to point out that in the same period when the forty-two previously diagnosed cases of SIDS led to charges in a court, there were in fact 25,000 total cases of deaths which were diagnosed as SIDS (White 1999). Those who have attempted to quantify the problem have argued that the proportion of homicides among the SIDS cases ranges from somewhere around 1 per cent (McClain et al. 1993) to perhaps as much as 10 to 20 per cent (Emery 1993).

At the same time, in the words of one authority: 'There is no disagreement that some infants who die suddenly and unexpectedly do so from known causes, and that one of those causes is homicide' (Bergman 1997: 120).

One of the critical tasks for medical researchers is to provide some clear guidelines to distinguish child homicides from the presumably much larger number of deaths where the cause has been SIDS. Reese (1993), for one, has suggested a set of procedures by which fatal physical assaults on children might be distinguished from cases of SIDS. Similarly, the American Academy of Pediatrics (1999) urged a number of important reforms in the investigation, review and treatment of unexplained deaths of infants. Much more work in this direction is needed in order to protect grieving parents from the double blow of the death of their infant child as the result of SIDS and unfounded suspicion that their intentional actions were responsible for the death. Nevertheless, it needs to be acknowledged that some unknown (but presumably small) number of homicides are mistakenly diagnosed as SIDS and will therefore not be included in any tally of known child homicides.

*Unproved or Unprovable Fatal Physical Assaults*

Some child deaths that are the result of physical assault, or abuse, by adults (nearly always family members) may be classified as accidents. Even though the features of some child deaths may be quite similar to other homicides, the available evidence may not be deemed strong enough to support a successful criminal prosecution. Consider the following case from the present files:

> Roger O. (aged 20) had lived with Lorri M. (aged 18) and her 7-month-old son, Charles, for the previous six months. Their relationship was strained by their lack of money, both were unemployed, and they did not have the money for the rent of the caravan in which they were living. Charles was known to be 'always sick', and at the time of the events surrounding his death had been suffering both from teething and constipation (the week before he had suffered from a virus).
>
> On the day of his death, Lorri dressed Charles to take him shopping. Roger started an argument, saying that he thought it was too cold for Charles to be taken out. Lorri relented and left Charles in Roger's care. Roger's account of what then followed was that he and the baby were on the bed together, while Roger was reading a book.

After a period of time, when he looked up from his book, Charles was on the floor and had ceased breathing. Roger then stated that he attempted mouth-to-mouth resuscitation, and that the baby's head was 'wobbling' and that he was 'arching his back'. Charles was taken to hospital, where he died shortly after.

At the hospital, Roger was crying and head-butting the wall, assuming that he would be blamed for the injuries. An autopsy revealed severe head injuries not consistent with a simple fall. Further, it revealed that Charles had suffered severe injuries previously, including a broken arm approximately ten days beforehand. Neither Roger nor Lorri could explain the earlier injuries. While the medical evidence and opinion indicate that Roger's explanation of these events is improbable, Roger was not charged with the homicide, and the Coroner was unable to determine if the death was by 'unlawful killing, misadventure or otherwise'. [Case No. 85-1758]

This death is remarkably similar to many child-killings by fatal assault, both in terms of the injuries responsible for the death, and the pattern of prior abuse shown by the earlier injuries uncovered through the autopsy. The extensive injuries suffered by the victim were not consistent with the story told by the adults. Where the parent or parents and their families maintain their silence, however, it may be difficult to establish the evidence needed for a prosecution. This case was not treated as a homicide by the police or by the Coroner, and is consequently not considered a homicide within the present files.

Some of the same elements are found in the following account:

Delbert K. (aged 19) had been living with Ruth S. and her three children for six months. He was thought to be an excellent parent to the children and he actively participated in child-care duties. One day, upon returning home from picking up the eldest child from school, Ruth found Delbert near hysteria, and the 2-year-old, Velma, clearly near death. Delbert at first claimed that he had heard Velma talking in her cot, and when he went to pick her up she accidentally fell; he later changed the story, saying that the baby had fallen when trying to climb out of her cot.

Velma died the next day in hospital. Six doctors were involved, and they did not believe Delbert. The injuries observed were not consistent with his story. The medical evidence suggested that the death was the result of brain damage caused by violent, repetitive shaking. Velma's vertebrae were also fractured, and she had bruises on her head and body. Further, the autopsy also revealed old scratches and bruises, and haemorrhages that were at least ten days old.

Corroborative evidence was available from a friend, who had observed Delbert violently striking another of the children a few days before this episode, and Velma's biological father had also observed bruising on one of the children, and had even confronted Ruth over the matter.

The police initially classified the death as accidental, but after the autopsy the case was re-opened. The Coroner found that Delbert had contributed to Velma's death, and Delbert was charged with murder and bailed on that charge. One month later, a *nolle prosequi* was entered [that is, the prosecution decided not to prosecute the case] as it was deemed that the evidence was 'inadequate to disprove that the death was other than accidental'. [Case No. 86-1973]

Given the combination of medical evidence and the Coroner's conclusion, this case was treated as a homicide in the present research.

In many respects these two cases look alike. In both there were injuries that could not be explained by the stories told by the stepfather. The autopsy revealed that both children had experienced severe injuries prior to the fatal incident. However, the combination of medical evidence and the Coroner's finding in the second case led us to conclude that the death was a homicide, while in the other it is necessary to back away and conclude that we are unable to establish that this clearly suspicious death is a homicide. In essence, cases were included if a finding of homicide was consistent with the conclusion of either the police or the Coroner.

On the other hand, some initially suspicious cases seem on the basis of the pattern of the evidence to be safely considered as accidental deaths, as in the following case:

It was established at autopsy that Ellie M. (19 months) died of severe brain injuries that were externally caused. All of the evidence pointed to the fact that the parents were devoted and caring. The child at the time the symptoms were noted was in the care of a babysitter who was determined to be a qualified and experienced day-care worker. Some questions were raised about this death because the surgeon who attended 'was concerned as to the possible cause of the injury that was not readily apparent'. The post-mortem examination 'revealed a subdural haemorrhage resulting in severe brain injury, with signs of earlier haemorrhage which could have occurred days earlier with little external manifestation'. On the basis of the evidence at hand, the Coroner concluded that the infant had 'received impeccable care' from both parents and the babysitter and that 'the particular normal childhood incident which triggered the fatal haemorrhage cannot be determined on the evidence before the inquest'. [Case No. 90-4126]

An autopsy can usually determine whether the child died of natural causes, or if the death was a result of injuries or some form of trauma. In this case, although a mystery remains as to the exact cause of the injuries resulting in death, the available evidence suggested to the Coroner an accident rather than a deliberate killing. As this case suggests, there are instances where the causal factors are apparently external to the child, yet it is not possible to determine definitively whether the death was the result of intentional actions on the part of one or more adults.

Some cases are ambiguous as to whether or not they should be classified as an accident or a homicide. One such case, which was ultimately not considered as a homicide in this research, is the following:

Q.T. (age 14, unemployed) had been born in Vietnam. One weekday night, a friend came to visit him. After talking for a few minutes, Q.T. asked his mother if he could go out for the evening. The mother gave permission, but asked him not to stay out late. She did not see Q.T. again until the friend brought him home unconscious at about 9 p.m. the following night. When they were unable to revive him, they attempted to summon an ambulance. This took some time because of language difficulties, and by the time the ambulance arrived, Q.T. was dead. The autopsy revealed that death was a result of broncho-pneumonia in association with intravenous usage of heroin or morphine. Throughout, language difficulties posed a problem for the investigation, although the police finally concluded that there were 'no suspicious circumstances surrounding the death'. The Coroner at the inquest found that he was unable to 'determine if the intravenous injections were self-administered or otherwise'. [Case No. 85-3327]

In this instance, while the injections might have been administered by others, the general weight of the available evidence led the police to the conclusion that this death might reasonably be treated as something other than a homicide. There remains, however, the possibility that others injected the drugs, but since neither the police nor the Coroner considered there was sufficient evidence to reach such a conclusion, the case was not included as a homicide in the present research.

The following case illustrates that a homicide database is subject to ongoing changes:

At 7 a.m. on a summer morning the body of a 13-year-old girl was found on a well-known surfing beach along the western coastline of

Victoria. Police arrived and found the body face down on the sand, partially clothed. There were signs that sharks had attacked the body while it was in the water. Initial identification was made from photographic documents found in the girl's tracksuit pants. Forensic analysis indicated that there had been some consumption of alcohol prior to the death. The autopsy revealed brain injuries prior to death, as well as 'injuries to the neck suggestive of the application of compressive force'. The death was classified as an apparent drowning. The whereabouts of the deceased prior to her death are not known. The general absence of suspicious circumstances led the police and the Coroner to treat this as a case of accidental death. [Case No. 92-4137]

Some features of this account strongly suggest homicide. The body was clothed when it was found, indicating that the child had not accidentally drowned while swimming. The injuries prior to death may indicate violence leading to a homicide. However, there are a number of alternative explanations. The death might have occurred when the child fell from some rocks into the water, or she may have stumbled over one of the nearby cliffs.

On the basis of initial findings and the conclusions of the police and Coroner, the case was excluded in the early stages of the research. Late into the research, however, new information emerged and police were again investigating the case as a homicide, so it was included in the research.

These cases demonstrate that there can never be, given the present state of knowledge and of medical and judicial practice, a definitive, accurate number indicating the exact level of child homicide (or homicide in general, for that matter). Any set of existing data will suffer to some degree from a problem of under-reporting of the total volume of child homicide and perhaps an under-representation of some forms of child homicide.

### Some Cautionary Notes

In the text which follows, the individual cases are presented as narratives. We have written these narratives as a result of consulting a number of different documents, including the witness statements, which were used to provide wherever possible the actual words of the participants in the events which led up to the homicide. Inevitably, these accounts represent a particular construction of the events as they took place. We have tried wherever possible to balance accounts, especially where there are disputes about the sequence of events in the violence. It may be, however, that the views of key participants are not represented, and certainly it must be acknowledged that the voice of the victim was not directly accessible. In the Japanese film *Rashomon*, a number of different tales of rape and murder are told by the central actors (including an account provided by the victim, rendered by a shaman). The point of the movie is that, while these stories are markedly different one from another, each is in fact an account of the same rape and murder. Narratives, the movie warns, are influenced by the standpoint of the teller, and, in the present case, from the standpoint of the compiler of the account as well. We recognise the nature of this problem, and have drawn for these accounts on as much textual material as could be found. To the best of our knowledge, the case studies represent an accurate summary of the key events in the homicide.

There is a second problem that also needs to be recognised. While the study covers a reasonable span of time (1985–95) in Victoria, Australia, there are social factors, and forms of homicide, that are not present in the ninety cases that have been identified. We have not found, for instance, examples of killings by nannies, deaths as a result of Munchausen syndrome by proxy, school shootings, or cases where very young children kill other young children, as in the Bulger case in England in the early 1990s. In order to round out the picture of child homicide, some discussion of these missing parts of the puzzle of child homicide is included in Chapter 7. It is also recognised that Australia does not have the same pattern of intense ghetto life of the African–American and Latino populations found in the major cities of the United States, which contribute so directly to the distinctive patterns of homicide in that country. Although we will include some of the important patterns of ghetto violence in Chapter 7 in a discussion of street gang violence, there are much wider effects of ghetto life that are reflected in the general patterns of violence, which will not be found in an Australian study. The patterns of violence in Australia are much more consistent with patterns of violence found in the United Kingdom and Western Europe (Polk and Weitekamp 1999).

Also, Victoria differs somewhat from other Australian states in that Aboriginal and Torres Strait Islander people constitute a much smaller proportion of the population than is found in, say, Western Australia or Queensland. Within Australia, the Aboriginal population is distinctively at risk when the topic of homicide is considered, their rates being up to seven times higher than the non-Aboriginal population (James and Carcach 1998). States with lower proportions of Aboriginal and Torres Strait Islander people, such as Victoria and Tasmania, thereby have a somewhat different pattern of homicide victimisation than is found in the Northern Territory, Queensland, Western Australia or South Australia.

### Forms of Child Homicide in this Research

The ordering of data and observations further defines the subject of the research. The groupings of the child homicides for the purpose of discussion here evolved from the data analysis. Overall, a distinguishing feature was the immediate context of the events, defined in terms of whether the homicide occurred within, or outside, the family network. Chapters 3–5 examine filicides (a child homicide committed by the child's biological or de facto parent), that is, they occurred within the family context (58 cases). Chapter 6 examines non-filicides that occurred outside a family situation (32 cases).

A second dimension that emerged from the analysis of the scenarios was the sex of the offender. Within the context of family child homicides, the content of the case studies indicated clear differences in situations where women were the offenders, in contrast to men. Chapters 3 and 4 will consider those filicides where women are the offenders, and Chapter 5 will address those where men are responsible for the lethal violence. When the focus shifts to the killings of children outside the family, in virtually all cases the offender is male (to be addressed in Chapter 6).

Within the two broad context groupings, there are themes specific to that context (Table 2.1). Filicides, for example, include neonaticides, fatal physical assaults, attempted and completed suicides, and cases of exceptional psychiatric disturbance. Within the non-filicides, the first cluster of groupings consist of masculine scenarios of violence that are found in adult homicides (Polk 1994; Smith 2000), including male-on-female violence as a result of jealousy or control, mostly male-on-male violence in honour contests, homicide in the course of other crime, and conflict resolution through the planned use of violence. In addition, in child killing outside the family, groupings were necessary for killings which resulted from accidental shootings, and those which arose out of sexual exploitation.

In both of the broad context groupings it has been necessary to provide for a category of 'distinctive' killings. These are homicides which take place within the relevant context (family or non-family), but where the social dynamics are so unusual or different that the cases cannot be considered within the available thematic groupings (there were four such cases in the present group of filicides, and three in the non-filicides). These few cases in essence pose 'mysteries' for our analysis: despite a considerable amount of case narrative material, it is

**Table 2.1** Distribution of child homicide by social context and form of child killing, Victoria, 1985–1995

| Forms of child homicide | No. of cases |
|---|---|
| **Filicides** | |
| The killing of children by a parent (Chapters 3–5) | 58 |
| *Neonaticides:* the killing of a newborn child within the first 24 hours of birth | 11 |
| *Fatal Physical Assaults:* a child death resulting from a severe physical assault | 19 |
| *Attempted Suicide, Suicide:* a filicide accompanied by the suicide or attempted suicide by the parent | 18 |
| *Exceptional Psychiatric Disturbance:* the offender believed they were compelled by external forces to kill their child | 6 |
| *Distinctive:* a group of cases that are significantly different from all other cases | 4 |
| **Non-Filicides** | |
| The killing of children by an offender who is not the parent, and is not otherwise in a responsible caring role in relation to the child (Chapter 6) | 32 |
| *Honour Contests* | 7 |
| *Homicide in the Course of Another Crime* | 4 |
| *Conflict Resolution* | 3 |
| *Sexual Exploitation* | 4 |
| *Jealousy and Control* | 4 |
| *Accidental Shooting* | 2 |
| *Distinctive* | 3 |
| *Unknown* | 5 |

still difficult to discern the exact nature of the social relationships between victim and offender, and the way that these social dynamics contribute to the lethal event.

Finally, as is always to be expected in files such as these, there are five cases where important circumstances of the death are unknown. These are clearly homicides, as determined by the cause of death at the autopsy. Furthermore, there are enough facts present to indicate with virtual certainty that the death was not the act of another family member, yet little else is known (as in the case, for example, of two young teenagers found stabbed to death in woods next to a remote stretch of highway). Accordingly, we have been able to consider these as examples of non-filicides, but other than this determination, we indicate that other circumstances are 'unknown'.

Specific details of analysis are presented in Chapters 3–6. This case study analysis allowed for consideration of a number of features of the immediate context and circumstances of the cases. In Chapter 7 we shift to consider the broader themes and issues that emerge across the cases. Although the present investigation covers a reasonably long period (1985–95) we recognise that with only ninety cases there will be forms of child homicide not found within our case narratives. Accordingly, in this chapter we consider forms of child homicide that have been identified in other research, which throw light on important issues of child homicide that merit investigation, but which are not found in our data (for example, homicides resulting from street gang violence).

In the final chapter, we consider the theoretical implications of the observations made throughout the book. It becomes evident as one reads through the analysis and the cases that child homicide takes many forms. At the broadest level, it varies with social context and with the sex of the offender, and as will be seen, the age of the victim. But these factors alone are but crude indicators of the complexity of these events, as will become evident in our exploration of the cases.

# CHAPTER 3

# *Neonaticide*

'I was worried about what the people in town would have said.'
*Mother*

A children's welfare organisation is pasting posters on
public rubbish bins across Italy urging reluctant mothers
not to throw their newborn babies away. The fliers depict
a wide-eyed, winsome baby with its head sticking out of a
dustbin. Plastered across the drawing is the appeal: 'I'm
a baby! Take me to the hospital or a safe place.'
*Age, 3 July 1998, p. 10*

In approaching the study of children as victims of homicide, we argue
that the analysis must negotiate through, first, the social context (whether
the killing occurs within or outside the family) and second, the sex of the
offender. We begin the investigative project by looking at killings of
children by their mothers (and we shall see that when women kill
children, they are, in the present case studies at least, always the natural
mothers of the child victims). In this chapter we look at those killings
where the mother kills her newborn baby in its first hours of life.

The term 'neonaticide', that is the killing of a child within the first
twenty-four hours of birth, first entered the published literature in 1970
in an examination of the murder of newborn infants (Resnick 1970),
but the problem itself is hardly a new one. The killing of unwanted
infants was common in ancient Greek and Roman societies, even being
defended by such writers as Seneca and Pliny the Elder (Langer 1974).
Oedipus, and Romulus and Remus, were notable survivors in literature
of attempts to kill shortly after birth. Historically, it was not uncommon
in Inuit communities for infants with congenital deformities, and one of
a set of twins, to be killed. In China, well into the nineteenth and some

31

claim into the twentieth century, female infants were killed at birth because of the future burden of paying their marriage portion and because they could not transmit the family name. Some American Indians, it is reported, routinely killed 'half-breeds' at birth (Resnick 1970). One report asserted that, as recently as the early nineteenth century, up to one-third of live-born infants were killed or abandoned by their parents (Wissow 1998: 1239).

In nineteenth-century England, a growing horror of the large-scale killing of unwanted infants at birth contributed to the development of a long series of political manoeuvres which ultimately led to the definition and implementation of a new criminal offence of 'infanticide' (Behlmer 1979). The mood of the period is captured in the observations of William Burke Ryan:

> In the calm evening walk we see in the distance the suspicious-looking bundle, and the mangled infant is within. By the canal side, or in the water, we find the dead child. In the solitude of the wood we are horrified by the ghastly sight; and if we betake ourselves to the rapid rail in order to escape the pollution, we find at our journey's end that the mouldering remains of a murdered innocent have been our travelling companion, and that the odour from the unsuspected parcel truly indicates what may be found within. [William Burke Ryan, *Infanticide: Its Law, Prevalence, Prevention and History*, 1862, pp. 45–46, cited by Behlmer 1979: 404]

Unfortunately, as we enter into this discussion we must recognise that some confusion is possible in reading the literature because of the frequent mingling of the terms 'infanticide' and 'neonaticide'. As Resnick observed:

> In the literature, all child murders by parents are usually lumped together under the term 'infanticide.' In the author's opinion, there are two distinct types of child murder. 'Neonaticide' is defined as the killing of a neonate on the day of its birth. 'Filicide' is operationally defined as the murder of a son or daughter older than 24 hours. [Resnick 1970: 58]

Historically, there has been a broad reach to the term 'infanticide', the phenomenon being the focus of numerous anthropological, historical and legal commentaries. Consider this typical example:

> Infanticide has been practiced since prehistoric times. Children have been thrown into rivers and burning pits, 'potted' in jars to starve

to death, exposed on hillsides and in streets, suffocated, mutilated, and beaten to death. Bones of infants dug up by archeologists, with inscriptions identifying them as first-born sons of noble families, date all the way back to Jericho of 7,000 B.C. Hiel the Bethelite built Jericho with his youngest son buried in the foundation. Indeed, sealing children in wells, foundations, and bridges to strengthen their structure was common from the wall of Jericho to Germany in 1843 ... In the Grecian states of old infanticide was not only permitted but enforced by law. A Spartan lawgiver decreed that all infants be examined by the older men of the community. If found to be deformed or weak the child was thrown into a deep cavern at the foot of Mount Taygetus ... The practice was defended by Aristotle and Plato as a means of getting rid of deformed children and preventing an excess of population. [Montag and Montag 1979: 368]

Although this shows that across cultures and time there has been acceptance of the practice of killing infants, in some instances, as where neonates are exposed, the text refers to what Resnick would consider 'neonaticide'. In other circumstances, as where children were sealed into structures, it is not exactly clear what the age of the infant might be. There is, in short, the possibility of misunderstanding with respect to how the terms are used, since at times infanticide includes neonaticide, while in other sections the events clearly involve infants who have lived well beyond the one-day boundary that defines neonaticide.

One of the important arenas where such a confusion of terms will be found is in commentaries on law and legal process. In the United Kingdom and Australia, however else the term is used, infanticide at law is a specific offence involving the killing of a child, exclusively by the mother, before the child reaches the age of one year. As a consequence, when the case of a child that has been killed within twenty-four hours of its birth (a neonaticide for our purposes) is considered in the courts, the specific legal charge that may be laid is that of infanticide. What is described in social scientific terms as a 'neonaticide' comes to be treated in law as 'infanticide':

The second place where this confusion is found is in discussion by historians and anthropologists. As illustrated in the statement by Montag and Montag, authors may choose to retain the term 'infanticide' in their analysis of the killings of infants across a range of age categories, extending the term to cover those cases which here will be considered as neonaticides. For a recent example, Lowenstein (1997) considered within a review of infanticide the exposure by ancient Spartans of 'misformed or handicapped' neonates, and the deliberate killing by Susan Smith in South Carolina of her two young sons, as well as mothers who batter their children, which can occur commonly at ages up to at least 3 years old.

The tern 'infanticide', whether defined by law or in the usage of social commentators, is a more inclusive term than 'neonaticide'. Readers should keep in mind, then, that material on issues related to infanticide (1) may contain discussions which have an important contribution to make to the understanding of neonaticide, but that (2) much of such material may deal with events that are quite different from the circumstances that relate to a death which occurs within twenty-four hours of the birth.

### Neonaticides with Known Offenders

In Victoria between 1985 and 1995, there were eleven infants (12 per cent of the total child homicides) who were determined to have died in the first twenty-four hours of life. In six of these cases, information is available about the circumstances that resulted in the homicide, including the identity of those responsible for the death. All of these cases involve infants whose birth was unwanted by the mother.

> Alice Price (17 years of age, unmarried) gave birth in the toilet of the family home. Her parents were home at the time. She placed the body in a plastic bag and left it in the laundry. Her mother found the bag the next morning. Her family had thought she had put on a bit of weight, but her sister with whom she shared a bedroom noted that, 'At no time did I realise that Alice might be pregnant.' Alice did not see a doctor during or after the pregnancy. Sex education had not been discussed in the family. Alice stated to police, 'I was in bed and I started getting pains in the stomach. I went to the toilet but nothing happened. I went back to bed … the pains got really bad and I went back to the toilet. I got into the room and started to pull down my pants and the baby came … I didn't know I was pregnant. I was scared … I thought about being pregnant a couple of times but I didn't think I was … I effectively closed my mind. I didn't want to know. I was hoping it would go away.' Alice thought that her partner would leave her and that the family would be ashamed. She was also scared of her father's physical abuse in disciplining her. [Case No. 85-1369]

Neonaticides are often characterised by the total denial of the pregnancy, as evidenced in this case. Most often the young women do not seek any kind of medical advice regarding the pregnancy. The psychiatrist in one case reported: 'I believe that she genuinely pushed the thought of pregnancy out of her mind. At no stage during the pregnancy did she ever give it a serious thought. As far as she was concerned she was not pregnant' (Case Nos. 85-2886/7). In other cases where the pregnancy is at some point acknowledged by the woman, she nevertheless effectively denies it to herself, 'just hoping it would go away':

> Amy Johnson (19 years) stated, 'I denied to myself that I was pregnant. I knew deep down that I was, but I put it to one side and hoped that it would go away. I just went on as though I wasn't pregnant.' When asked why she didn't seek help during labour, she stated 'I didn't think to.' [Case No. 86-0001]

The woman's self-denial of the pregnancy is reinforced for her by the lack of visible physiological changes normally expected with pregnancy. There are reports in the literature where mothers actually lose weight over the course of the pregnancy, and even experience monthly vaginal shows of blood (Brozovsky and Falit 1971: 679). Thus in these cases the pregnancy is rarely suspected even by close family and friends. In two cases, the pregnancy was not apparent to the male partners of the young women even though they continued to have sexual relations (Case Nos. 85-2886/7, 85-1369). As suggested in the first case narrative above, neither Alice's parents, siblings nor boyfriend recognised that she was pregnant:

> Mary Price, mother of several children, including Alice, noticed one Friday morning a plastic bag that had been placed on top of the family freezer. When she looked inside, she found the body of a baby. She then confronted Alice, who at first attempted to avoid the discussion, but finally called her mother into her bedroom, saying: 'Mum, I've had a baby.' Mary had not known her daughter was pregnant. A younger sister later observed that, while she had noticed that Alice had put on weight, 'At no time did I realise that Alice might be pregnant.' Her boyfriend, John, had also noticed that Alice was putting on weight, but when asked she denied that she was pregnant. John stated that, when he later questioned her, she 'said that she hadn't told me about being pregnant or having the baby because she thought that I would leave her'. He also observed that Alice was 'so scared on the night of the birth that she didn't really know what she was doing'. [Case No. 85-1369]

Many young women continue in their ordinary routines with work-mates, never acknowledging the pregnancy. All of the women in the investigation by Wallace (1986) continued in their usual activities as students or workers. When questioned by those close to them, the women were able to explain away their weight gain by factors such as a problem of fluid retention.

In the case of Rosie M., the pregnancy was not only not evident to close family, but also was not detected in medical examinations.

Rose M. (aged 15) was watching television alone in a caravan situated at the back of her parents' home late one Saturday night, when she first felt the birth coming on. She stated later: 'I felt like I wanted to go to the toilet, so I stood up and got a cramp in my side, and that's when the baby came ... First the baby's head popped out and then I realised I was having a baby ... it wouldn't breathe ... I was confused ... I was upset that it wasn't breathing ... sitting there holding it ... I just didn't know what to do.'

Rosie reported that the birth was quick, and that she only pushed once. Apart from the first cramp, she did not experience any pain. She was not aware that her vagina had ripped. The baby neither cried nor moved. Rosie severed the umbilical cord with a pair of garden shears that were in the caravan. She then wrapped the body in a towel, placed it in a plastic bag and buried it behind the incinerator.

Five days beforehand, Rosie had been prescribed tablets for fluid retention and had been placed on a diet by her doctor. The physician stated: 'Rosie to me was certainly not obviously pregnant.'

Three days before the birth, Rosie was in a car accident, and received bruising to her abdomen and legs. She also experienced vaginal bleeding. Again she was taken to a doctor, and again the examining physician apparently did not realise that she was pregnant.

Rosie was able to conceal her pregnancy throughout from her family. Her father was one of the few who suspected that she might have been pregnant, but his suspicions were dispelled after she had been examined by her doctor. Rosie shared a room and dressed in front of her sister, the sister merely noting that Rosie had put on weight on her hips and buttocks. Rosie claims that she menstruated throughout her pregnancy, and her sister confirmed that Rosie had used her supply of tampons every month.

On the day after the birth, Rosie's father took her to hospital, believing that she was ill due to the car accident. The examining doctor realised that she had recently given birth. Rosie was extremely anaemic and had retained the placenta. The doctor indicated that she would have died very soon if she had not received medical attention.

Although denying it at first, Rosie eventually admitted the birth and subsequent burial. She was extremely vague about the whole matter. [Case No. 85-2679]

The failure of physicians to realise that Rosie was pregnant, even days before birth, may sound extraordinary, but in fact has been observed elsewhere:

> The denying attitude of the patient is so pervasive that it affects not only her perceptions and those of her family, but those of teachers, employers and even physicians. During the 5th month, Nancy [one of the cases examined in the study] in one of her rare moments of suspecting that she was pregnant, consulted her physicians. A pregnancy test was ordered and returned positive. A month later she reported to her doctor the vaginal spotting. The doctor accepted her statement and ordered no further investigation. He apparently did not perceive any abdominal protuberance, although she was in her 5th month. Gerchow points out that in these cases it is not uncommon for the patient's physician to miss the pregnancy and arrive instead at the patient's wished-for diagnosis. [Brozovsky and Falit 1971: 679]

Other commentators share the assumption expressed here that the young woman's denial of her pregnancy is responsible for the limited physiological changes and the consequent failure of doctors to identify the pregnancy:

> the suggestion that a woman's self-denial may be so strong that she convinces others she is not pregnant remains an interesting feature of these cases. In some cases, this denial was so strong that it was maintained right up until the actual birth of the child. When labour pains begin, several of the women failed to associate such pain with the impending birth. [Wallace 1986: 118]

An alternative explanation, of course, is that the limited physiological changes are factors that enable or facilitate the young woman's denial, even to herself, of an unwanted pregnancy. Consistent with their self-denial of the pregnancy, the women rarely prepared for the birth. Frequently the birth was precipitate and the little pain, if any, that was experienced was incorrectly interpreted as a desire to urinate or defecate. Birth therefore is most frequently given in locations that are close at hand, such as toilets or bedrooms, even in some cases when others were in the house. Bartholomew and Milte (1978) examined in some detail a case of a 16-year-old Australian who worked up to the day of the birth, giving birth to the child in a cubicle in a toilet while at work.

It is uncommon for these women to make elaborate plans to conceal the offence. The baby is most often strangled or suffocated immediately after birth and then put in a bag and placed out of sight and out of mind in a nearby location: under the bed, in the garbage bin, in the dirty clothes basket, in the laundry (as in Alice's case noted above), or wrapped in a blanket in a wardrobe.

Having given birth alone and without assistance, and in the context of their self-denial of the pregnancy, the women are often subsequently confused about the event. For example, Silverman and Kennedy (1988: 125) report a Canadian case in which a 16-year-old who had a child alone was afraid of the consequences of discovery; she strangled or suffocated the infant, but was too confused to remember what she did. The body was left in a garbage bag in a truck full of garbage.

Often in these accounts a sense of confusion is combined with fear:

> I put the baby in my clothing wardrobe. I did that because I was scared, and I didn't know what else to do. … I didn't try to help the baby to live. I don't know if I wanted the baby to die. I was scared. I didn't know what to do. I didn't really want the baby. I don't know what I was going to do with it, the body I mean. [Case No. 88-3128]

In the Australian context, Wallace has observed similarly the vagueness and confusion in the women's understanding of what happened after the birth:

> The denial so tenaciously clung to during pregnancy is no longer tenable when the child is born … A lonely, precipitous [sic] delivery to a young girl would be a terrifying experience. Small wonder that most of these women were very vague about what actually happened at the time of the delivery. Some were disassociated or distant and a couple had no recall as to how the child had died. [Wallace 1986: 118]

While most homicides involve tensions strung at an exceptional level, and while narratives of different scenarios often feature some amount of confusion, there is a quality of confusion and disorientation among these mothers that stands apart from that observed in other forms of homicide. A theme which runs through these accounts is that of difficulties experienced by the pregnant woman in communicating with other family members about the circumstances of sexuality and the pregnancy, as has been noted by others who described the circumstances of one such offender (age 18):

> Mrs A. would usually deal with her anger and dysphoria by avoiding others, adding that her family would not want to discuss her relationships with men or sexuality. Mrs A. stated that her family not only considered abortion sinful but made it clear that alternative

methods of birth control were not open for discussion. [Silva et al. 1998: 1113]

Single young women commit the majority of neonaticides. In some cases, the women are older, and they are in few instances married (Resnick 1970; Alder and Baker 1997). In the present research the seven identified mothers were unmarried: four were teenagers and three were in their twenties. Of the older women, one was a 28-year-old woman who was a recently arrived migrant from a culture in which illegitimate birth could result in stoning to death (Case No. 93-0607). A second woman was a 21-year-old who was engaged to be married, had been told little of contraception, and was intent on planning her forthcoming wedding (Case Nos. 85-2886/7). The third neonaticide by an older woman involved a 29-year-old who lived in a small country town; she was from a deeply religious family, was extensively involved in community and church activities, and had a history of heavy alcohol consumption. She was thoroughly confused about the event, but did comment, 'I didn't know what else to do. I was worried about what the people in the town would have said.' (Case No. AG96-85)

## Neonaticides Where the Circumstances of the Death are Unknown

Of the total of eleven neonaticide deaths, little is known about five (almost half of the eleven neonaticides) other than the discovery of a body of a neonate. Although perhaps not as visible as in nineteenth-century England, in contemporary Western society 'suspicious-looking bundles' are sometimes discovered:

A group of children playing in a laneway in Essendon came across a bundle wrapped up in plastic bags. As they poked and explored the bag with sticks and a wooden garden stake, they broke open the top of the bag, revealing the face and head of a dead infant approximately one day old. Although in the circumstances it was difficult to identify the cause of death, it appeared from the presence of paper stuffed in the mouth and throat that it resulted from 'asphyxia due to upper airways obstruction'. Despite extensive media campaigns, the identity of the infant, and further circumstances surrounding the death, were not forthcoming. [Case No. 88-4188]

Other neonate bodies were found in a plastic bag floating in a dam (Case No. 92-9999), in a sanitary bin (Case No. 90-1432), and buried in the backyard of a home (Case No. 90-2327). Another body was found in the effluent from a sewage farm:

The deceased was located at the Ararat Sewerage Farm. The body of a premature baby (around thirty weeks of development) entered the sewerage farm through the sewerage system. The baby had been born recently, within twenty-four hours of the discovery of the remains. The placenta and cord were still attached. The baby was caught in the grille unit used to stop large objects entering the system. The mother's identity was never established. [Case No. 92-2993]

The finding of 'bodies in sewers' is not an isolated phenomenon unique to Australia. In the United States Piers notes:

A doctoral candidate in the social sciences at one of the large mid-western universities, who was teaching courses in the social sciences to employees of a large city sewer system, learned from these employees that, during the previous year, four corpses of newborns had been found in the sewer screen. The newborns had been thrown directly after birth into the sewers, a preferred place for children's corpses for millennia. No identification or investigation was attempted in these cases of infant death. [Piers 1978: 14]

Modern sewerage and waste disposal systems have expanded considerably the possible locations for the disposal of the bodies of infants. Dumpsters and other public waste disposal systems are often sites for the discovery of these bodies, but they are found across a wide range of locations. In Italy, a recent account indicated that:

Around 13 babies, most of them dead, have been found abandoned in Italy so far this year … As well as those found in bins, the grim call includes one newborn discovered dead in a wardrobe, others buried among garbage in Milan and Rome and another stashed alive in a cardboard box. [*Age*, 3 July 1998, p. 10]

Similar findings are recorded in the United Kingdom and the United States. Rose (1986) begins his analysis of infanticide in England with the following description:

In January 1984 a baby's body was found in a plastic bag, deposited in a litter bin in Sutton, Surrey. In March came news of the discovery of a badly burned body of a new-born baby in a field at Bramford, Ipswich. A few weeks later the mutilated body of a baby was found in a refuse skip on a factory site at Misterton, Doncaster. [Rose 1986: 1]

In the United States, Adelson notes:

In Cleveland ... as in any metropolitan community, the finding of
dead newly-born children in sewers, alleys, incinerators, trash dumps,
streams, lakes, parcel lockers, women's public lavatories and the like is
a frequent occurrence. Rarely is there adequate evidence to point to
or even give a lead to those responsible. [Adelson 1959: 61]

Contemporary life offers a number of possible ways of disposing of the
tragically small bundle that constitutes the body of an infant at its birth.
Such cases, where very little is known about the death, including the
identity of the perpetrator, pose a number of problems for the analyst. In
a strict sense, some of these may not be homicides, since it may not be
knowable if the child was born alive, or if born alive, whether the death
was the result of 'natural causes' or deliberate actions by the unknown
perpetrators. In one of the cases in the present study where the body was
found in a refuse bin, the company responsible for the bin was unable to
provide any details regarding from where the body might have come. In
this case the Coroner observed that:

a person or persons unknown contributed to the death of the
deceased in circumstances where the deceased almost immediately
after her birth was dumped and abandoned and left to die. It does not
necessarily follow that the mother of the deceased contributed
although that is probable. On the evidence, I am unable to establish
what if any involvement she had in the events leading to the death of
the deceased. [Case No. 90-1432]

The obstacles that are presented by these cases for any potential
investigation and identification are overwhelming. Unlike other human
victims, the deceased has not evolved a social identity that creates the
possibility of tracing them. Further, the surrounding family and social
networks that might otherwise have reported a missing body may in
fact be responsible for the death, and thus hardly likely to call on the
authorities about the killing. Despite the fact that so little is known about
the circumstances of the child's death, in this study we elected to consider the finding of these bodies as examples of neonaticides. The death
of the child is not in dispute, and the circumstances are sufficiently
suspicious to warrant their inclusion.

### The Motivations for Neonaticide

Resnick (1970: 1416) concluded from cases of neonaticide in the United
States that 'The stigma of having an illegitimate child is the primary
reason for neonaticide in unmarried women today.' As indicated above,

for some women this stigma is associated with some significant repercussions other than simply social disgrace. One may wonder, from the
point of view of these women, whether much has changed since an
observation quoted by Resnick from an early nineteenth-century writer,
who commented:

> A delicate female, knowing the value of a chaste reputation, and the
> infamy and disgrace attendant upon the loss of that indispensable
> character ... resolves ... rather than encounter the indifference of
> the world, and banishment from society, to sacrifice what on more
> fortunate occasions, it would have been her pride to cherish. [Resnick
> 1970: 1416]

In a context of potential strong negative repercussions for them of
pregnancy, none of these women wanted to be pregnant.

Drawing upon his reading of the research literature, Resnick (1970)
suggests a passive–active dimension to characterise the ways women deal
with the situation of an unwanted birth. At one extreme of this continuum are the women who deny they are pregnant to others and to
themselves, and who make no advance preparations either for the care,
or killing, of the child. At the opposite extreme of the continuum,
Resnick suggests, the offenders appear to be more active in the events
surrounding the killing. For example, historical accounts of infanticide
in England and Australia in previous centuries (Langer 1974; Sauer
1978; Behlmer 1979; Laster 1989) document the deaths of newborn
infants that were carried out relatively deliberately and thoughtfully by
the mother or other closely involved parties.

A classic example is the sixteenth-century 'Parker's case' (described by
Hoffer and Hull 1981: 11), in which a clergyman (George Parker), a
midwife (Jane Saway) and 'the recipient of the clergyman's adulterous
advances' (Helena Millicent) were all convicted of murder and hanged
for having conspired to kill Millicent's child at birth. All three were
convicted, although it was established in the course of the trial that it was
the midwife who did the actual killing.

An inverse relationship has been observed between the availability
of safe and effective contraception, especially abortion techniques, and
such deliberate acts of infanticide, particularly neonaticide (Wallace
1986: 25; Laster 1989: 156; Allen 1990: 38, 98, 110, 164). The killing of
newborn infants has also been a method of purposively eliminating
devalued or unwanted children – those lacking a socially accepted father,
deformed infants, infants possessing an undesirable physical characteristic such as the wrong skin colour or sex, and those conceived by rape
(Jones 1980: 51; Rose 1986; Mendlowicz et al. 1998).

There is little evidence in the present cases of women carefully planning, before the birth, the death of the child and the disposal of the body
and other evidence. It is likely that even today, with a larger collection of
cases and more information about some of the unknown cases, that at
least some of the neonaticides might involve clear intentionality in the
death of the newborn infant. Indeed, in November 1996 national
newspapers in the United States carried a story of the death of a newborn
that was of this form. That case involved two high school teenagers who
killed their newborn baby in an attempt to avoid the scandal that would
result from disclosure of the birth (in July 1998 the two were sentenced
to short terms in prison). However, it is probable that there will be few
such cases of deliberate killing where women have available an array of
birth control techniques and procedures as well as readily available (and
relatively safe) procedures of abortion, all of which can be done well
before a woman faces the trauma of an unanticipated birth as did the
women we have seen in these case narratives.

## Neonaticides and the Law

Historically, in English and Australian law the prosecution of neonaticides has posed a particular set of problems in terms of the nature
of the evidence required. There are now, as there have been in earlier
times, what Walker (1968: 126) refers to as the 'practical difficulties' in
proving murder in cases of neonaticide: the baby might have been still-
born, or the woman, if alone at the birth, might have been so exhausted
by the labour that she was unable to properly tend to the child. In any
legal proceeding taken against a mother who has killed a neonate, a
central issue to be established by the prosecution is that the child was
alive at birth, this being a matter which can quickly become complicated
from either the legal or medical point of view. One issue, for example,
is whether or not the child 'had achieved an existence wholly distinct
from its mother', which must be demonstrated in order for a charge to
proceed (Behlmer 1979: 411).

In most jurisdictions, Australian law requires that a child is considered
to have been born alive if it 'has breathed' and if it has 'been wholly born
into the world' (Bartholomew and Milte 1978: 5). This can lead to a
number of technical issues, especially in terms of establishing, well after
the death of the newborn, if the child has actually breathed. In many of
the present case narratives it would be impossible to determine whether
or not the child had been born alive. Often a long period had elapsed
before the discovery of the body, and by that time the advanced decom-
position made it impossible to find definitive evidence which would
sustain a charge of criminal homicide. The net result of such difficulties

is that during the period of this study (and in sharp contrast to practices in the nineteenth century, see for example, Laster 1989), none of these women in Victoria was prosecuted on a charge of either murder or manslaughter. In fact the only prosecutions noted were in the case of Alice, where she, her mother and brother were charged with 'concealment of a birth'.

## Problems with Estimating the Level of Neonaticide

The present data, in combination with that observed elsewhere, suggests further that a significant, unknown, and unknowable amount of neonaticide goes undiscovered. There is an accidental quality to many of the discoveries of the bodies of neonates, especially in and around the contemporary garbage disposal devices, which raises a question about the number who are disposed of and not discovered. Among the present cases, and in the report of Wallace (1986: 119), are examples of women who have been successful in hiding a previous neonaticide, only to have the earlier death disclosed when a further homicide is discovered. Consequently there is every reason to believe that there is consistent underreporting of the total volume of child homicide. In the Australian national homicide reporting program, for example, there were but two neonaticides reported in the whole of the country in the three-year period 1990–92 (Strang 1994). Given that the present data suggest there was an average of at least three or four in a period of that length for Victoria alone, it seems quite likely that such official data seriously underestimate the level of this form of child killing.

## Conclusion

Whatever the accuracy of the official figures, it is clear that this form of child homicide constitutes a major and significant pattern that requires consideration in any study of lethal violence where children are victims. The National Committee on Violence in Australia (1990) underscored the fact that individuals were at their greatest risk of being victims of homicide in the first year of life, and a major component of these deaths will be neonaticides. A study in England and Wales found that, among infants under the age of 1 year, the greatest period of risk was in the first twenty-four hours of birth (Marks and Kumar 1993: 333). These first hours are dangerous for at least some children, and much more needs to be known about the attendant circumstances.

As a violent offence, the sex distribution of this form of child homicide is distinctive. Neonaticide is definitively an act of women. None of the known offenders in Victoria was a male (although in the case of Alice, noted above, her brother was brought into court along with her mother, charged with the crime of concealing a birth). In the New South Wales study (Wallace 1986: 117), of fifteen neonaticides where charges were laid (out of a total of seventeen known cases), all involved the mother of the child (ten women in all). An investigation in England and Wales reported that, among a somewhat larger group of neonaticides, there were forty-five mothers and only three fathers who were considered as suspects (Marks and Kumar 1993: 333). As Wallace (1986: 117) observed: 'Men are only rarely involved in neonaticide.' In one of the few large studies, Resnick (1970) found that, of 168 total cases, in only two was the father held solely responsible for the neonaticide. Resnick went on to comment: 'Although it is not uncommon for fathers to murder older children, it is rare for a father to kill a newborn infant. Fathers have neither the motive nor the opportunity of mothers' (p. 1417).

The extent of the killing of newborn babies is probably the least knowable of any form of homicide. However, the available evidence suggests that the practice is not as widespread in contemporary Australia as it was in previous periods. The availability of contraception and abortion in any society is likely to decrease the number of such killings.

Nevertheless, in the present study neonaticides constituted a significant proportion (12 per cent) of all child homicides. In all of these cases where details were known, the women were deeply fearful of the repercussions of a pregnancy, so they never acknowledged to themselves that they were pregnant, nor could they come to terms with the fact that they had given birth. The baby was killed immediately after birth, frequently in an effort to stop it from crying, and then placed out of sight and out of mind. While the circumstances of the pregnancy, the birth, and the aftermath of neonaticides suggest that an unusual psychological process took place, the records examined in this research did not indicate that any of the women had a prior history or signs of psychiatric illness, either immediately before, or after, the event.

The observation in other research that this form of child homicide is most often committed by young women has prompted the conclusion that the 'socio-pyschological factor that mediates the event is immaturity' (Silverman and Kennedy 1988: 115). However, in the present study not all of the women were in their teenage years. In general they are women trapped in a web of circumstances whereby they are unable to face the consequences of the unwanted pregnancy. The woman, even to herself, acknowledges neither the pregnancy nor the birth. Unprepared for the birth, the mother kills the newborn infant or it dies from neglect. In general, these scenarios reveal the burden of responsibility for contraception that is borne by women in our society, and the continuing negative consequences for women of unplanned, single parenthood.

# CHAPTER 4

# *Mothers Who Kill Their Children*

More than two-thirds of the women in the present files who killed their children (sixteen of twenty-two) did so when the children had passed beyond the first hours of life. Although wicked stepmothers feature in a variety of folk myths and images (Daly and Wilson 1998), it is striking among this group of women that all were the natural mothers of the children who were killed. It is sometimes assumed in our society that one of the closest social bonds that can be forged is between the natural mother and her child, yet the tragic accounts of child homicide make clear that even within this relationship things can, and do, go horribly wrong. The two most common scenarios in which mothers killed their young children were, first, those in which the child was killed in a complex homicide-suicide event; and second, cases of fatal physical assault where in most instances the child was either battered or shaken to death.

## Maternal Filicide-Suicides

As we move through the various stages of life, and especially in the early adult years, life can impose heavy burdens of responsibility and, at times, pain. For some, these burdens are no longer bearable, and for them suicide becomes a way of seeking relief. But what if you come to that point, and you are a mother? In some circumstances when women finally decide to take their own lives, they also determine that it is in their children's best interests that they be taken with them. Different sentiments can form the basis of this decision. For some mothers the fear is that once they are gone there will not be anyone else able to care adequately for their children. Other mothers may be more pushed by the perceived need to save themselves and their children from the circumstances which they believe are unbearable for both of them.

Most of the mothers in the present investigation who killed their children as part of their own suicide plans expressed some combination or version of these themes in their explanations, often in suicide notes, for their action. Consistent with their view of the world and their rationale for taking their own and their children's lives, the mothers in these incidents most often take the lives of all of their children (in no case was the husband killed). In all these cases, the mother's understandings and feelings regarding her relationship with her children and the nature of her responsibilities for them play a significant part in the unfolding of events.

Mothers who kill themselves and their children are not the unwilling or relatively new young mothers who kill their newborn child or whose children die as a consequence of physical abuse. These mothers are older, ranging in age from 18 years to 35 years, with four of the mothers being in their early thirties. Their children also tend to be older than in the other circumstances in which mothers kill their children: the children were aged between 18 months and 10 years, with an average age of 4 years. For example,

Cindy was aged 24 years when she killed herself and her two children, aged 5 and 2 years. She had earlier been involved in a car accident and had suffered a severe neck injury that resulted in ongoing severe headaches and nausea. The son received severe brain damage in the same accident. Both Cindy and her husband made several trips to the United States to try to treat the son's brain damage: this left them financially drained. Cindy complained of insufficient help from her husband in handling the son. Over the years she had been admitted to psychiatric hospitals three times and had previously attempted suicide twice. Her husband had left her and moved in with another woman. Her Greek parents blamed her for her marriage break-up. Cindy felt that she had no one to talk to and ultimately would not go to psychiatrists or psychologists for further help, for fear of further hospitalisation and separation from her children. On the previous night she had talked to the babysitter about suicide and said that she loved her kids too much to leave them behind. In a suicide note to her parents she said, 'I don't feel I am murdering my children but saving them from sorrow and pain without their father … it's the only way out … all I ever wanted was a happy marriage with happy, healthy children … I have tried very hard … I can't leave my children behind. At least with God there will be peace and happiness and no pain, so I will take them where they will be happy, and I will be there to take care of them.' [Case Nos. 85-2886/7]

The terms 'altruism' or 'misguided altruism' have been used to describe the motivation in cases such as this, in which the mother expresses a belief that the children are 'better off dead' (d'Orban 1979; Resnick 1969, 1970; Wallace 1986; Wilczynski, 1997). Resnick (1970: 1414) found that altruism was possibly the most common motive for maternal filicide.

In most of these narratives there appears to be a mixture of overlapping concerns. The mother finds her life so unbearable that she cannot go on living and cannot bear to leave her children behind, believing that no one could look after them as well. At the same time there is indication in some cases that the mother is concerned about the well-being of the child specifically and that these concerns form part of her own unhappiness.

> Kimiko Kato arrived in Australia from Japan to join her husband who had arrived a year earlier to take up a consultant position with a computer company in Melbourne. Apparently she became homesick for her family and friends in Tokyo and was concerned about her son being able to assimilate into the Australian way of life. She was depressed and had earlier threatened to take her life. At the inquest the Coroner noted, 'It appears that suicide was seen as the only solution for her, because she believed that to return home would be seen as failure in the eyes of her friends and relatives'. She drove her car off the end of a pier with herself and son inside; both died. [Case No. 92-3425]

Another mother's concerns included a fear that the father was assaulting the child.

> Tina Tsekouras (35 years) was upset about her de facto Marco having an affair while he was in Greece. A friend said Tina spoke about it previously and was considering committing suicide: 'She had never got over the fact that Marco had the affair … When Tina accidentally found out about Marco's affair she was "shattered", it ruined her trust and affected her confidence.'
>
> When Tina and Marco separated, Tina was advised that she would not have sole custody of her daughter Brook (3 years). Tina wanted to keep Marco away from them, as she was concerned that Marco might be assaulting Brook. Friends said 'She could not bear the thought of Brook being with Marco because she could not trust him.'
>
> Tina was also having problems at work. She talked of committing suicide on several different occasions, commenting that she could always end it and take Brook with her if things became too bad.

Tina drove with Brook to a coastal car park and ran a vacuum hose from an exhaust pipe into the car and started the engine. They were both found dead in the rear seat of the vehicle, the child secured in a child's seat restraint. [Case No. 88-3345]

Cultural conflict and isolation were more often a feature of the lives of these women than of the other women in the study. Three of the six women were born outside of Australia and another woman's parents were Greek. In two of these cases, conflicts with the spouse involved the wife's unhappiness as a consequence of her husband's infidelity while on a visit to their home country (Case Nos. 88-0016/27, 88-3345): in one of these cases the spouse returned bringing his new partner with him to the family home (Case Nos. 88-0016/27). Social isolation as a consequence of ethnicity is apparent in the Kato case above. Having arrived in Australia from Japan almost a year before the murder-suicide, the mother was unsettled, still somewhat unconnected to the Australian community, worried about her son's assimilation into Australian culture, and unable to speak with others in the Japanese community about her difficulties (Case No. 92-3425).

Problems in their relationship with their male partner or spouse are significant factors in the circumstances of these women. Physical violence against the women by their male partner was reported frequently in these filicide-suicide cases (four of the six cases).

Rosa Murphy (18 years) was living with her de facto, who was exceptionally violent towards her. The violence in the relationship was one of the factors that contributed to Rosa losing custody of her daughter (2 years). After expressing concern that she was unlikely to regain custody of her daughter, given her circumstances, including the violence in her relationship with her spouse, Rosa threw her daughter and then herself from the balcony of a high-rise block of public housing flats. [Case No. 87-3206]

Separation from their spouse, who was in most cases also the biological father of the child, was a significant feature of the context at the time when some women killed their children. In one case the mother had left her husband (Case Nos. 88-0016/0027), while in the other two cases the woman's current spouse had recently left her (Case No. 93-2465, and Case Nos. 85-2886/2887).

The marriage of Sita Goswami (31 years) was 'stormy', with violence by both spouses. Her husband is reported to have married another woman while overseas and brought her back to live with the family in

Australia, but Sita chased her from the house. After another fight in December, Sita took her two children (aged 7 years and 18 months) and left her husband to live in another apartment. In January she returned to the family home, and after another fight with her husband, Sita killed herself and the children by pouring kerosene over them and setting it alight. [Case Nos. 88-0016/27]

Sita's husband suggested that she might have killed the children to hurt him by ensuring that he could not have them. Retaliation homicide has been identified as a distinctive form of child homicide in other research (Ewing 1997; McKee and Shea 1998; Wilczynski 1997). Ewing (1997: 99) notes that the Greek myth of the Medea (in which a mother kills her two sons as a means of hurting her unfaithful husband) is often used as an example of this form of child homicide. In contemporary times, in some cultures such as in Hong Kong (personal communication R. Broadhurst, 4 September 2000), similar scenarios feature quite prominently in child homicides. Such a scenario is graphically portrayed in contemporary literature in Amy Tan's *Joy Luck Club*. However, as will be seen in the next chapter, expressed motivation of this form arises more often in accounts of paternal filicide. While mothers other than Sita were distressed as the result of their husband's relationship with another woman, none of the other women in this research indicated that the killing of the children was a means of retaliating against the child's father.

Separation from their spouse and the father of their children had both emotional and financial implications for the women. Coping alone with the distress of the factors leading up to the separation itself, the women also faced a range of other difficult and pressing circumstances. In one of these narratives (Case No. 87-3206), the mother's doctor noted that 'She felt trapped by her life circumstances and her only escape was to take her life.' The words of the Coroner in regard to this case captured the nature of the lives of many of the women who committed murder-suicide when he noted the 'violence, hopelessness and despair' that appeared to run through this case study.

While it is probable that the break-up of their relationship with their spouse would result in financial insecurity, in general this was not a focus of the women's expressed concerns. Unlike several of the women who killed their children in fatal assaults (discussed in the next section), these women were not dependent upon government social service benefits or otherwise living on the economic margins.

One of these narratives differs from the others in that, although it was a serious attempt, the suicide was not successful. Despite this difference, the case captures the complexity of the mixture of the women's emotions and their explanations for these events, which blend their own loneliness and unhappiness with their despair about the future of both themselves and their children.

Joanne Gunsten (33 years) attempted suicide by slashing her wrists with a knife. When police arrived, she was lying on the floor in the bedroom, and they initially believed she was dead. She then resisted medical aid, saying, 'I don't want to live, I want to die. What have I got to live for?' Joanne was divorced from the father of her three children, who had physically abused her. She had been living in a 'stormy' de facto relationship, but her partner had very recently left her. Joanne did not believe that she would be able to support the children, financially or otherwise, by herself. She strangled her son (10 years) to death and had attempted to kill her other two children, before attempting to kill herself.

Mrs Gunsten reported suffering depression, insomnia, poor appetite and poor concentration. She said she had not been coping and did not want to be a single mother. 'I can't provide for the children on my own, I resent people telling me that I can, I told them that I did not want to look after the kids.' She believed the children would be better off dead: 'They have nothing to live for with people walking out of their lives.'

Joanne said, 'See, my major dilemma through all this is – is that – is that I want to die. If I died my children would be left on their own.' … 'I wanted to die and I wanted to take the three children with me.' Asked her reasons for attempting to kill the children, she replied, 'There's no way in the world I could have provided for those children physically, mentally, emotionally and financially on my own, yet everybody told me I could and I know I don't have the capacity.' In relation to her feelings for her children, Joanne said, 'I love them very, very dearly and I – I – I just couldn't provide for them.' [Case No. 93-2465]

Such expressions indicate that these were mothers who in their view loved and cared for their children. In most cases there is no evidence of previous systematic abuse of the children. There were two exceptions: Sita (see above, Case Nos. 88-0016/27) was reported to have a violent temper and to sometimes take this out on her husband and children; and Cindy (Case Nos. 85-2886/7) reported hitting her children and had sought assistance from a health clinic to prevent her from causing further harm to them.

In some cases the mother's efforts to 'care' for the children are reflected in the planning and preparations to ensure that she is successful in her efforts to take both her own and her children's lives, and in the detailed instructions stipulated in suicide letters regarding burial. For example:

> Cindy wrote numerous letters to other people. She also left instructions regarding details for their funerals, expressing the wish that they be buried in white coffins, with [her son] placed to her left and [her daughter] to her right. She had bought new suits for the burial. These were placed on the couch ready for the undertaker. [Case Nos. 85-2886/7]

These may be emotional events, but they are not irrational in their execution. They are most often planned and prepared for in advance. In keeping with the mothers' expressed care for their children, the events are most often organised in ways to ensure the success of the action and with minimal direct violence.

These were women whose lives were not easy: violent spouses, financial difficulties, separation from spouses, a handicapped child, fears of the spouse sexually assaulting the child, and fears of the loss of custody of the child. The difficulty these women were having coping with their lives is indicated by four of the six having previously attempted suicide and a fifth who had threatened suicide. Four of the women had also consulted a psychiatrist: one woman had been hospitalised on three occasions (Case Nos. 85-2886/7). One mother was at the time a client of a psychiatric assessment and community treatment program, who had visited her the previous Saturday night. The caseworker reported that 'the case progress was good up until then and I was confident that Joanne had overcome her homicidal/suicidal tendencies' (Case No. 93-2465).

Overall, these cases involved women, most often over 30 years of age with two or more young children, who felt they could no longer cope with their difficult circumstances and so took their own and their children's lives. They often expressed the view that their actions were in the best interests of the children: 'I wanted them to be at peace.' These were women who had been deserted by their male partner, and the father of their children. Feeling alone in the world, they planned a desperate act, having decided that it was the only option left for them to bring peace and happiness to themselves and their children. In these cases we see the dark side of the burden of 'motherhood' as it is socially and culturally constructed. In particular these are women who believed that only a mother could properly care for her children, and that as the mother they were ultimately responsible for the well-being of their children.

## Fatal Assault

One form of child killing which has received considerable media coverage and provoked public outcry in recent years in Victoria occurs when a young child dies as the result of a physical beating by the parent or carer. In most such homicides the perpetrator is the male step-parent or guardian. Of the nineteen parents and carers in this research identified as the perpetrators of child assault homicides, fourteen were male. In two cases the perpetrator could not be identified (see Chapter 2). Nevertheless, some children are killed as a result of physical assault by their mothers. This is not surprising when considered in the context of estimations that '70% of physical assaults against children are perpetrated by women' (Dougherty 1993: 92). Silverman and Kennedy (1993: 180) identified this form of filicide as one of two main patterns of maternal filicide, describing it as 'child abuse gone awry'. In the present study, five mothers killed their child in this way. In two of these cases the male partner was also implicated in the child's death.

The filicides of this form in which the mother alone was found to be the perpetrator present three different scenarios. The first case is consistent with a pattern identified in other research, in which a young, inexperienced woman kills her first child in its first year of life.

The pregnancy of Jane Evatt (19 years) had not been medically identified until forty-eight hours before she gave birth. She went into sudden labour after she discovered she was pregnant. Laurie was born prematurely and was kept in hospital for six weeks. He had only been home for ten days when he was killed. Jane gave different explanations for Laurie's injuries, claiming that he had fallen off a bed, and later that he had accidentally bumped into a coffee table. However, the Coroner found that the injuries sustained by Laurie would have required the application of considerable force, and it was unlikely they were the result of accidental mismanagement. Although Jane admitted that she had been treating Laurie roughly, the Coroner noted that there were few signs that he had been abused or roughly handled prior to the events that led to his death. Jane explained that she was angry and upset that she had been left alone, and expressed concern that her de facto husband might not be returning. A psychiatric report noted the lack of ante-natal care and concluded: '[Laurie's] death resulted from an attack by a mother who was deeply depressed as a result of the child's birth, severely lacking in coping strategies, totally unprepared for a mothering role and totally unable to tolerate a crying infant, since his crying stimulated awareness of her own intense distress. ... Her attempts to stop him crying probably led to his death.' [Case No. 89-3804]

This case is typical of such cases, in that the women were generally living in de facto relationships of relatively short duration. In virtually all narratives, the mother kills the child when it fails to respond to her efforts to stop its crying, or to obey some other of her demands. Although there is little evidence of extensive prior abuse of the child in this case (perhaps because it was so young), most such cases entail a prior history of physical abuse of the child:

> Marjorie Casa (26 years) was Romanian and spoke little English. She was extremely isolated: her family had remained in Romania. She had five children ranging from 9 months to 9 years old. Her husband worked full-time, and neither he nor his family helped with the children. Complaints by her neighbours about the children crying caused Marjorie much distress. Both parents described the baby as 'nervous', 'irritable', and 'always crying'. Marjorie was ex-tremely frustrated and had little sleep due to her baby's incessant crying.
>   On the evening of the death of Myrna Casa (9 months), the baby was vomiting as her mother was attempting to feed her, the 2-year-old was also crying to be fed and changed, and the other three children's behaviour was such that Marjorie had sent them to their rooms. Des-pite 'all sorts' of calming methods the baby did not stop crying.
>   Doctors believe that Myrna was struck with a heavy, flat object. Marjorie tried to revive her baby and sought help from a neighbour who rang an ambulance. Myrna died from a fractured skull, sub-dural haemorrhage and brain damage. Although, according to her husband, Marjorie had treated all of the children well, the autopsy revealed fractures and trauma that were estimated to have occurred months before. [Case No. 86-2754]

Jane Evatt was inexperienced, but Marjorie Casa was an older mother with more experience in child raising; nevertheless she was exhausted and frustrated having to cope with a number of young children with little assistance and in economically stretched circumstances. As is more often the situation in fatal assault cases involving the male guardian, others did not know of the prior abuse of this child victim until the autopsy revealed earlier injuries.

A third case is different again, in that both the mother and the daughter she kills are somewhat older than in the previous cases, and both the mother and her male de facto are intellectually disabled. In this case there was evidence that the prior physical abuse had been observed by, or was suspected by, others.

> Raelene (33 years) and her daughter, Andrea (4 years), were living with Ken. Both Ken and Raelene were intellectually disabled. Raelene's partner in a previous relationship noted that she was strict with his children and would go 'over the top' in her disciplining of them: he left Raelene because he was 'fed up' with the yelling and hitting. A social worker with the Intellectual Disability Service, who had been assisting Raelene with her parenting, noted that she 'did try really hard to be a good mother'. However, 'under stress, [Raelene] loses the ability to cope'.
>
> Concerned about injuries to Andrea, the social worker notified Children's Protective Services, who subsequently visited the family. Andrea implicated Ken as the cause of her bruising. Ken subsequently left: Raelene blamed Andrea and was very angry with her. Ken and Raelene continued to see each other. From March 1994 until five days before Andrea's death, Protective Services regularly visited the family. At that point it was decided that the risk of harm was reduced.
>
> There are different versions about what happened on the morning of Andrea's death, but from Raelene's accounts she was apparently upset that Andrea had wet her bed and so she shook her: 'I shook her far too hard.' Then she claims that Andrea fell backwards, hitting her bottom and head. She then put Andrea to bed and went to the shop, leaving the children with Ken. When she returned, they checked Andrea who was like a 'limp rag', so they called an ambulance. [Case No. 94-1581]

In both this case and two others (95-1263 and 87-5430) described below, the prior abuse of the child was known to child protection or health authorities, or the consequent injuries to the child had been noted and commented on by friends or relatives. Other studies have similarly noted that it is not uncommon for government agencies and services to be aware of such cases before the child is killed (see also Cheung 1986; d'Orban 1979; Oberman 1996; Wilczynski 1997). In the United States, one study found that 46 per cent of fatalities from abuse or neglect had been (or were at the time of the death) under investigation by child protection agencies (Ewing 1997: 95). The involvement of child protection and health agencies in these cases is consistent with the economic circumstances of these women, who tended to be in economically deprived situations relative to other women in the research. There are many distressing components in these stories, not least of which is the ultimate futility of the mothers' efforts to seek help.

Perhaps not unexpectedly, women who kill their children as part of a pattern of physical assault are frequently reported also to be physically violent with other children. In the narrative above, Raelene was reported to be violent towards her previous de facto's children (Case No. 94-1581). In the following two cases, the women were also physically violent towards their other children.

The death of Bree (8 months) was initially treated as a case of sudden infant death syndrome. However, the autopsy revealed extensive recent head injuries (no older than twenty-four hours) resulting from at least two, and possibly seven, severe blows to the skull. There were also a number of older injuries (including a broken rib three to four weeks old), as well as signs of neglect. A homicide investigation was therefore undertaken. Bree's mother, Marie, and her de facto, Don, acknowledged amphetamine use. Marie's ex-husband, Bree's father, said 'As a mother, I would say that Marie didn't really care too much. If Lisa [Bree's sister] misbehaved at all, Marie would just lash out and hit her. She wouldn't care where she hit her or how hard she hit her.' He also claimed that he saw Marie shake Bree for crying and say 'Shut up you little bastard' before throwing her onto the bed. Don was reported by his previous wife as being 'the best father that my children could hope to have'.

On the night before Bree's death, Marie noticed that she had a stiff neck and a spongy lump on her head. Don wanted to take the baby to hospital immediately but Marie suggested they wait until the next morning. Marie admits she was 'stoned' that night. The Coroner was unable to determine exactly what circumstances led to Bree's death. He observed that only two people, Marie and Don, had the opportunity to inflict the head injuries, and that both were negligent in not taking Bree to a hospital for medical treatment. He concluded that both contributed to the cause of death. [Case No. 87-5430]

In a similar case, both the mother and her de facto husband, who was not the father of the child, were again found to have contributed to the child's death.

At the time of his death Sean (19 months) and his two brothers (4 years, 10 months) were living with their mother Rhonda (30 years) and her de facto, Len, in a public housing flat. Sean was the fifth of Rhonda's seven sons. It was alleged that Rhonda and Len were responsible for the severe head injuries that resulted in Sean's death. On arrival at the hospital, Sean was found to have face, head, back and chest injuries of various ages. Both adults admitted previously hitting Sean.

Rhonda was noted as having a low level of intellectual functioning and had herself been raised in unstable family circumstances, the victim of long-term physical and sexual violence.

According to a doctor, who had referred her to a psychiatrist and not the child welfare agency, she had previously tried to suffocate her youngest child. Two of Rhonda's previous de facto husbands and her husband, from whom she was separated, claimed Rhonda was violent towards her children. For example, claims were made that she held her son by the neck under the water in the bath; 'shoved the food down his mouth, making him choke and making him cry'; held a pillow over a baby's face; and threw pieces of cutlery at her son. Two of her former partners said they had left her because of her treatment of the children. Her former mother-in-law said that Rhonda had repeatedly claimed that she couldn't cope with the children. At the time of Sean's death, a medical examination found that his 10-month-old brother had suffered a fractured rib and possibly a fractured wrist a few weeks previously. In the past, two children had been placed in the custody of their grandmother and another had been adopted following a child welfare investigation instigated when he was taken to hospital with a broken leg.

Four days before his death, friends had noticed bruising on Sean: Rhonda asked if they could look after him for a while, but they refused. The next day Rhonda wrote to Sean's father asking him to take Sean because he was being 'a major problem'.

The accounts by Rhonda and Len of the events leading to Sean's death vary. Both reported that the child was 'fitting' (Rhonda), or 'went funny and was shaking' after having been bathed by Len. Len reported that he hit Sean and he fell back and hit his head on the floor. Rhonda says she shook Sean when he was 'fitting' and put him back into his cot. They discussed calling a doctor, but Rhonda was worried that they would get 'caught for child abuse'; they nevertheless called a doctor. Both Rhonda and Len were charged by the police with murder, but only Rhonda was brought to trial. [Case No. 95-1263]

The trials related to this case captured the attention of the media, and people tried to understand how such an event could occur. Rhonda's own childhood was a tragic story, including extensive physical and sexual abuse. Both Rhonda, and Marie in the previous account, could be depicted as extremely disadvantaged and perhaps 'damaged' women. Certainly their stories, on the one hand, elicited public sympathy. On the other hand, these women used violence as a means of coping with their situation; these were violent women, and their violence was directed towards their children over long periods.

## Extreme Psychiatric Disturbance

A mother killing her child is so inconsistent with our modern understandings of motherhood, that we might want to believe that she has to be 'mad'. However, other research findings indicate that most mothers who kill their children have not been diagnosed with a psychiatric illness. For example, a study of eighty-nine women charged with infanticide found that no more than twenty-four were mentally ill (d'Orban 1979), and another found that only four of a sample of forty-six maternal infanticide cases involved women who had been medically diagnosed with chronic mental disabilities.

Despite evidence that there is no clear relationship between mental disorder and criminal behaviour (Monahan and Steadman 1982), violence and mental illness are often conflated in popular media presentations. However Mouzos (1999: 4) found in her analysis of Australian homicides during a nine-year period that 'the overall prevalence of mental disorder amongst homicide offenders appears to be significantly less than that in the general population'.

In the present research, just over half of the women whose stories were discussed as filicide-suicides had consulted a psychiatrist, including one woman who had been hospitalised on three occasions for her psychiatric illness. More of the women in this study had been treated for psychiatric illness than the men. This is consistent with the finding by Mouzos (1994: 4) in her study of homicide more generally in Australia that 'a greater proportion of mentally disordered offenders were women'. However, in interpreting these observations, we need to recognise the contentious issue of the definition of mental illness and the influence of the client's sex on ascriptions of mental disorder (Chesler 1974). Given the tendency of the medical profession and the women themselves to understand their difficulties in personal pathological terms, to seek to understand these events solely in terms of the mother's illness would be to deny other significant aspects of her life circumstances.

At the same time there were some women whose actions appeared to be more directly a consequence of their illness. Noting that defining mental disorder is a contentious issue, Mouzos (1999) draws upon the National Mental Health Strategy to distinguish two main categories of mental disorder: psychotic and non-psychotic. Mouzos notes, 'People experiencing an acute stage of a psychotic illness ... lose touch with reality. Their ability to make sense of thoughts, feelings and external information is seriously affected. They may develop delusions or experience hallucinations. They may be depressed or elated out of all proportion to their life circumstances' (p. 2). It is difficult, given the data at hand in the present case narratives, to establish whether or not a person is psychotic. However, the situation of three of the women was distinguishable along these lines from the other women in the study. These women killed while they were in a state of extreme psychological disturbance in which they were 'hearing voices' or believed that other 'forces' directed them to kill their child.

These scenarios had much in common with the murder-suicides. In fact, two of these women claimed they had made futile attempts to commit suicide at the time they killed their daughters. Pam Clarence said she tried to drown herself in the bath with her daughter: 'I tried very hard to drown but it doesn't work' (Case No. 94-1163). Sheila Keith 'indicated that she tried to kill herself after killing her child by poking the knife into herself, but she indicated that it would not go in' (Psychiatrist's report, Case No. 91-0863). However, while their own death was a central aspect of the women's explanations in the murder-suicides, in these three cases the women were also delusional and their explanations for their behaviour centred on references to higher forces or other beings.

Joan Peters (34 years) began to display symptoms of paranoia, believing that the family home was bugged and the intimate details of their lives were being broadcast, a couple of years before she killed her only daughter. During that period she attempted to commit suicide with her daughter (4 years) by jumping off the top of a shopping centre roof with Kim in her arms. Joan suffered serious injuries, requiring hospitalisation for five months, and Kim suffered a leg injury. Following this incident, Joan was diagnosed by a psychiatrist as suffering from a schizophrenic illness and was placed in a psychiatric hospital for two months.

Joan's husband stopped work to watch over her at home. However, he states that their relationship disintegrated and they lost all communication, and notes that Joan's behaviour was 'strange', and she seemed to feel that everyone was 'against her and wanted her out of the way'. Her husband gave evidence that, about three weeks prior to the murder, he noticed his wife was deteriorating, but was afraid to confront her with this in case it 'sent her off'. Joan had ceased her medication two months earlier without her doctor's permission.

Concerned that his wife and daughter had failed to attend a pre-arranged birthday party, Joan's husband returned home. On entering the kitchen he saw Joan kneeling over their daughter's body and pulling her by the hair. She looked up at him and shouted, 'I am the God incarnate. I have cleansed the demons.' When he tried to get her away, she said, 'I am the God, I haven't killed her, look at your daughter.' When the police arrived, Joan had to be physically subdued. Despite police efforts, she would not let go of her daughter's hair, and eventually the hair had to be cut away to release her grasp.

Joan stated in a police interview that a voice from God had told her to exorcise her daughter: 'The voice took over. It kept roaring and roaring and the stuff all over me.' She said 'it just told me what to do' and it said, 'I am the Lord your God, you must kill your daughter'. She went on, 'it was the look of her eyes': she saw 'evil' in her daughter's eyes. According to the psychiatrist in charge of Joan's treatment, she was suffering acute schizophrenia at the time of her admission, and although aware that she had killed her daughter, was unaware that this was wrong. [Case No. 88-4727]

Most often these women had histories of psychiatric illness with previous psychiatric treatment and hospitalisation over extended periods. Other 'forces' directed their actions. At the same time, like the women who committed suicide, their explanations also indicated that they believed that the act was in the best interest of the child.

Sheila Keith (40 years) came to Australia from South Africa with her husband. Her husband reported that in the four years before she stabbed her 5-year-old daughter to death with a kitchen knife, she had been displaying behavioural problems, was depressed and aggressive. As a result she had been treated over a period of time at a psychiatric centre and had been placed in a psychiatric hospital on two occasions.

In police interviews, Sheila indicated that she killed her daughter as part of a suicide pact and thought her husband was killing himself as well. She intended to kill herself also. Believing the world was going to end and that everybody would die, she killed her daughter first to save her the pain at the end of the world. She explained her behaviour as – 'Really it was some force that was forcing me to do it. I – I didn't do it intentionally, please.' Sheila said, 'I feel good that she's gone. She is better off where she is. I'm not upset, I feel okay, she's much better off now.' [Case No. 91-0863]

Not surprisingly, these disturbed mothers showed signs of having trouble in their parenting relationships. One mother was reported to have been aggressive and violent towards her other two children, and the 'erratic' behaviour of another mother had contributed to her losing custody of her daughter. However, other people or the women themselves maintained that the child they killed was special to them, that they were especially bonded to the child. Sheila's husband claimed that, although she could show a great deal of aggression toward the two older children when she was ill, 'It was strange, however, that she never showed any ill will at all toward [Anne]. [Anne] was her favourite' (Case No. 91-0863). A similar theme can be found in the following narrative:

Pam Clarence was wet when police spoke to her at her house the morning after she had drowned her 6-year-old daughter in the bath-tub. She claimed that a shadow had told her to get in the bath with her daughter. 'The shadow took my hand and put it on [Sophie] and told me to get in as well. It was painful, God it hurt.' She repeatedly spoke of black shadows and how she had been 'in the bath since last night fighting the spirits'. In a letter to another daughter about the event, Pam said she and Sophie were 'bonded', while others had 'rejected' her. In a police interview, she said, 'I would never have hurt [Sophie], never, never, never. I loved her too much ... I knew I was dying and wanted her to come with me ... I just wanted her to be with me and she wanted to be with me.' [Case No. 94-1163]

Whereas women who commit murder-suicide tend to take all of their children with them, these women tended to take the life of the child to whom they felt closest, most often the youngest. There was more often some form of direct violence in these homicides not found in the maternal filicide-suicides: one mother drowned her child in a bathtub; another stabbed her daughter to death, and the third child died as the result of beating.

As with the maternal filicide-suicide cases, two of these women – still living with the husband who was the father of their child – claimed that their husbands were abusive or violent towards them: the claim was denied by the husbands and, according to the women, ignored by the police. In the year before the offence, one mother reported to the police that her husband was abusing her. The police believed she was unwell and that these were paranoid delusions.

Sheila Keith gave evidence to the police and to a psychiatrist that her husband was violent and aggressive to herself and the children when he was drunk, including sexually assaulting her with considerable violence. She told the psychiatrist she had gone to the police about her husband's violence, but they would not assist her. In a police interview, asked whether hers was a happy family, she replied, 'Never happy family from the start, never, never happy, had it hard, really hard.' Her husband on the other hand gave evidence that she was aggressive and somewhat violent towards the two older children and him when she did not take her medication. He maintained that the marriage was a happy and normal one at first, but then his wife became aggressive toward him and this culminated in her receiving psychiatric treatment. [Case No. 91-0863]

Both of these women had also sought help and treatment from psychiatrists in recent years. Pam Clarence (Case No. 94-1163) was reported by her husband, from whom she was separated, to be a 'very heavy drinker'; she had also been to a psychiatrist and the police in the past to seek help for her problems. At the time she killed her daughter, she was concerned about custody of her daughter, her finances, and where she was going to live. She wrote in letters to her other daughter that she did not know where they were going to sleep, she had no money and felt 'rejected': 'I sang out for help so many times and the only help I got was police coming through my house at 11 p.m. at night.' In a police interview, she said, 'Not one person offered any help. Even when we were haunted in that house every night.'

Overall, these women were older, in their mid-thirties to early forties, and generally had a history of psychiatric illness. In the midst of their illness they believed that they were compelled by external forces to take the life of one of their children. Like the women who committed murder-suicide, these women believed that their actions were in the best interests of a child to whom they believed they were particularly bonded.

### Distinctive Cases

Up to this point, it has been possible to group the cases of maternal filicide in such a way that their shared features contribute to an under-standing of the circumstances that resulted in the death. One of the persistent puzzles imposed by a large set of empirical data is deciding how to handle cases that do not fit into any of the common patterns. In the present research there are two such cases, which nevertheless raise important issues for consideration. The first is the only one in this study in which postnatal depression was posited explicitly as a significant factor in the homicide. It is also one of two cases in this research in which the child's death was initially classified as resulting from sudden infant death syndrome (SIDS) .

Sheree Slater was reported as having had 'a chaotic family background with deprivation and violence'. Reported to be of 'extremely low intelligence', she had left school by age 15. By the time she was 20 years of age, she had given birth to three children in less than twenty-seven months. Sheree is reported to have coped well as a mother until the birth of her third child, after which her behaviour was described as irrational and she was diagnosed as suffering postnatal depression.

Her husband then left her for a short time. In a seriously depressed state and after having inflicted injuries to her face with a knife, she was admitted to hospital and the children were fostered. On her release, her husband returned and she was coping reasonably well until her youngest son had convulsions and was diagnosed as having diabetes. Sheree found the procedure of extracting blood from her son for testing very stressful. She was observed by police acting irrationally during this time. Sheree suffocated her son (8 months) soon after, although at the time the death was diagnosed as a case of SIDS. Sheree later indicated she had been finding it difficult to look after three children, was concerned about her son's health, and was upset about injecting him.

Within a couple of weeks of her son's death, Sheree took an overdose of sleeping pills and was admitted to a psychiatric centre. Within a fortnight, her second child was admitted to hospital with symptoms similar to those of the dead boy. One week later, Sheree suffocated her daughter. Her explanations are unclear, but she expressed concern that her daughter would suffer as her son had. Some resentment towards her husband is indicated by her comments regarding her husband finding their dead daughter: 'Now he knows what I went through with Matthew.' Psychiatric reports indicated that she was 'seriously psychiatrically disturbed' at the time of the two deaths. [Case Nos. 89-2009/1676]

It is evident that Sheree, like many other mothers, was depressed after the birth of her third child. More contentious is the degree to which the killing of her children can be accounted for by reference to an illness, 'postnatal depression'. While childbirth may be a precipitating factor, increasingly it is being recognised that, rather than hormonal changes or other physiological factors, the mother's circumstances are significant for understanding this phenomenon. Sheree Slater's situation is a classic example of the sort of environmental circumstances that are considered relevant to postnatal depression: the stress of coping with a difficult or unwanted baby; lack of financial and personal support; and anxiety about being able to cope with the child-rearing (Baker 1991: 22).

A second distinctive case in this research is also unusual in terms of the forms of child homicide identified in other research. The case involves the death of a child as a consequence of her parents' well-intentioned but misguided actions.

Cassandra Everet (3 years) had a series of colds. As treatment her parents put her on a fast for twenty-seven days. Cassandra died of terminal pneumonia and malnutrition. The mother (26 years) and father (24 years), both trained nurses, were committed to a version of naturopathy which the father had largely taught himself. Both their children were considered well cared for, apart from concerns expressed about their diets, which left them anaemic and under-weight. The mother maintained, 'we didn't believe there was a risk, and we certainly wouldn't have done it if we thought there was any risk to her life.' [Case No. 85-1464]

This case shows that the actions of loving and caring parents can result in the death of their children. Thus, while the child in this account was essentially starved to death, it would be a mistake simply to consider this as a case of 'neglect', since clearly the child was in general far from neglected. Some parents have other than conventional notions of health care and medical treatment, and although in general there may be a view that such parents are eccentric or misguided, the concerns sharpen when the practices lead to life-threatening actions. The contemporary state may intervene if it becomes aware that the child's life is actually at great risk, as in cases where parents for religious reasons will not permit standard life-saving treatments by conventional medicine. In the case of Cassandra, the level of risk unfortunately did not become apparent soon enough, either to the parents or the authorities.

## Conclusion

The diversity and complexity evident in these cases of maternal filicide suggest that present conceptualisations and understandings are inade-quate. The conclusion of Silverman and Kennedy (1988: 123) seems particularly apt in regard to these findings: 'Female perpetrated homi-cide is not a monolithic act that can be easily explained by one frame-work.' At the same time, in all the diverse scenarios in the present research, all of the women were the biological mothers of the children they killed. As we shall see in the next chapter, this is quite different to the child homicides committed by men in the family context.

In part, the diversity in the nature of maternal filicides revealed in this research is a consequence of the data source, which included women who committed suicide. These women would not be included in studies using prison or arrest data. Therefore it is not surprising that, while these women made up a significant proportion of the cases in this study, their stories have not been the subject of as much attention as neonaticides and cases such as those discussed in this chapter as fatal assaults. For example, Silverman and Kennedy identify two main forms of maternal filicides: infanticides in which the 'socio-psychological factor that medi-ates the event is immaturity' (1988: 115), and non-infanticides that are

essentially 'child abuse gone awry' (1993: 180). The murder-suicides
identified in this study fit neither of these categories. The cases are
not consistent with the infanticides defined by Silverman and Kennedy
(the children were generally older than 12 months of age), and the
mothers were generally older, and therefore more mature, than the
other mothers in this study. Neither were the cases of murder-suicide
consistent with the second category offered by Silverman and Kennedy.
These mothers were generally not known to have previously abused their
children; rather, these mothers most often killed their children out of
a deep sense of caring, bonding, and personal responsibility for their
well-being.

Acts of violence by women tend to be described and understood as
highly emotional events. Although the present narratives provide some
support for such a view, this does not mean that women's violence is
necessarily the result of a sudden loss of control. The mothers generally
explain their fatal assaults as sudden eruptions in the face of the frustration of a crying child. However, they express concern also about what
the neighbours will think, about the child disturbing their neighbours or
their de facto husband, about their sheer frustration in light of their
overall circumstances. Usually the fatal assault is not the first assault on
the child, so the event cannot be understood and explained solely in
terms of the emotions of the single event.

In contrast, in the filicide-suicides the mothers tend to carefully plan
and orchestrate the event. These are mothers who are reported to be
particularly devoted and caring. The final moment might be a highly
emotional event, but the preparation is, from the mother's point of view,
quite rational. From their standpoint, they are taking the only action that
is left to them to assure the happiness of their children. Suicide appears
to be the focal point in these events, with the mother deciding that
neither she nor her children can deal with their present circumstances.
A fundamental assumption made by these mothers is that their children
will not be sufficiently well cared for without their mother.

While the children killed by their mothers in fatal assaults tend to be
under 2 years of age, the children whose mother takes their lives along
with her own tend to be older, averaging closer to 10 years of age. These
mothers most often have been living in a 'family' situation for some
years with the children's father when either the marriage breaks up, or
the mother decides she can no longer cope with the circumstances of the
marriage. Violence against the mother by her husband is often an issue
in these situations.

The murder-suicides and the exceptional psychiatric disturbance
cases were similar, in that the mothers were more likely than in the fatal
assaults to report having suffered violence from their husbands. However

the observation is not consistent across the cases. This suggests that, although women's own experiences of violence may be a significant factor in the life circumstances of some women who kill their children, not all women who do so have been physically abused. However, official documents in criminal justice files are not to be relied upon as sources of information regarding the incidence of domestic violence. It may very well be the case that domestic violence was more widespread across the cases than was apparent in the files used in this research. While acknowledging the significance of contemporary debates about the relationship between women's experiences of violence and their own violent actions, it is not possible to draw any definitive conclusions from the present narratives regarding such relationships, and this is as an issue warranting further research.

The idea of a mother killing her children is so inconsistent with everyday understandings, or perhaps myths, about mothers and their relationship with their children, that the action itself might be considered evidence of 'madness'. While histories of psychiatric illness were not characteristic of the women in this study, two of the women were of notably low intelligence. Women who killed themselves and their children tended to have sought psychiatric treatment at some point. Further, some of the women who had had more extensive psychiatric treatment were having delusions at the time they killed their child. In general, these were also women who were coping with a range of exceptionally difficult circumstances, which frequently included problems with their husband such as violence, separation, and custody battles. The situation of these women needs to be further considered in light of research and literature on the pathologising and medicalising of women's problems, both by women themselves and the people from whom they seek assistance.

Other people knew the situation of many of these women. Women who committed suicide and women with exceptional psychiatric disturbance were at the time being treated by medical professionals, or had been treated in the past. Their ultimate situation and actions indicate the need for further analysis of the ramifications of psychiatric treatment for women. Also, it was not uncommon for women whose children died as the result of a fatal assault to be known by others (friends, relatives, doctors, child protection agencies) to be having problems raising their children and to have been violent towards their children. The mothers in the fatal assault cases were more likely than other mothers in this research to be unemployed or in particularly difficult economic circumstances. These were mothers who were living on the margins of society: they were frequently on social welfare benefits; public welfare or health professionals were involved with the case; and alcohol and drug use were more often mentioned as a feature of the women's lives. In more ways than one, it was not only their mothers, but also the community that failed these children. These cases clearly indicate the need to review our responses, both as individuals and as a community, to indications of violence towards children.

# CHAPTER 5

# *Male Family Members Who Kill Children*

While filicide is unique among homicides in terms of the high proportion of women offenders, many of the lethal events involving children that take place within the family context are caused by men. Among the present accounts, the number of child homicides in the family context accounted for by men (24) is slightly higher than those observed for women (22). These numbers may appear similar, but important differences in the events emerge through the case narratives.

Perhaps the most outstanding difference is in terms of the offender's relationship to the child. In all of the cases discussed in the previous chapter, the women were the biological mothers of the children who were killed. When we turn to look more closely at the children killed by men in the family context, we find that over half of the perpetrators were the de facto partner of the child's mother. Nine of the twenty-three men were the biological fathers of the children they killed. However, the child homicides in which the biological father is the offender differ in a number of dimensions from those committed by the mother's de facto spouse.

## Fatal Assaults

The single most prevalent form of men killing children is referred to in this study as a fatal assault. Over half (55 per cent, 11 of 20) of the men in this study who killed children in the family setting committed this offence. Other research has similarly found that men are most often responsible for this form of child homicide (Ewing 1997: 95). Ewing cites a Colorado study that found '80 percent of deaths from head and body trauma were attributed to male perpetrators' (p. 96).

A characteristic of these cases is the apparent intent to punish or discipline, rather than to kill the child. Ewing (1997: 97) characterises these events as 'corporal punishment run amok'. In many cases the male attempted to resuscitate the child and sought urgent medical attention (Case Nos. 93-1674, 94-0698, 94-2205, 86-1973, and 87-0500). For example, one father ran from the house carrying the baby and screaming 'Save my baby for God's sake' (Case No. 87-1304).

At the same time, autopsy reports revealed that the children's injuries were extensive. A post-mortem found Doug Versaci had died from extensive internal injuries that were described by the forensic pathologist as similar to those usually found in victims of serious motor accidents (Case No. 90-3384). The injuries suffered by Anita White (14 months) included a fractured skull, haemorrhages and bruising to head and neck, which were deemed to have required a severe amount of force and again were described as like those received in a car accident (Case No. 94-2205). An autopsy report in a third case noted:

> The deceased has been the victim of a number of injuries in the recent past. In the week prior to his death he has received: a fractured skull; fractured right 10th and 11th ribs; a deep laceration on each of the upper and lower lips; injury in the region of the pancreas, the root of the small bowel mesentery and the retroperitoneum. [Case No. 93-1674]

These cases generally involved the person who was responsible for caring for the child at the time, lashing out in response to the behaviour, most often the crying, of an individual child. Thus these events always involved the death of one child. In explaining their actions, both the men (and the women) who commit this offence tended to speak in terms of the circumstances of the immediate event: frustration, just having had enough, and trying to get the child to stop crying. Two triggers of these events have been identified in other research: toilet training difficulties among toddlers, and colic among infants (Ewing 1997: 97). In most cases there was evidence of prior physical abuse of the child and on the occasion in question, this extreme physical violence resulted in the child's death. For example,

> Kathy Mathews, a senior high school student, was 17 years old and the mother of Jacob (15 months). Kathy had been living at home with her parents until three weeks prior to the incident, when she moved into a nearby caravan park with Trevor Henderson. On the day the baby died, Kathy left Jacob with Trevor while she went to buy some food for tea. According to Trevor, Jacob was sitting on a chair in the annexe, eating a sandwich and watching television, when he left to take a bag of rubbish to the bin. When he returned, Jacob was choking, so he

stood him up and put his fingers down the child's throat to try to clear his mouth. He held the child under one arm and banged on his back. When Jacob appeared to improve, Trevor stood him up, but he fell backwards hitting his head on the concrete floor. The child looked so white, Trevor shook him and gave him little taps on the face: he was breathing but making strained noises. Trevor put the baby in his pusher to wait for his mother to return. When he felt he could not wait any longer for Kathy to return, he began to walk to the hospital with Jacob. When Jacob went 'floppy', he tried to resuscitate him and applied hard pressure with both his hands to Jacob's stomach. Two women passing by eventually gave them a lift to the hospital.

The Coroner found that multiple injuries inflicted by Trevor contributed to Jacob's death. The autopsy revealed that, in the week or so prior to his death, he received a fractured skull, fractured ribs, laceration to his lips, and injury to the pancreas area. There were also some injuries that might have occurred in the days prior to his death. The injuries to the abdomen were described as severe and 'of a degree occasionally seen in a car accident where there has been severe compression or crushing of the abdomen'.

Before Kathy left her parents' home, bruising had been observed on Jacob, and the government child protection agency had investigated. Jacob was a client of the department at the time of his death. Social workers continued to visit Kathy and the baby after they moved to the caravan park and, observing injuries, discussed possible actions with Kathy. Kathy's parents had also asked her about injuries that they observed on Jacob, which she explained as accidents. Both Trevor and Kathy denied that Trevor ever hurt the child. Kathy did acknowledge to the social workers that Trevor was rough with her, and neighbours also reported the sounds of Trevor severely assaulting Kathy. [Case No. 93-1674]

In general, fatal assaults occurred in families consisting of young adults and young children. The men ranged in age from 18 to 38 years, with an average age of 26, and just over half were 23 years of age or younger. All but one child (who was 4 years of age) killed by a male custodial adult were 2 years old or younger: 54 per cent were under 18 months. In general, these young families were coping with stressful circumstances: references to 'money troubles' and arguments over money, unemployment and reliance on social service benefits are not uncommon; and drug and alcohol use were frequently mentioned.

One of the most consistent features of fatal assaults is that the male perpetrator is generally a stepfather, or living in a de facto relationship with the mother, not the child's biological father. In the present research the mother's de facto spouse committed the fatal assaults in thirteen of the fifteen cases. In most cases, the mother and her partner had been together for less than six months, in some cases for less than one month. However, two biological fathers in this study did kill their child in this way. One of the biological fathers accused his wife of frequent infidelity and denied paternity of the child, whom he had abused over a period of time (Case No. 87-1304). Another biological father was intellectually impaired and was caring for a drug-dependent partner (Case No. 90-1633). The significance of paternity as a factor in fatal assaults is captured in the comments of a mother who noted 'that Rick always reminded me that Rebecca and Jessica [the victim] were my children not his ... He was different with Anita to what he was with Rebecca and Jessica' (Case No. 94-2205).

A sense is developed through these scenarios of a mother attempting to juggle the demands of her child and her new partner. Sometimes the new partner resents the time the mother spends with her child. Other research has identified jealousy of the child's relationship with the mother as one of the motivating factors in child homicide (Baker 1991; Wilczynski 1997). The following case displays indications of this situation.

The alleged offender's cell mate reported, 'He went on to say that on odd occasions he was put off by Christopher because Margaret spent more time with Christopher and every time he cried Ron took it out on him [Christopher] because he continuously cried in his presence and it got on his nerves. He also told me that the child would always shy away from him and that's why he always tried to put him to bed himself. He told me that he thought that might change things but it did not. [Case No. 93-1769]

Like Ron, most de facto spouses were reported by the mother to be involved in 'caring' for her children. In fact, some mothers indicated that the de facto played a significant role in the child-caring tasks:

He was known as an excellent stepfather who actively participated in the child-care duties. He claimed that he terminated his employment when shift work was introduced in order to maintain his family responsibilities. [Case No. 86-1973]

Dale appeared to get on well with Sam ... he would do everything for Sam ... At night, Dale would pick me up and Sam would already be in his pyjamas ready to go to bed after tea. I didn't have to do anything for Sam as Dale had already taken care of everything ... He virtually took over the care of Sam from the time we shifted in and seemed to be doing a good job of it. [Mother in Case No. 86-3184]

Dave has always been good with all of the kids, including Zac and Jed who aren't his. He would take them to the shops and walk them to school or kinder. [Case No. 94-0698]

The perpetrators frequently referred to their role in child-care and, unlike mothers who kill their children, these men tended not to under-estimate their abilities as child-carers:

I took over the role just like a real father. I used to take him shopping all the time and bought him most of his toys ... I went down the park with Sam ... he was good as gold, then he fuckin shit, put shit all over the place, then I belted him ... I hit him all over I guess ... I just punched him for a minute and a half ... then I picked him up and cuddled him ... I don't know why I got carried away like that.' The autopsy disclosed multiple bruises of different ages, indicating that Sam had been assaulted on a number of occasions preceding his death. [Case No. 86-3184]

This male is clearly attempting to portray himself as a caring parent, and one who is not violent in general. It should be noted, of course, that it is not uncommon for violent males to persistently deny their involvement in violence, even when that violence has brought them within the reach of the criminal justice system (Dobash and Dobash 1996).

In explaining or attempting to excuse their actions, the men focused on the frustrations of the immediate event and described their actions in instrumental terms. In some instances the objective given was to be able to get on with whatever he was doing, or simply to reduce the anxiety of the crying child.

Austin was sitting on the floor, eating a packet of chips, and he started crying. I picked him up and whacked him on the bum three or four times with an open hand. I put him down and he was still crying. I picked him up and shook him [to] shut him up ... I didn't lose my cool, I was just annoyed ... I was just annoyed because I couldn't hear the video. He was getting on my nerves. [Case No. 87-0500]

In other instances, the objectives appear to be related to asserting and maintaining authority and power over the child.

Neighbour: 'At times Caitlin [21 months] would stand up to him and refuse to do what she was told. I remember her saying "no" to Carnes on occasions, which made him even worse. He didn't like the children not doing what they were told.' Carnes himself spoke of her 'stubborn personality' and commented, 'I hit her ... I hit her hard ... but that's Caitlin. She was a ... she's a rough nut. I mean, if you don't make it hit home, it doesn't have any effect. She'll, you know, she'll just laugh it off. She'll wait till you're not looking and giggle about it.' [Case No. 91-2001]

Other explanations, while also instrumental, tended to emphasise the emotional element and the loss of control.

A fellow prisoner [Breen] of the perpetrator [Dennis] made a statement to the homicide squad in which he detailed Dennis's accounts of his violence towards the child. Regarding a split ear, which he had told the mother occurred as the result of the child falling out of bed, Dennis told Breen, 'I roughed him around, I didn't mean it, it just happened and I left him there as I didn't want Esther to know in case she left me.' Blister marks were revealed to be the result of Dennis hitting the child with a belt while the mother was in the shower. He talked of causing other injuries, including a broken ankle, pushing which caused a lump on the child's head, pinching and hitting with pieces of lattice across the legs. He spoke of the child getting on his nerves while he was trying to watch television: 'I just lost my cool and went off the deep end.' Regarding the event in which the child died, he spoke of the child crying all day and the mother leaving to go and get a video. He had been trying to watch television and so 'I put my hand over his mouth to try and stop him crying.' When the child continued to cry, Dennis's violence escalated dramatically: 'I didn't really mean to do it, I just lost it.' He then put the child to bed as if nothing was wrong. [Case No. 93-1769]

While the violence was often explained as a loss of control in light of specific events, losing control was not something unusual for these men, who were often described as being 'quick-tempered' (Case No. 91-2001). There is also evidence of violence against the female partner in ten of the fifteen cases, including one where the couple had separated with the woman reporting extreme violence at the hands of the partner. In families with more than one child, violence against siblings was also not uncommon. For example, in the Versaci case (No. 90-3384) a sister reported, 'Sometimes Pete smacked us so, so hard that we thought we were going to die.' Thus, for these men, despite the words of some to the contrary, the child murder was not an isolated incident of violent actions.

In these fatal assault cases, men were more likely than women to try to deny their actions or to cover them up. They created stories, such as

'I was just playing', the child was 'accident-prone' (Case Nos. 86-3184, 87-0500), or was accidentally dropped (Case No. 86-1973), the child fell down stairs (Case No. 87-1975), had 'fallen from her cot' (Case Nos. 94-2205, 94-0698) or had accidentally fallen and hit her head on a table (Case No. 90-1633). In Jacob's case, as we have seen, the child was said to have choked on a sandwich and the male minder had attempted to dislodge the blockage by putting his fingers down the child's throat and hitting him; the child also fell over on a concrete floor (Case No. 93-1674).

Men's denial of violence and their explanations for their violence towards children reveal a diverse and sometimes contradictory range of understandings of masculinity in relation to being a father, and the relationship between these understandings and violence. Most deny the violence and attempt to present themselves as caring fathers.

> When asked by police to describe his own personality, the male stated: 'I dunno, I'd say I'm a pretty normal sort of a fellow ... I'm patient to a point, you know. Then, I suppose then, I – I – I – get a little gr – I get a little aggression and go and scream and make my presence felt ... I mean, and, and, and I will if I have to, I will be violent, if I have to, to t – t – t – to keep the – to keep what I think is not good for the family, away from my family, 'cause they won't listen when I tell them to go away and leave me alone.' When later it was put to him that the story he gave was not consistent with the pattern of burns, with the implication that he might be in trouble: 'I don't believe that you can say that to me. I didn't hurt that little girl. I – like I said, I love her and I would never hurt her. I didn't spray her with hot water. What do you think I am, an animal? Eh? I wouldn't do that to somebody I like.' [Case 91-2001]

While the 'good father' is not violent towards children, and denies it where possible, violence can nevertheless be justified in terms of assuring authority over the child. In the privacy of the interaction between the man and the child, 'doing masculinity' may mean using violence to maintain and establish power, but in public it may mean denying such violence.

The child's mother most often did not question the story as told by her de facto spouse in denying responsibility for the child's injuries. In many instances this was facilitated by the fact that the event occurred while the mother was not present. The injuries were most often inflicted while the child was being minded for a relatively short period (e.g. the mother had gone shopping, or to collect other children from school).

> The mother stated: 'I have never seen Rick show any violence to the kids.' However, she noted there were occasions when she would return

home and Anita had bruises on her, and her partner sometimes took the girls to their rooms to punish them and admitted pulling their hair out. [Case No. 94-2205]

However, some mothers had also covered up or denied evidence of injuries inflicted on their children. For example in Jacob's case (Case No. 93-1674) the mother explained the bruising on her son, which was noted by her parents, as resulting from play with another youngster. Similarly, on a previous occasion an injury had been explained to a police officer as resulting from play with a 2-year-old cousin. When confronted by a doctor with fears that injuries were caused by beatings at home, she denied the allegation. In another case:

The mother had in the past told social workers that 'the boy was clumsy', and on another occasion that her other son had inflicted the injuries, or that she didn't know how the bruising occurred. A neighbour told a social worker that she could sometimes hear the cries of the children above the sound of her television set. The mother also said that both were responsible for disciplining children and giggled as she told of children being told by Versaci to stand in a corner with their hands above their head. The Coroner concluded, 'Tragically not only did she abandon her children to persistent physical abuse by leaving them in that environment and remaining silent, but she also persisted in a line of conduct designed to direct attention away from her de facto.' [Case No. 90-3384]

The Coroner found in one of these deaths that the mother contributed to the death of the child by failing to obtain medical treatment for the child after she had received scalds and burns to 30 per cent of her body (Case No. 91-2001).

The mother's denial was in some cases facilitated not only by the violence occurring when she was not present but also by her partner offering explanations for the injuries. In one case the mother found the explanations for the injuries she had observed were plausible, given that, 'I spoke to [her son] and he didn't tell me anything different so I had no reason to disbelieve [her de facto] … It didn't even occur to me that he might be mistreating [her son]' (Case No. 86-3184). The acceptability of such explanations was sometimes reinforced by medical examinations that did not challenge the accounts of the injuries. For example:

The mother took the child to the emergency department of a hospital, where she reported that the child had been unwell and that his hair was falling out in clumps. Medical personnel found that the child was pale and had some bruises that were felt to be consistent with the explanations provided by the parents. Blood tests were taken, as there was some concern about his blood clotting. They believed Christopher to be recovering from a viral infection and that his diet should be improved, but did not find the bruises significant. [Case No. 93-1769]

The mothers at times failed to acknowledge the evidence of violence in terms of visible injuries to the child that were observed by others:

The violence occurred when the mother was not present. When the mother observed injuries to the child (including missing hair, lumps on his head, and bruises on his legs), she accepted the explanations given by her de facto. She said that it was only with hindsight that she became suspicious. But other relatives noticed that Jacob seemed to be constantly bruised and injured, including burn marks. The mother's brother commented, 'What stands out to me is that both Trevor and Kathy never seemed to worry about the injuries, as if it was an everyday thing.' [Case No. 93-1674]

It appears therefore that in some cases the mothers did not object or comment, and thereby gave tacit approval for the aggressive and sometimes violent treatment of their children. For example, in one case (No. 91-2001) a neighbour commented, 'There were numerous other occasions when John disciplined the two girls whilst I was present. As I said, he used to yell and scream at them for the smallest of things. I just couldn't believe that Cora would let someone treat her children like that.'

Fear for their own safety may have influenced what some mothers 'knew':

The de facto father had also been violent towards other children and the mother of the child. He denied having caused injuries that led to the death of the child, and the mother initially supported his account of the events. She initially claimed that he was not violent and that he was a good father. After the death of the child, in a later statement, the mother reported that the male had accused her of acting as a police informant and assaulted her. In this later statement she also said, 'It was always when we argued and then he became violent. He has also made threats towards my family and me. He has stated that if he cannot get me he will get somebody to do this for him. The reason I have not come forward with these details is because of my fear of John. I am still very scared of what John will do and believe that I am taking a risk making this statement.' [Case No. 91-2001]

A protective order had previously been granted to Child Protective Services because of Jenkins' violence. In her statement to police, the mother [Julie] noted that, after she began living with Ross Jenkins, Brendan started vomiting after meals and was bruised. In a later statement she said, 'I am scared of him. I wanted to believe what Ross said about Brendan falling down the stairs but I really didn't believe him, especially after the doctors. I just didn't really want to believe that he could have done it.' A neighbour commented, 'Whenever Ross was around Julie was terrified of him.' [Case No. 87-1975]

Not only mothers but also others, such as neighbours who observed or strongly suspected the violence, did not report the behaviour in part because of fear for their own safety.

A near neighbour often heard yelling and very loud smacking coming from the house. She said, 'The smacking was so loud it made me sick and cringe. These smacks would have hurt an adult.' After the death she said, 'I broke up and cried my heart out. I blamed myself for not ringing up and telling somebody, but I was too scared what this male person might do.' [Case No. 91-2001]

Further comments by this neighbour suggest another reason for the mother's failure to acknowledge or report the violence towards her child.

Once she heard a woman from the premises yell out, 'Stop it, don't do it, leave her alone!' No reply was heard from the male and the smacking continued. 'In fact when she yelled out, the smacks became louder and more severe.' [Case No. 91-2001]

Thus, it may be that fear of further or even worse violence against their children also prohibited some mothers from reporting the violence.

Mothers may also be reluctant to report because they fear they will be held responsible, or that they will lose custody of the child when the injuries are reported. When a police officer and a social worker went to visit Jacob Mathews to follow up reports of suspicious injuries, the child's grandmother is reported to have said, 'I suppose you have come to take the kids off us have you?' (Case No. 93-1674; see also Case No. 90-3384).

Overall, the men who killed children as the result of a pattern of physical assault were young men living with the mother of the child in an economically marginal situation. That is, their relationship to the child was a consequence of their relationship with the mother. While these men tended to describe the killing of the child as a loss of control in response to the immediate actions of the child, they had assaulted the child on more than one occasion and generally had also been violent to other children and the mother. The homicides were generally represented by the perpetrator as events in which anger and frustration resulted in his losing his control and punishing the child, as a means both of stopping the behaviour that was offending him and of asserting his authority.

### Filicide-Suicide

Cases of paternal filicide in which the father also either attempted or was successful in committing suicide are distinguishable from the fatal assaults on a number of dimensions. Perhaps the most apparent difference is that, in all but one instance, men who commit filicide-suicide are the biological fathers of the children they kill. Separation and custody battles are a feature of these cases. These fathers tend to be older (in their thirties) than the mother's de facto spouses in the fatal assaults, and the child victims also tend to be older. In most instances these men are not reported to have been previously physically violent towards their children. Whereas in the fatal assaults the parent lashes out and kills one child, in these cases the father kills all of his children, and sometimes his wife as well.

While the paternal filicide-suicides share some features, again there is some internal variation. In particular, the scenarios tend to be distinguishable in terms of the degree to which the mother is the key object of the father's actions. In the attempted suicides, the fathers tended to express concern about their children, and feelings of their own pain and loss. In most of the instances in which the fathers were successful in killing themselves and their families, feelings of jealousy, anger and rage are more dominant.

### 'Nothing can happen to her now'

Misguided 'altruism' is a term that has been used in previous research (Resnick 1970; Wilczynski 1997) to identify cases in which the parent indicated, either in a suicide note or in prior comments to friends and relatives, that they believed that the filicide was in the best interests of the children. A not uncommon sentiment in such cases is that 'They're better off dead'. For example:

> Ted was 10 years old and his sister Eleanor was 13 years old when their father, Matthew (41 years), killed them. Matthew and his wife Mona were in the process of divorce, including ongoing custody battles. Having had custody of the children for the previous eleven months, Matthew killed them the day after the court gave Mona sole custody.

After killing the children and writing a suicide note, he took some medication, cut his wrist and attempted to electrocute himself: he survived. He admitted his action to the police, saying, 'I killed my children because we have been living in hell, the situation is horrendous and we've been tormented.' [Case Nos. 88-0541/2]

Another father who killed his only daughter said, 'Well, if she's dead – she's all right, nothing can happen to her. ... I wouldn't have to worry about my daughter any more' (Case No. 91-2514).

However, the men's comments suggest an awareness that the mother would also suffer as a consequence of the action, and was to some extent a target of the action. The Coroner's Record of Investigation notes in the case of Matthew (Case Nos. 88-0541/2, outlined above) that the offender had previously threatened suicide 'in order to force Mona [his wife] to accede to circumstances he sought'. He had indicated 'if he couldn't have Mona then no one would', that he would do anything not to lose Mona, and that he would use the children to prevent the loss of Mona. In Case Nos. 89-5280/1, in which the father killed his two children, the mother wrote to the prosecutor indicating that she believed that her husband's actions were designed in part so that she would be 'left with nothing'. Vindictiveness towards the wife is also suggested in the third case:

*Police officer:* How did you feel about [your wife's] attitude to you?
*Father:* Lousy, quite selfish.
*Police officer:* Hmmm.
*Father:* Vindictive.
*Police officer:* And what did you decide to do about that?
*Father:* What I did, kill my daughter. [Case No. 91-2514]

In two cases there is some evidence of prior violence and threats of violence against the mother (Case Nos. 88-0541/2, 89-5280/1). However, there is not necessarily a previous pattern of violence towards the children, as where it was observed that 'Adam was a caring father towards Elizabeth and he was never violent towards us' (Mother, Case No. 91-2514). Another mother told the police on the day of the homicide, that 'he wouldn't hurt them' (Case Nos. 88-0541/2). Yet another mother told police: 'At no stage did I believe he would hurt his own children'; however, in later accounts, she reported that the father had previously been violent towards one of the children (Case Nos. 89-5280/1).

Like Matthew, the other fathers also reported attempting suicide at the time they killed their children. One father cut the gas pipe to the hot water service, and turned on the gas stove and the space heater before splashing petrol through the house. He then stabbed himself twice before setting the house alight (Case Nos. 89 5280/1). Another father 'cuddled up' to his daughter in her bed after shooting her twice in the head with a nail gun. He reports attempting to shoot himself with the same gun to the chest, but the gun misfired (Case No. 91-2514).

In each of these cases, the parents had separated and there were ongoing battles over the custody of the children. By their own accounts, these men felt 'hopelessness, helplessness and uselessness' (Psychiatrist's report, Case Nos. 89-5280/1). One father said, 'I thought I was doing the only thing I could do, that was left, the only possibility' (Police interview, Case No. 91-2514) and another that 'I am a very lonely person ... I couldn't cope any longer' (Case Nos. 88-0541/2). They were also reported by psychiatrists to be men with 'few if any close friends' and who felt 'alone and lonely' (Psychiatrist's reports, Case Nos. 91-2514, 89-5280/1).

There are, then, indications of feelings of powerlessness, of matters having gone beyond their control, of pain as a result of the loss of children, and of anger at female partners. The murder of their children is described by these men as an emotional outburst in the face of their own pain.

> *Father:* I just became emotional. I just couldn't take any more. My kids were being tormented.
> *Police officer:* What was your intention when you hit Eleanor and Ted?
> *Father:* I just wanted it finished, I've been through so much.
> *Police officer:* Did you realise by hitting your children you would probably kill them?
> *Father:* Yes, I know, I wanted them killed. I've been through so much and I couldn't take any more. [Record of interview, Case Nos. 88-0541/2]

Although these homicides are often depicted by the men as emotional outbursts, in two of the three cases there was evidence of some preparation: a steel pole had been previously sharpened, and a particular form of nail gun had been purchased (Case Nos. 89-5280/1, 91-2514).

While the fatal assaults involved men in their twenties, these men were older – 38, 32 and 41 years of age – and so were the children: 13 and 10 years, 8 and 5 years, and 8 years (Case Nos. 88-0541/2, 89-5280/1, 91-2514).

These homicides also differ from the maternal filicides in which the mothers expressed the belief that what they were doing was in the child's best interest. In the mothers' situation, it appears suicide features prominently in their motivation. The mother believed that the world had gone wrong for both her and her children, and that if she were to suicide, they would suffer even more. In comparison, in the accounts in this research, the fathers who expressed concern for their children as their primary motivation did not successfully commit suicide. This suggests that suicide was not as significant in the motivations of these fathers.

*Mother as Object, Child as Pawn*

In three cases, it seems that the mother was the ultimate object of the father's violence. These are situations in which there had been a history of jealousy and violence against the mother. Violence against the children had been used as a means of controlling the behaviour of the mother.

In two of the cases, the father successfully committed suicide (Case Nos. 89-3903, 86-1274); in the third he survived (Case No. 88-0190). In each case the father killed the mother as well as the children. This is a distinctively male pattern of filicide: in none of the maternal filicides did the mother kill her children and her husband. In two of these cases the killer was the biological father (Case Nos. 89-3903, 88-0190) and in one, the de facto spouse of the mother of the child (Case No. 86-1274). In the latter case, the male killed himself, his de facto wife and her child. In a departure from the pattern of the other paternal filicide-suicides, the perpetrator did not take his biological son, who also lived with them, on the journey that ended with the homicide. However, we do see in this scenario the pattern of jealousy and violence against his de facto spouse.

Karen (11 years old) had only moved in with her mother Vera (aged 29) three months before her death. Bob (aged 41) and his son Martin (15 years) were living with Vera. Vera and Bob's relationship had been 'on and off' for the past four years. She was a particularly attractive woman, and he was jealous. According to Vera's sister, 'He was always following her around when she went out on her own … I have seen him assault her when he was sober. It was generally when he got jealous and accused her of seeing other men.' Bob was also jealous of the relationship Vera had with Karen and Martin.

Vera's family and friends report that, over the years, Bob had beaten, bitten and scratched Vera on numerous occasions. Vera's eyes were frequently blackened. Bob threatened her with knives so often that she would hide all the large knives in the house and would carry a knife in her bag for protection from him. She had been hospitalised as a result of injuries inflicted by Bob. On that occasion, he left her unconscious in a gutter; she had cuts and bruises over her entire body.

On another occasion, Bob 'knocked her out' and left her locked in his van for days.

Vera left him several times, but returned to him due to his threats towards her and harassment of her family and friends. Vera's sister noted that Vera 'was scared stiff of him'.

Bob bought a caravan and a four-wheel-drive vehicle. He allowed Martin to remain in the house with a friend, but took Vera and Karen for a 'holiday' against their will. A week before they departed, Bob bought a gun under a false name and without a licence.

In January, just before noon, the charred remains of one large and one small body were discovered inside a burnt-out caravan. Bob had apparently shot Vera and Karen in the head, poured petrol over the vehicle and caravan, set fire to them, entered the caravan and shot himself in the mouth. [Case No. 86-1274]

In other cases, the perpetrator was the biological father of the children. As in the previous case, it appears that it is the husband's relationship with his wife that is central to his actions that result in the death of his daughter. His relationship with his wife is violent, and jealousy and anger at separation are significant factors. However, unlike the other cases described above, his wife escapes, and although his actions in the scene leading to his daughter's death endanger his own life, he also survives.

Peter (age 36) and Kylie had two children, Mike (age 16) and Lia (age 12). The family had fled to Victoria from Queensland, with Peter changing his surname, to avoid apprehension by police for charges of inflicting grievous bodily harm and offences of a sexual nature allegedly committed against his wife.

After moving to Victoria, Peter continued his violence towards his wife. He threatened to kill her and 'to cut [Mike's] and [Lia's] throats' in front of her if she tried to get help. In November Kylie left, but Peter forcibly kept the children. In December, the children fled from the house while Peter was gone, and they went to live with their mother.

The following January Peter met Kylie and the children at their factory to discuss the custody of Lia. An argument transpired, and Peter produced a shotgun that he placed under Kylie's throat and taunted her, calling her a 'whore' and saying she brainwashed the children. He then pointed the gun at Mike and told him he was a 'lying, snivelling prick'. He fired the gun at him, but it was unloaded.

Peter told Kylie he would take her back to her house to get Lia's clothing. En route they stopped at a petrol station, where Kylie and Mike escaped and called the police. Peter fled with Lia in his vehicle.

A high-speed police chase ended when Peter's vehicle crashed into a police van. As a constable approached his vehicle, Peter pointed the gun at Lia and discharged it. She died instantly from severe shotgun wounds to the head. [Case No. 88-0190]

In each of these cases separation, or the threat of separation, appears to be an important issue for the father. In Case No. 86-1274, the wife had left on several occasions, but her husband's threats of violence contributed to her return and he threatened further violence against the children if she left again. In the third case of paternal filicide-suicide of this form, the wife had left and there were ongoing battles over her return and the custody of the children (Case No. 89-3903). In this account the father shot the mother five times in the face before turning to shoot his 8-month-old daughter in the face. He then drove to a nearby paddock where, after a period of drinking and confrontation with police, he shot himself.

If there were indications of emotions of pain and loss in regard to the children in the attempted suicide case discussed earlier in this chapter, most of these male filicide-suicide scenarios are filled with emotions of anger and possessive jealousy. In maternal suicide-filicide, it was the suicide that featured quite strongly as a significant factor in the motivation. This seems to be less so in the present scenarios. The most powerful motivating factors seem to be in relation to harming and establishing ultimate control over the wife. These male filicide-suicides are more consistent with the retaliatory child homicides identified in other research (Ewing 1997; McKee and Shea 1998; Wilczynski 1997). In an early study of murder-suicide, West (1966: 145) noted: 'Overt signs of previous hostility towards their victims, and conscious motives of jealousy, vindictiveness, and resentment, were much more frequently displayed by the male offenders, among whom the rejected loves, jealous husbands, and violent tempered men formed a sizeable group.'

At the same time, while themes of control and possession of the female partner are evident in these cases, we have to address the fact that in all but one of these cases the perpetrator also killed himself along with the children. Unlike the women who suicide, these men tended not to leave notes, and had not spoken with others about their intentions in relation to their own life, so we know very little about their reasons for these filicide-suicides. However, while issues of control and possession are evidently significant in these events, the fact that the man then kills himself as well suggests that we need to be considering the further complexity, or multi-layering, of these homicides.

Early theories of murder-suicide postulated that the suicide in such cases might be a way of avoiding punishment (West 1966: 145). Or it might be that the homicide and the suicide are both the ultimate expressions of control: these killers not only take their children's and partners' lives, but they ensure that no one else can hurt them in response to their actions. On the other hand, the suicide might suggest that there is something here about the 'possession' or control of wife and family that runs deeper in connection with self-definitions and understandings of themselves as men. Familicide is rarely, and not at all in this research, a form of homicide committed by women. Ewing (1997: 135) suggests that men responsible for familicide tend to have a notion of family that entails them having control. At the same time, this introduces contradictions. From their perspective, they are the centre of the family: they are both 'overcontrolling and yet overly dependent on family members or partners' (p. 134). When their position of control is challenged, they feel personally threatened. Ewing suggests that a man's fear of losing control over his wife and family is not the only issue in familicides: 'His concern is more often with losing control over all aspects of his life, or at least those that he most values. He is a man who, in his own eyes, is, or is about to become, a failure' (p. 135).

This analysis would seem to be particularly pertinent to a final case of familicide, which is quite unlike the others in the present study in that there was no evidence of prior violence towards the wife or children. The case involves a man who killed himself, his wife and two children. To friends close to the family, they appeared to be a close unit. The father was a small business proprietor who had run into financial difficulties and believed that he was at the end of his rope (Case Nos. 88-0558/9). While this is a distinctive scenario in our data, Ewing (1997: 135) suggests that it is the 'more common pattern among filicide-suicides'. These are situations in which the father suffers a significant reversal in his circumstances that threatens his ability to continue caring for his family. 'Faced with such overwhelming threats to their roles as providers, controllers, and central figures in the lives of their families, each of these men became desperate, depressed, suicidal, and homicidal' (p. 135).

## Extreme Psychiatric Disturbance

Most of the mothers who committed filicide-suicide had at some point sought psychiatric treatment, but this was not the case for the men who killed or attempted to kill themselves and their children. However, this cannot necessarily be read as indicating that women's behaviour is more likely to be the result of psychiatric illness than men's. Women are generally more likely to seek medical advice than men; they are more likely to accept explanations for their life problems in terms of personal deficiencies; and their coping difficulties are more likely to be understood as evidence of psychiatric illness.

There was nevertheless a case in our files that involved a father with ongoing psychiatric ill health.

In July 1994, Irene (10 years), Karina (7 years) and Carl (5 years) all died, along with their mother and father, in a house fire started by their father. Irene died from a gunshot wound to the head, while all the others apparently died from fire exposure. Their father, Grant (38 years), had placed receptacles of inflammable liquid in two bedrooms and an accelerant in another bedroom. The bodies had been doused in petrol.

Grant had been treated for paranoid delusional thinking and depression, and had been admitted to a psychiatric hospital from March 1989 to July 1990. He had continued to be treated by a psychiatrist and had an appointment for later in the month. He had been prescribed anti-psychotic medication. However, he had a history of not taking his medication, and his psychiatrist believed that prior to the fire he had stopped taking it, which resulted in a psychotic state. The toxicology report showed no evidence of anti-psychotic or anti-depressant medication in his blood.

He had indicated to his psychiatrist and his GP that he had marital problems and was angry with his wife for obtaining an intervention order against him. Family members reported frequent arguments about money (Grant was on an invalid pension). His wife had been distressed about her husband's behaviour, such as throwing objects at her. One neighbour said, 'Nellie would do everything to avoid upsetting Grant, as he reacted very strongly if things didn't go his way.' A friend of his wife's described Grant's physical and mental abuse of his wife, whom he threatened with death if she left them. Grant's first wife (from a two-month marriage) said he struck her and was possessive and jealous. She ended the marriage, despite Grant's threats he would kill her parents and burn their house if she did so.

The police had previously attended the house after reports of a 'domestic situation', including one occasion when a child was heard screaming. The Department of Human Services had also been notified about the worries for the children's welfare. Inquiries were made, but no protective concerns regarding the children were identified. The department decided there was insufficient information to suggest the children were at risk.

Neighbours, friends and members of the family's church reported 'bizarre' behaviour by Grant. They believed the children were prisoners in their home as they were not often seen. Arguments were heard from the house. Grant once told a neighbour that the family had been naughty and he had locked them up in the house. The house was surrounded by a high metal fence, and large dogs were kept in the yard. [Case Nos. 94-1851/2/3]

It is clear that Grant was suffering a psychiatric illness. At the same time, similar to the other filicide-suicides in which the key target of the father's actions is the mother, there is a prior history of violence and abuse of the children's mother.

## A Distinctive Case

While most of the cases examined thus far in each of the chapters have involved the deaths of children in their pre-teenage years, the following case involved a 16-year-old.

Wallace Kennett (55 years) shot Jason (16 years), the son of his de facto wife, after she had announced to her son her intention to marry Wallace. Upon hearing the news, her son 'went wild', pushing and threatening his mother and demanding she leave Wallace. Wallace reported that Jason 'was raving on about getting some of his mates to come around and wreck the flat and told his mother she was as good as dead'. A fight between the two males ensued, with Jason kicking Wallace as he continued to make threats. Breaking off the fight, Wallace went into another room, and fetched a gun and then shot the son to death. When asked why he shot Jason, Wallace replied, 'Because he was becoming violent.' William's final words to the police were, 'I'm very upset. I'm tragically upset and I just – I'm terribly sorry it's happened.' [Case No. 86-3037]

This case has some similarities with others observed here. The killer, a male, is not the natural father of the victim, but one who could be assumed to stand in the role of either stepfather or de facto partner of the victim's mother. Beyond this, however, it diverges sharply, and is one of the only cases in these files where a homicide is classified as taking place within the family where the victim is a teenager. The actual dynamics of the violence have nothing in common with the other filicides of this chapter. Rather, they share more characteristics with the adult male-on-male pattern of violence outlined in the following chapter. This homicide also serves as a reminder that, in extensive files such as these, cases with unique configurations of factors are likely to emerge.

## Conclusion

While there are differences between the child homicide scenarios considered in the previous chapter and this one, there are nevertheless similarities in terms of the material circumstances of the men and women who committed these offences. In general, these are men and women with limited economic and social resources. There are some exceptions, but most often they are at the lower end of the socio-economic spectrum. The immediate situation of the homicide is set in the context of stretched economic resources and the consequent personal and familial stresses. Partly because of their economic circumstances, they are often also people who feel personally and socially isolated. They come to believe that only they can resolve the situation that confronts them and that there is only one option available to them. At the same time, it is apparent in the cases considered in these chapters that the sex of the offender and their relationship to the child figure prominently in the form and nature of the homicide.

When a child dies as the result of a fatal assault, the person responsible is most likely to be a man, and in all cases in this research, that man is not the child's biological father, but a man in a de facto relationship with the child's mother. A significant fact that frames the killing of children by men in the family context is whether or not the man is the biological father of the child. Biological fathers are not the ones who fly into a rage at an apparently disobedient child. Of the two biological fathers involved in such cases, one questioned his paternity of the child he killed, and the other was intellectually impaired. This is in contrast to the fatal assaults committed by women, which in this research were all committed by the biological mother of the child.

When biological fathers do kill their children, it is most often in a situation in which they are separated from the child's mother, or they perceive a threat of separation. While the children killed in fatal assaults tend to be under 2 years of age, there is a wider age range (average age of 10 years) of children killed by their biological father. In part this is because these events usually occur after a family unit has been in place for some years. These are very tragic events because they generally involve more than one child and one or both parents as victims. These homicides are likely to take one of two forms. In the first, the father indicates concern about his children's welfare and, at the time of killing them, attempts to take his own life. In a second, the mother of the child appears to be the father's principal target; these are often situations in which there has been a history of violence against the wife and/or the children. In this research, these men most often took their own lives as well as those of their wife and children. This form of homicide, familicide, is almost exclusively committed by men (Daly and Wilson 1988).

These observations, along with the observations in the previous chapter of the significance of expectations regarding motherhood for maternal filicide, draw attention to the need for further consideration of the structure and understandings of motherhood and fatherhood in our society. We know little about the meaning and experience of being a father for men. The scenarios of paternal filicide considered in this research show that further exploration of these matters is essential to an understanding of these events. Threats to the man's control and possession of his wife in particular, and in some cases children, appear to be trigger events in many of these scenarios. However, different men with different identities, different emotions and different objectives are visible in these stories; angry men, men filled with despair, men who have given no previous indications of willingness to use violence, and men who regularly use violence. We also see indications of the complex and sometimes contradictory nature of individual men's accounts of themselves: there are men who express anger, pain, and hopelessness, men who are controlling and dependent, or aggressive and caring. There are men who are ready to use violence to establish their authority in relation to children but who reject the use of violence against children in public. Overall one is left with the feeling that there is still much more we need to explore in terms of the complexity and multi-layering of men's understandings of themselves in relation to their wives, their children, children in their care, and wider audiences.

## CHAPTER 6

# *Killing Outside the Family*

The killing of children most often occurs within the family circle, but there is a significant proportion of such killings where the offender is outside any kinship or family child-caring network. In fact, within the present study, roughly one-third (32 of the 90 victims, or 36 per cent) of the homicides were the result of actions of persons other than family members. A number of striking differences emerge when these non-family homicides are compared with filicides. First, the offenders are virtually all male (26 of the 27 known offenders). Second, the victims are distinctly older than filicide victims (whereas most filicide victims are under the age of 6, most of the non-family victims are teenagers, and the average age of this group is just over 14.5 years). While these two characteristics are important, they only hint at the issues that become clarified when the thematic material of the qualitative analysis is revealed. A large component of these killings appears to be youthful involvement in adult patterns of violence, but there are some elements of risk and vulnerability that are unique to childhood.

### Child Victims of Adult Masculine Scenarios of Violence

Many of the non-family homicides, especially those where the victim is close to adult years, are the result of young persons, technically in law still children, becoming swept up in adult scenarios of violence. Such cases most often involve a male offender, with research reporting consistently that the proportion of males among all homicide offenders ranges from 85 to 90 per cent (Wolfgang 1958; Wallace 1986; Falk 1990; Strang 1992; Silverman and Kennedy 1993). In addressing the characteristically male nature of homicide, Polk (1994) identified four distinctive scenarios of adult violence. These four scenarios account for eighteen of the thirty-two non-family homicide victims and form the starting point for our following analysis of child homicides outside the family. We begin by considering those scenarios that in general involved primarily male-on-male violence.

### When Boys Play Men's Games: Honour Contests

It is true that most homicide offenders are male; it is also the case that, in a majority of all adult homicides, *both* the victim and the offender are male. In a national study in Canada, homicides with both male victims and male offenders accounted for 53 per cent of all homicides (Silverman and Kennedy 1993), while an investigation in New South Wales (Australia) reports a virtually identical 54 per cent (Wallace 1986). In his analysis, Polk (1994) argued that there are three major scripts of violence within which most of these male-on-male homicides can be described: confrontational or honour contest violence, violence as a form of conflict resolution, and homicide in the course of other crime.

The first of these is 'confrontational' or 'honour contest' violence (Polk 1999), where typically males come together in a public space such as a pub, a party, a park, or a street or laneway adjacent to pubs or discos (use of alcohol is noted in the great majority of these cases). In the interaction that occurs, something happens which is taken as a threat to the honour or reputation of one of the males; it can be an insult, a jostle, perhaps a non-verbal challenge of some sort. Words are exchanged, whereby a challenge to combat is laid down and accepted. What follows then, typically, is a fight in the course of which lethal violence is employed; in some narratives, one or other of the parties may temporarily leave the scene to fetch a weapon. The death was not initially intended, but was a consequence of the rapid playing out of the challenge and resulting fight. Such contests of honour accounted for seven of the non-family homicides involving victims under the age of 18, in all of which both offender and victim were male. The dynamics typical of such events are illustrated in the following narrative:

Colin (age 17) was a member of a loosely organised group known as 'Bogans', while Charles (age 19) was identified as a 'Headbanger'. Both were at a disco in a local tennis centre, when a group of the Bogan males became involved in an argument with a group of girls who were hanging out with the Headbangers. After a brief exchange of taunts and insults, one of the girls punched Colin, who retaliated with a punch in return, and then the two began a pushing match. Charles came over and attempted to pull the girl away. Colin called

Charles a coward and a wimp, and began to throw punches at Charles. At this point, a general fight began between the two groups, involving ten or twelve people. Charles then pulled out a knife and stabbed Colin several times in the chest and abdomen. Colin died shortly after (his blood alcohol level was found to be 0.079 per cent). [Case No. 1931-87]

The scene for this event was a disco, where groups of males and females mingle and meet. The visible group identities ('Bogans' versus 'Headbangers') provide a focal point around which social friction occurs; as the groups pass in the space, friction can flare into violence. It is definitively a leisure scene, and one where alcohol plays a major role. As the conflict unfolds, there are the initial central actors and the social audience, but then the audience moves from backdrop into the centre of the conflict itself. Words which challenge the honour of males – in this case Charles was called a 'coward' and a 'wimp' – especially in front of his male and female peers, constitute a threat to his standing as a male which is not to be tolerated. The age groups in this conflict are mixed, with the age of the victim (17) falling within the present study parameters, while the perpetrator's age (19) falls slightly outside. Put another way, when some young adolescent males become involved in street and peer scenes, their social world is one where there is a mix of ages, some being somewhat older than the victim. This happened also in the following case:

At 6.30 p.m. on 1 August 1987, Elton (age 15), David, Angie and Helena arrived at the eighteenth birthday party of Paul. David had invited Elton, who did not know either Paul or his family. They sat down in the garage out the back (which was where the party was), and proceeded to drink beer. Elton stated later to police that he drank 'about ten stubbies' of beer and acknowledged that he was 'slightly' affected by alcohol consumption. After some time, Elton went inside to call up some mates to tell them to come to the party. On the way back to the garage, he and David tipped up a table, causing several glasses and bottles to break and some pot plants to fall in the pool. They then returned to the garage. Angela, who witnessed this, stated, 'Elton had been drinking but he knew what he was doing.' Paul's father warned all those in the garage that if he found out who had caused the damage, he would kick them out. Tommy (age 17) accused Elton of overturning the table in front of everyone, which caused Elton some discomfort. Tommy approached Elton and said, 'Anyone that knew the Goodalls wouldn't do something like that.' Elton said, 'You aren't suggesting I did it?', at which Tommy just repeated himself.

They moved closer to each other and appeared to be ready to fight, so a girl stepped between them and they settled down.

Tommy insisted that Elton apologise to Mr Goodall for the damage he'd done, but Elton refused. Tommy and a few others then dragged him over to Mr Goodall and forced Elton to say sorry, but it was said in a less than convincing manner. Mr Goodall said something to the effect of 'I don't like people destroying my property, please leave.' Elton and David became abusive to Mr Goodall. Tommy then said, 'It's all right, Mr Goodall, I'll see him off the property', and pulled Elton towards the driveway. Tommy and those helping him were saying things like 'On your way mate' to both Elton and David, who had also been asked to leave. Tommy was holding onto Elton's jumper and being 'fairly vocal'. Elton told him he could find his own way to the gate, but Tommy said that he wanted to make sure. Someone behind said, 'We'll get him when we get out the gate.' David claims that both he and Elton were punched and pushed as they were walking down the drive. According to one of the 'escorts', Elton and David were calling them names such as 'wimps' and 'dickheads'.

Once outside, Tommy shoved Elton, causing him to fall in the grass. Elton then punched Tommy and a scuffle ensued, in which Elton produced a knife and stabbed Tommy three times. Elton then ran away and was chased by Tommy's friends. Tommy was carried inside and died before medical help arrived. [Case No. 87-3307]

As in the previous narratives, the violence erupts in a public scene in which young males, some known, some unknown to each other, are drinking and at leisure. Something happens so that challenges are thrown about, and a combative mood begins to build (a few minutes before the fatal encounter, Elton was heard to say to a friend that he was 'going to have a fight', asking the friend to keep others away so that it could be 'one-on-one'). The early moves result in an overt confrontation in which a direct threat to Elton's honour is laid down, followed by moves on the part of a group of young males to forcibly eject him from the property. At this point, the interaction leads rapidly toward violence involving pushing, shoving, and a fight. That the encounter will prove lethal is not the outcome anticipated by any. Honour had been challenged, and violence will be used in its defence. The principals in these events are all young, the victim being 17, the offender just 15.

These confrontations can occur in various possible locations, including public parks and reserves, as found in the following account:

Matt's brothers and some friends were sitting drinking in the Bill Turner Reserve, Glenroy, on New Year's Eve, at about 8 p.m., when a group of males in a small Datsun pulled up and started abusing them. The car then drove off. Matt (age 16) arrived at about 9.30 p.m. with some others. Fifteen minutes later, the same Datsun drove up again, its passengers abusing and taunting the group in the park. The driver, Rickey (age 19) yelled out 'You fuckin' dogs' over and over, then drove off, only to return ten minutes later to repeat the abuse. One witness from the car says, 'They all started laughing at him. This seemed to upset Rickey.' This happened one more time and the car stopped about 3 metres from Matt's group, the passengers yelling 'dogs' and 'fuckwits' to the group outside. The whole group rushed at the car, and Paul threw a can of beer that went through the open window at the front. Several members of the group began kicking the car, and James (Matt's brother) did 'elbow drops' on the roof. According to James, Matt was not involved in this and just watched. He states, 'He just doesn't like getting into fights.' In the melee, one of the car's windows was smashed. There was much shouting and swearing but, according to James, no punches were thrown at this stage, and no one got out of the car. The passenger in the front seat of the car, however, claims that he was punched about four times. Suddenly, the car drove off, and Rickey shouted, 'We'll be back.'

According to one of the passengers in the red Datsun, Rickey was drunk, and seemed to be 'spinning out'. Rickey drove back to his place, where a group of his friends came out to inspect the damage to the car. They were so drunk that they could hardly walk. One of them asked, 'Who done it?' and Rickey answered, 'It was the guys in Justin Avenue.' The group became very aggressive at this and started yelling things like 'Whoever done this is gonna pay for it.' One ran to the back yard and came back with four cricket bats. Some friends came with him from the yard, where there was a party in progress. All fifteen (possibly sixteen) of them got into Rickey's Holden sedan or sat on the bonnet, and they drove off.

At about 11.30 p.m., the car stopped 6 metres from the group in the park and those in it yelled out, 'Come on you cunts' and 'Don't fuck with us.' Paul and a couple of Matt's group (but not Matt) had armed themselves with garden stakes in preparation for the attack. The people in and on the Holden climbed from the car and charged, one shouting, 'There's the cunts that got me brother.' About three of them were carrying stakes and another three had steel rubbish bins. Rickey was one of those with a stake, and he was doing most of the shouting. He was shouting things like 'Get back here you bastard and I'll knock shit out of you.' James grabbed Matt and told him to 'bolt'. Realising that they were far outnumbered, the group in the park scattered. Matt and his brother Ronald ran up a nearby street with about eight guys, all carrying tree stakes, chasing them. The brothers were separated in the chase. It appears that Matt threw a stake at Rickey and Neil. Rickey claims that Matt hit him with it, but a medical examination revealed only a small area of localised tenderness, which was 'not consistent with recent injury'. Rickey picked the stake up, chased Matt up a driveway, and hit him on the head with it. Matt fell to the ground, and Rickey hit him at least once more before decamping the scene at 11.45 p.m. Ronald recalls hearing some screaming, followed by silence, when everyone dispersed and left. One of Matt's brothers found him lying in the bushes in the garden, semi-conscious, helped him home and put him to bed. Matt was found dead (from extradural haemorrhage) the next morning. Even with the elapsed time, his blood alcohol content was still 0.02 per cent. Rickey appears to have initiated the fight, even though he denies this. [Case No. 89-0002]

Again the scene is a public one, in this case a local park. Two groups, both of whom had been drinking for some time, were involved; the provoking incidents were words passed back and forth between the groups. In this case, as is often true in these honour contest homicides, the ultimate victim is an individual who through most of the action has been well in the background of the unfolding events. As in the previous account, most of the other (and more central) actors were older, and in some respects it may be both relative size and age (16) which served to make Matt the target of the lethal violence from Rickey and his group.

One hidden feature of this narrative is that Rickey and the close circle of his friends were set apart clearly within the Glenroy community in terms of their ethnic identity (being Maori), this ethnicity being a feature of the friction between the groups. In another account, ethnicity also plays a role in the evolving conflict:

The dispute broke out between a group of 'Old Australian' and Vietnamese youths on St Kilda beach, just behind Luna Park. It had started, according to observers, when Donnie (age 16) and his friend Sam were walking up and down the beach 'looking for a fight'. They approached one young person and said: 'You fucking fat shit … do you want a fight?' The two apparently moved on after this boy backed off, saying he didn't want to fight. Donnie and Sam, as they moved away from the one encounter, found themselves among a crowd of Vietnamese young people.

In the jostling, the conflict shifted to the Vietnamese. Taunted, one of the Vietnamese boys kicked Sam 'in the guts'. The two Anglo boys drew out their knives and threatened the Vietnamese youths. The Vietnamese girls broke up this initial confrontation, and the two clusters separated.

The Vietnamese group moved off some distance, while the Anglo boys stood around, playing with their knives, and showing off. One of the smaller Vietnamese lads walked over and offered his hand, trying to smooth things over. The Anglo boys responded by telling him to 'piss off', saying, 'We'll keep on fighting.'

The Vietnamese group decided to leave. The Anglo boys went to the nearby changing rooms. Donnie moved up and challenged the Vietnamese youth who had kicked his friend, again pulling out his knife. The Vietnamese boy pulled out an even bigger knife. At this point, apparently, Donnie put his knife down with the intent of engaging in a fistfight to even things up. As he was doing so, Tan V. (age 14) slipped up from behind and stabbed Donnie once with his knife, then quickly dashed away. Donnie collapsed and died before medical help could be summoned. [Case No. 86-4189]

Again, the conflict is played out in a leisure scene, in this case a beach. The ultimate victim was the individual who precipitated the action (making this an example of what Wolfgang (1958) referred to as 'victim-precipitated' homicide). Notably in this case the major protagonists were all young, with the offender (age 14) being even younger than his victim (16).

Sometimes in an honour contest that results in lethal violence, the ultimate victim is an innocent party not involved in the interactional dynamics that produced the violence, but becomes involved only through misfortune:

It was early on New Year's morning, and two groups of teenagers were doing 'wheelies' and otherwise causing trouble with their cars in a car park near the Barwon River. Three men approached the cars, and 'told off' the teenagers, who allege that in addition they had damaged their cars by breaking off their external mirrors. The men then walked off down the road in the direction of a nearby caravan park.

The youths decided that they wouldn't 'let them get away with that'. With a cry of 'let's show them', the two cars took off in pursuit. The two cars made a pass at the men, and insults were hurled back and forth. The cars went past, then turned for a second run at the men at very high speed. The three men were able to leap out of the way, but the leading car swerved onto the shoulder, and the driver lost control. As the car spun well off the road, a student named Charles (age 17), who was walking home from a party with friends (and who had not taken part in any of the events which precipitated his death), was struck and killed instantly. [Case No. 87-0035]

The cause of this fatality was a contest that erupted when the teenage group provoked by the older males engaged in reckless action that resulted in the death of the young victim who had taken no part in the central events of this drama. The paths which lead to lethal violence can take many twists and bends, and sometimes the ultimate victim has little connection with the escalating steps taken by other males who engage in highly risky behaviour once they have been provoked.

Each of these scenarios has involved young victims, but the dynamics here are similar to confrontations observed among older males, though generally not much older than their mid-twenties. The scenes typically are settings of leisure where males congregate. There is a form of social circulation involved, the movement involving the passage of a mixture of friends, acquaintances and strangers. To the outsider, the lethal events can be set off by what appears to be the most trivial of provocations. Much has been made of the role of such trivial events in sparking this scenario of violence:

> The typical 'trivial altercation' homicide in America is an affair of honor with strong resemblances to the affairs of honor that have been described in other cultures ... The precipitating insult may appear petty, but it is usually a deliberate provocation (or is perceived to be), and hence constitutes a public challenge that cannot be shrugged off. It often takes the form of disparagement of the challenged party's manhood: his nerve, strength or savvy, or the virtue of his wife, girl-friend or female relatives. [Wilson and Daly 1985: 69]

Wolfgang was one of the early observers of the phenomenon of the apparent triviality of events that provoke some homicides:

> Despite diligent efforts to discern the exact and precise factors involved in an altercation or domestic quarrel, police officers are often unable to acquire information other than the fact that a trivial argument developed, or an insult was suffered by one or both of the parties. [Wolfgang 1958: 188]

It seems clear, however, that what is trivial to a respectable observer may be quite central to the marginal actor's sense of his male status. Daly and Wilson (1988) have argued along similar lines, that for some men it is important that they maintain their sense of honour, that they not allow themselves to be 'pushed around', that they maintain a 'credible threat of violence' (p. 128). For the male players in the homicide drama, the challenge to manhood is far from a trivial matter. And, in the present circumstances, the tragedy is that males at an early age (the average age of the seven victims of this scenario was 17) learn the moves consistent with this scenario, and young people well below full adulthood can become involved in the escalating violence, often triggered by what appear to be minor provocations, which results in the death of a young man.

### Violence as a Method for Conflict Resolution

The second of these male-on-male themes involves three cases which developed out of the use of violence as a device for the resolution of conflict. In these scenes, individuals who most often are exceptionally marginal in both an economic and social sense find themselves in a dispute (frequently involving a debt owed to a criminal associate) which they are unable to resolve with the available informal means. Because of their social status (within the criminal subculture, for example) they are unable to resort to the legitimate formal dispute-resolution procedures. Such individuals may find themselves calling upon violence as an ultimate device for settling their differences. As is true generally of this form of homicide, all of the cases in this research involved male victims and male offenders. The following is typical:

Greg M. (age 17), an apprentice, supplemented his income by dealing speed. It was common knowledge that he usually carried a knife with a 30-centimetre blade in a pouch that he wore around his waist. He also often carried an iron bar. David L. (also aged 17) had been unemployed for months. He met Greg for the first time when he received sixty dollars' worth of speed from Greg on credit. Over a month later Greg 'shot up speed' and then left his home with a friend in order to 'score' some more. They ran across David and his friend at a local 7-11 store. Greg demanded the sixty dollars he was owed. David explained twice that he could not pay it until the following Thursday when he received his cheque. Greg threatened that if David did not have the money in half an hour he would be back with his 'mates' and there would be bloodshed (not realising that the blood would be his own). After attempting to poke David in the stomach with his ubiquitous iron bar, Greg left.

David, after going home briefly for tea, armed himself with a tomahawk from his father's garage. He then met five of his friends at a park. When shown the tomahawk, one of David's friends exclaimed, 'That could kill someone.' David replied that he needed it for protection from Greg and his 'mates', but he would only use the 'back end'. Greg and a friend then arrived. After unsuccessfully demanding his money, Greg produced the iron bar and screamed, 'You're fucked then.' David replied, 'Come on, cunt' and pulled out the tomahawk from his jacket. They screamed and swung their weapons at each other. David struck Greg in the arm with the tomahawk.

From this point on the reports are inconsistent. Greg either dropped the iron bar or threw it at David, hitting him in the chest. Greg then produced his knife and threw it at David. David picked up the knife. Greg grabbed David and they struggled. Greg was stabbed once in the back. David dropped the knife in the park as he left. He returned home and replaced the tomahawk in the garage. An ambulance rushed Greg to hospital, where he died less than an hour later. [Case No. 85-1900]

This has some of the appearance of an honour contest homicide, but the events are not as spontaneous as the fights that arise out of threats to male status. The central issue was the debt that David was unable to pay, and the violence employed initially by Greg was the mechanism to try either to force payment or to punish his debtor. There is an element of intentionality about the violence that is not a common feature of the rapidly flaring confrontations described above. The importance of this theme of conflict resolved through violence is found in the following account as well:

The day before the homicide, Saul P. (age 17) was intercepted by the police at the Doncaster Shopping Centre with several of his friends when one of the group attempted to obtain a refund for a stolen quilt cover. As they were being questioned, Saul asked to make a telephone call, and he tried to phone his girlfriend at their house. Jackie U. (male, age 19) was at the house and took the call. Somehow in the confusion, Jackie was left with the impression that Saul had informed on him while being questioned by the police. What Saul said to a friend after being released by the police was that he had called the house to warn them; he thought they ought 'to clean up the unit because the police were going to do a raid' (according to later testimony of one of Saul's mates).

Jackie was a big youth, and noted for his violent temper. His friend Jimmy G. (also 19) had a similar reputation. One of Saul's group had recently had an encounter with Jackie, and described him as 'an ox and I know he would have pulverised me. I describe Jackie as a thug and pushy, very overpowering.' Another said of the pair that they were 'violent, aggressive bullies. When they are together they think that no one can get in their way.'

The next evening (after a long day of drinking and drug use), Jackie and Jimmy went to Saul's residence. They immediately sought him out, calling him an informer, a 'dog'. A witness stated that Saul kept trying to say, 'Let me explain, let me explain.' The two were in no mood for explanation, and started to systematically beat Saul. At one point he was hit with such force that his head put a hole in a masonite wall. Saul was quickly rendered unconscious, and died of head injuries early the next morning,. When questioned by the police the next day, Jackie said that he was 'shitted off with [Saul] for having dobbed me in to the police the other day and telling them where I was.' There is no comfort in this banal tale that Saul had not informed on either Jackie or Jimmy. [Case No. 92-0695]

This narrative is a bit closer than the previous one to the honour contest scenario in its central dynamics. One might view the perception of Jackie that he had been dobbed in by Saul as a challenge to his honour and reputation. On the other hand, consistent with other conflict resolution events, the violence here is clearly intentional. The telephone call had created a grievance, one which was responded to with what was clearly planned and wilful violence. As with the previous scenario, this masculine pattern of calling upon violence as a device to bring a conflict to a conclusion is one that does not often have youthful participants. The three victims of this pattern of violence were all male, and their average age was 16.

### Homicide in the Course of Other Crime

Another of the scenarios identified by Polk (1994) is that in which the death arises in the course of another crime. There were four narratives in this investigation which fit this scenario. In all these cases, the offenders were male, but the nature of this form of masculine risk-taking is that on occasion the victim is female, as in two of the accounts that follow. A typical occurrence within this pattern is the 'double victim', where the victim (a female in this instance) of what is initially an armed robbery is then killed during the course of the robbery:

The body of Sally Tracey (age 14) along with that of her father, a gun shop owner, and a shop assistant were found inside the burned-out gun shop. Medical examination revealed that the three had died from gunshot wounds. As a result of police investigation, Joel Lucas (age 24) was charged with and later convicted of the homicides. He had apparently gone to the shop when he thought only the owner would be present, intending to kill him and steal guns, but ended up killing the other two when he found them at the scene. Although he initially denied the killings, he admitted committing both the robbery and the burning of the shop. He later admitted to a fellow inmate that he was responsible for the homicides, and when questioned about the death of the girl, was reported to have said, 'She shouldn't have been there in the first place.' [Case No. 93-2637]

While deaths in the course of other crimes are not in themselves unusual, what is unusual is the age of this victim. The offender, of course, is a male, and an older one at that. It is inherent in the routine of crimes such as armed robbery or burglary that those victimised are older males who are in possession of the goods that are the target of the crime. As this case demonstrates, children can stray into these scenes. In this narrative, the child victim happened to be spending time in her father's shop, and the lives of both father and daughter were forfeit in the course of the robbery.

A second form is the 'reverse victim', where the offender of the initial crime becomes the victim of the lethal violence. The case in our files involved a teenager who was engaged in a late-night burglary:

Kenny (age 17) previously had broken into a toy store in Keilor and stolen several models that he had attempted to sell to his friends. He returned to the store early one morning, determined to steal more of the toys. When he kicked the door open, the store alarm went off, awakening the proprietor who was living on the premises. The owner then picked up his rifle, and confronted Kenny. In the exchange, a shot was fired which ripped into Kenny's abdomen. Kenny ran out of the shop, moaning and clutching his stomach. He collapsed and died shortly after. [Case No. 88-0151]

In common with other offenders within this scenario, Kenny undertook the exceptional risks that are involved in serious criminal activity. Events arising in the course of other crime account for 16 per cent of all Victorian homicides (Polk 1994), but it is rare that this style of violence will involve children, including teenagers, as either the initial offender or the victim. The decision to engage in dangerous criminal activity is connected to exceptional risk-taking behaviour, which is more likely to be a feature of adult than youthful life.

The average age of the victims of this form of child homicide was 16. One form of this type of homicide which is more associated with youthful risk-taking behaviour involves events related to motor vehicle speed.

One such case is a death in a motor car, which under most circumstances would not fall within the boundaries of this research. In this case, however, the car had been stolen. The victim was a teenage girl (age 16) who was a passenger in a car that crashed. The driver was a boy (age 17), who had stolen the car and taken a group of friends for a joy ride: he lost control of the car when driving at speeds in excess of 175 kilometres per hour (Case No. 90-4153).

## Accidental Shootings

There were two killings involving children as victims in the years of this study which were apparently treated as 'accidental shootings', but which from the sparse information seemed to involve more than would ordinarily be implied by this term. While this scenario is not part of the scheme suggested by Polk (1994), it is included here as a way of rounding out the accounts which involved male-on-male violence. Both of the cases are difficult to describe because of the absence of detail, although it is possible to state that in both cases the offenders were male, as were the victims. The killings took place in rural Victoria, and as a consequence did not go through the routine process of investigation leading to the inquest, since in such cases the coroner's inquest may be held in the country, with one of the magistrates from a country town serving as the Coroner. The records of such cases tend to be scanty. In one of these:

> In the middle of a bright, summer day, Ronnie Knox (age 16) and a group of his friends in the country town were shooting with a single-barrel 20-gauge shotgun. After wandering about and firing several shots, they were approached by another group of boys, including Stan McKay (age 12). An argument broke out between the boys, and Ronnie grabbed the gun, pointed it at Stan, and fired. He said later that he thought that one of the other boys had taken the remaining cartridges out of the gun (apparently a red cigarette lighter had been discarded by one of the group, and Ronnie mistook its shape and colour for a shotgun cartridge). The loaded gun fired, hitting Stan in the head and chest, killing him instantly. [Case No. 85-0001]

Ronnie states that he did not know the gun was loaded. There was an argument, however, and the gun, loaded or not, was employed as a weapon in the dispute. Somewhat similar dynamics are involved in the other case:

> David Scanlon (age 11) was sitting in a friend's lounge room with four other boys watching what was referred to as a Rambo-style

movie. At the end of the movie, one of the youths, Jackie Young (age 16), went to his brother's room and took up a .22 rifle and a magazine with live ammunition. He then came back into the room and proceeded to point the rifle around at the other boys. When he sighted in on David, he pulled the trigger, killing David instantly. [Case No. 86-0002]

Both of these cases involved young males (as both victim and offender), and both offenders were clearly using guns not just improperly, but in a threatening way. These were not cases of individuals being wounded with a gun which was being cleaned, or when one of a group tripped while going through a fence. There was an aggressive use of the weapon that goes beyond a simple tragic accident. And, in fact, while there is no record of action taken against Ronnie in the first of these cases, Jackie, the offender in the second, was convicted of manslaughter and given a term of two and half years in a youth training centre.

### Intimate Partner Violence

We were able to identify three discernible patterns of violence which involved females as victims where the sexuality of the girl played a role in the pattern of victimisation. The first of these results from the fact that, as girls mature into their teenage years, some move into adult-like intimate relationships with male partners. For some of these young women, this means exposure at a young age to the rage that results from the jealousy or 'sexual proprietariness' (Daly and Wilson 1988) of their male partners. There were three cases of female victims killed by a male partner in the present data that involved this particular theme of male violence: one was a couple who had been living together (Case No. 88-2850); in another the man was a boarder in the young woman's family home (Case No. 88-4396); and in the third, the couple were not living together but had been going out together for nine months and were planning to start a family (Case 86-3143). These are cases in which two young people (the average age of the victims was 16, and the offenders' average age was 21) are very close to each other before the young woman decides to end the relationship.

George S. (age 18) boarded in the house of the family of Kelly T. (age 16). Kelly had been George's girlfriend for some months. Their relationship was described as 'non-sexual', more an adolescent boyfriend–girlfriend type of relationship. George found it difficult to express his feelings, but it was obvious that he was 'keen' on Kelly and jealous of her. He was described as being attached to Kelly and very caring, and as having developed an 'immature obsession' with her. However, Kelly did not have the same feelings for George. He found this difficult to accept and became very depressed. While at times he appeared possessive and jealous, at no point did he hit, verbally abuse or threaten Kelly.

At Christmas time, however, Kelly decided that she no longer wanted to maintain that relationship, although she still wanted to be 'friends' with George. Still deeply in love with Kelly, George then went through a difficult period, alternating between highs when Kelly would treat him well, to deep lows when she would assert her independence, especially in terms of making clear her interest in going out with other boys.

After several months the matter suddenly came to head, with no warning in terms of any forms of previous violence. One evening George, Kelly and Kelly's parents went together to a local party. Kelly made clear her interest in another boy at the party, a boy whom she had seen previously. This threw George into a moody tailspin. Upon returning with the family group from the party, he stayed up brooding after the others went to bed. After a couple of hours, he went out into the back yard and picked up a piece of moulded concrete lawn edging. He returned to the house, and by his account he then went into Kelly's bedroom. He looked at her for some time as she slept before hitting her twice in the head with the piece of concrete. Afterwards, when he began to realise the enormity of his actions, he tried to set fire to Kelly's bedroom in an attempt to cover up what he had done. The deception fooled no one, and George readily admitted causing the death when interviewed by police later that morning. [Case No. 86-4396]

This case has much in common with accounts of homicide among older males that involved possessive rage, including the attempt of the female partner to withdraw from the relationship, the jealousy as she attracts the attention of other males, and the brooding rage and despair that spills into violence. Further, as is true in many of the cases involving older victims, the violence does not necessarily erupt spontaneously in the course of an argument (Polk 1994). It follows a period of reflection, and thus shows elements of 'malice aforethought' that is quite common in killings by males of their female sexual intimates.

An element of difference between the cases in this study, which involve young couples, and those in other research which involve older adults (Polk 1994), is the absence of a prior history of physical violence by the male partner. There was no such history of violence in the above case; nor is there in the following case, in which it was the young woman's threatened termination of the relationship which again led to the violent reaction of her male partner.

> Betty S. (16) had been going out with Greg M. (20) for nine months. They had formed a sexual relationship, and were attempting to start a family. They were reported to be an affectionate couple with no indications of any prior violence on the part of Greg. There had been some arguments regarding Greg's long spell of unemployment. On their way home, after an evening out drinking, an argument broke out over Greg's unemployment. Betty announced for the first time that she wanted to end the relationship. Greg became further depressed on the drive home and said to another passenger in the car, 'What have I got to lose by shooting Betty and myself?' Upon arriving home, Greg told Betty he would give her until two o'clock to 'think it over'. When she had made no response, in the early hours of the morning he shot her in the head and neck. [Case No. 86-3143]

While elements of anger and rage may be involved in the final taking of Betty's life, there are also suggestions that Greg was distraught and in a state of despair at the potential loss of his partner. Similar emotions are also evident in the following story, in which the young man also took his own life:

> Both Muriel H. (age 17) and Perry V. (age 26) were known to be heavy drug users. Perry used both amphetamines and morphine, while Muriel used amphetamines. They had lived together for some time, but about two months previously Muriel had moved out of Perry's household. Muriel thought he was too possessive. Perry took the separation very hard. He pestered Muriel to move back in with him, and on one occasion was observed striking her in the course of one of their arguments. Muriel would, however, occasionally stop by and spend time with Perry. We cannot know what transpired between Perry and Muriel on the final, and fatal, visit she paid to him, but what could be established later was that Perry first stabbed Muriel to death, then set fire to his house, resulting in his own death. Post-mortem examinations showed that both had been using drugs (Muriel amphetamines, Perry both morphine and amphetamines). [Case No. 88-2850]

In common with many of the homicides arising out of sexual intimacy, there is here both the threat to the male posed by the separation of the woman, as well as evidence of prior violence. At the same time it is an unusual case, in that many of the depressive murder-suicides committed by men involve an elderly male taking the life of his similarly elderly female partner. The scenario is nevertheless consistent with a common pattern of male proprietary violence toward their female sexual intimates (Daly and Wilson 1988; Polk 1994).

A final case of the homicide of a teenage victim in the context of an intimate personal relationship is distinctive, in that the victim was a 16-year-old male and the offender was an 18-year-old female.

> The relationship between Trish and Lucas had been somewhat stormy, with some reports of physical violence by Trish towards Lucas. Nevertheless, once Trish had left the relationship and was living elsewhere, Lucas continually contacted her about getting back together. Trish was increasingly annoyed by this ongoing pestering behaviour. The homicide occurred in the kitchen of Trish's residence, where an argument once again erupted between them, and Trish picked up a nearby knife and stabbed him once in the chest. [Case No. 93-2233]

Once again a significant element in the unfolding of this scenario was the unwillingness of the male to accept his female partner's wishes to terminate the relationship, the 'proprietariness' theme as it has been termed by Daly and Wilson (1988). However, the account is distinctive in this research, and in homicide research more generally, in that it is the man who is the victim. There are no cases in this investigation in which a young woman kills her partner who leaves or threatens to leave her; in fact, this is an uncommon scenario in homicides generally (Polk 1994).

## Children as Victims of Violence Evolving from Sexual Exploitation

Examination of the thematic material in the cases revealed other ways in which the evolving sexuality of girls becomes the focal point of male violence. One of these is situations where children become the victims of sexual assault or abuse, and consequent to that their lives are forfeit as well. Men were the offenders in all four of these cases (although in one case there was a female accomplice), and the four victims were female. The men were all significantly older (average age 40) than their much younger victims (average age 11) who, in all but one case, were not yet in their teenage years.

In the following case the homicide occurs at the time of the sexual assault:

> Molly M. (age 17) disappeared after a birthday at her house in Oxley. It was two years before the full story came to be known. Over a period

of months after the disappearance, a male Richard M. (age 36 at the time) admitted to a number of different persons that he had killed Molly and buried her body in the bush. When finally interviewed by the police, Richard stated that he and his de facto Sally E. had taken Molly to the residence after the party. Once there, Richard made sexual advances to Molly, which she resisted. Richard then forcibly raped Molly, afterwards stabbing her to death. Molly's body was located after Richard confessed the rape and murder to the police. [Case No. 91-3839]

This case is unusual in that, while the principal offender was an older male, a woman friend of the offender played a role in the events as they unfolded. In many of these cases, the sexual assault of the young person carries with it such peril of disclosure that the perpetrator in the course of the action strikes out and takes the life of the victim. This can be seen as well in the following case where the victim is well below the age of puberty, and thus the perceived danger to the perpetrator is even more extreme:

The mother of Kathy G. (age 8) awoke at about 3.30 in the morning after hearing sounds in the house. When she checked the house, she found that Kathy was missing. She called the police immediately, and they shortly after found Kathy's body in a nearby street. The girl had been abducted, sexually assaulted, then killed. A former intimate of the mother, who knew the household well, was charged with the crime later that day. [Case No. 92-3911]

This case demonstrated how often the danger to children is posed by persons who are known to the victim and family. In such cases children can become the targets of sexual desire and obsession, but the sexual possession of such a young child poses a danger if she lives to tell her tale (particularly when the perpetrator is a family intimate who can be readily identified by the child). Another variant of this tragedy, where the child is killed in a vain attempt to silence testimony, is found in the following narrative:

R.L. (age 46, unemployed) had not had great luck in his life. A police report described him as having 'a long criminal history including offences relating to violence and dishonesty ... He appears to be a person of little education, with an alcohol abuse problem extending over a long period of time.' From 1983 to 1985 he served a term in prison.

Over recent years R.L. had formed a friendship with the C. family (both of the parents of the C. household had lengthy criminal histories themselves). Upon his release from prison, the attachment with the C.'s was close enough that for a period of time R.L. rented a bungalow located at the back of their residence.

Isolated from other kinds of contacts with women, R.L. over the months and years developed a close relationship with a daughter of the household, Tammy C. (age 12). This had developed into what the police in their subsequent report described as an 'unhealthy relationship', that is, R.L. had sex with Tammy.

This was a dangerous game to play because of its potential consequences. Perhaps to protect himself, R.L. moved away from the C. household. He continued to see the family, including Tammy, however.

The peril was increased when Tammy became pregnant, a fact which was discovered when she suffered a miscarriage. Tammy refused to reveal the identity of the father to her mother. She did, however, tell two of her young friends that R.L. was the father, and further, that he had threatened to kill her if she revealed that he had been involved with her sexually.

Apparently becoming apprehensive that the whole affair was coming unstuck, R.L. phoned Tammy while she was having her birthday party. He asked Tammy to come over later because he had an additional present. When Tammy arrived, he produced a shotgun and shot her once in the head, killing her instantly. R.L. then phoned Tammy's mother and asked her to come over as well. Upon her arrival, he held the gun to her head, threatening to shoot her and the rest of the family as well. R.L. then attempted to choke Tammy's mother to death, but she was able to break away and alert the police. [Case No. 86-1199]

The source of this homicide resided in the sexual relationship. In this case, as in the previous one, the offender was faced with the consequences of engaging in sex with a child where the sexual victimisation could carry serious social penalties. In the fear and confusion (certainly aggravated by the general incompetence of this male), the child was killed in a clumsy attempt to blot out the facts of the sexual crime.

In each of the above instances, the offender was known to the victim's parents. We began the book with another scenario in which the offender was a stranger to his young victim and her family. In these circumstances if the offender elects to deny the crime, even where the evidence is overwhelming, little may be known about the details of the crime itself:

Shirl Bennett (age 6) disappeared after riding her bicycle up to a local milk bar on an errand for her mother. Her badly decomposed body was found in a storm drain some three months later. Allan Shaw (age 56) was charged, and convicted of the murder. While Shaw denied any guilt in the case (and therefore little can be established regarding what happened to provoke the murder of the child), the circumstantial case was strong, and he had a history of prior sexual offences. Given Shaw's denial, the available facts are scanty. A 6-year-old neighbour testified that he had seen an adult male get out of a car as Shirl was cycling toward the milk bar, ordering her to stop and to 'come here'. The child states that the man then picked Shirl up and put her in the car, and drove off (the child stated that he did think that Shirl wanted to go with the man). Two adults claimed that they had seen a child who was clearly distressed, in a car that matched the description of Shaw's vehicle, in the minutes after the initial abduction. At the trial, a fellow inmate who had shared a cell with Shaw testified that Shaw had confessed to the crime, stating that in his account, Shaw had said that during the time of the abduction, Shirl had pleaded with him, 'Take me home to mummy. I want mummy.' In handing down a maximum sentence of life without parole, the trial judge stated that: 'What you did was every child's fear and every parent's nightmare.' [Case No. 91-3189, supplemented with material from Hobbs and Rule 1997]

In all of these accounts the vulnerability of the young female victims rested with men whose sexuality was directed towards girls or young women. At times acts such as these approach what Cameron and Frazer (1987) have termed 'sexual terrorism', and they speak of the effect that such murders have on the female population: 'A generalised fear of the lurking sex beast is instilled in women from their early years; it is death we fear, just as much as rape, and sadistic killers haunt our very worst nightmares' (Cameron and Frazer 1987: 165).

For most young women, the gradual growing up into adulthood, including emerging sexuality, is a process of expanding fulfilment, one which inevitably means a movement away from the family of origin into a much wider world of multiple social connections. However, for a few young women that expanding world thrusts upon them a deadly encounter with the darkest side of male sexuality and violence. One potential source of such encounters is a serial killer.

## The Serial Killer

There is one example of known serial homicides in the present narratives. Although they are relatively rare events, these phenomena have been identified as a form of homicide in quite an extensive literature

(Cameron and Frazer 1987; Holmes and Holmes 1996; Geberth and Turco 1997; Hickey 1997; Egger 1998; Keppel and Walter 1999). In the present research, the case involved a victim (age 17) who was one of three female victims in a series of homicides by the one offender.

Nellie Robinson (age 17) was the third and last victim of the serial killer Peter Dixon. (Dixon's other victims were young women who were in their early twenties.) When Nellie had not returned home after school on a Friday afternoon, her parents became alarmed and notified police. Due to the previous two murders, a large group of volunteers was quickly assembled to search for the missing girl. Her body was found near the bike track that she normally used to come home from school. Her death was a result of stab wounds to the neck, and there were also injuries to her hands which were consistent with attempts at defence. When questioned in regard to these killings, the killer said:

'I've always wanted to kill. Since I was about 14. I've been stalking women ... since I was 17 ... Waiting for that opportunity. Waiting for the sign.'

When asked why his victims were women, he replied: 'Just hate 'em.'

'Beg your pardon?
'I hate 'em.'
'This particular girl, or girls in general?'
'General.'

Dixon confessed to the three murders, and was sentenced to life imprisonment with no minimum term (on appeal, a 30-year minimum term was set). [Case No. 93-2405]

Serial killers pose a particular problem for communities, and researchers. As was the case in the coastal region of southeast Melbourne where Peter Dixon killed his victims, the community in which such events occur lives with fear until the offender is apprehended: 'When a serial killer is stalking the streets of a city or town, those living in the area are under his spell. Headlines and stories in the press reveal the details of each victim's demise in the goriest detail permissible. Fear in the community is heightened' (Silverman and Kennedy 1993: 129). The fear is heightened by the fact that such killers are not readily recognisable in their communities. They are generally men who are otherwise able to live in the community and to present themselves as unremarkable (Hickey 1997). In the present narrative, the victims were all young women, and in this respect the offender is similar to killers like Ted Bundy or Christopher Wilder in the United States. But the life

circumstances and personal presentation of these men are not necessarily similar. Peter Dixon was described in many ways as being quite
ordinary; Chris Wilder, on the other hand, was described in the following
terms:

> Rich, sophisticated, handsome, charming, bright, highly admired –
> could such terms truly describe a serial killer? In Chris Wilder's case,
> and to the misfortune of eight attractive young females, these terms
> accurately described a man who tortured, raped, and murdered
> females in six or more states during 1984. Wilder's victims ranged in
> age from 17 to 24; evidence indicates that they experienced sadistic
> assault, rape, binding, and death from strangulation or stabbing.
> [Holmes and De Burgher 1988: 77]

As was true of Dixon's and Wilder's victims, Hickey (1990, 1997)
found that such killers were more likely to target women and children.
Although there are none in the present research, there are examples
elsewhere of serial killers who have focused exclusively on children as
their victims. In Staffordshire in the mid-1960s, Raymond Morris, the
'Cannock Chase Killer', killed three young girls, aged 5, 6 and 7, over a
two-year period. After the second killing, reflecting the impact these
killings can have on local communities, the Coroner issued the following
warning: 'This repugnant pervert is still at large. Children in this area
should not run about unaccompanied. While this murderer is at large no
child is safe' (Lucas 1970: 188). England has experienced even more
notorious instances of serial killing where killers whose victims were
children, including the Moors murderers Ian Brady and Myra Hindley in
the mid-1960s, and Fred and Rosemary West who were arrested in the
early 1990s (although some of the Wests' victims were adults).

Canada, too, has had to confront the tragedy of the serial killing of
children:

> In British Columbia between November, 1980 and August, 1981,
> Clifford Olson claimed the lives of eleven young people between the
> ages of 9 to 18 (although it is possible there were more victims).
> Olson had apparently variously sexually abused, beaten, strangled and
> stabbed his victims. Despite being put under police surveillance in
> July, 1981, Olson was able to kill four more victims. [Silverman and
> Kennedy 1993: 135]

The nature of serial killing poses a number of specific problems
for police investigators. The victims are selected 'by opportunity' in a
way that gives them a random appearance (for most killers there is

a characteristic patterning to victimisation). The choice of victims of such killers tends to be spread over a wide area. The fact that there is no link connecting the victim with the offender, among other things, makes serial killing one of the most difficult crimes to solve (Holmes and Holmes 1996; Geberth and Turco 1997; Egger 1998; Keppel and Walter 1999). Indeed, as the cases of the moors murderers and the Wests show, if the killers are able to successfully dispose of the bodies of their victims, police may not even be sure that such a killer is at work. In the Victorian case, Dixon was found when the police were able to work out the pattern of the killings. Also, they had the benefit of some luck in terms of identifying the offender in the aftermath of the killing of Nellie, with the result that Dixon was restricted to three victims.

### Distinctive Cases

As in any analysis of social phenomena, there are always examples of human behaviour that do not appear to mesh with observable patterns of similar behaviour. With the exception of the serial killers discussed above, the analysis of the narratives in this research has focused on the nature of the relationship between the victim and the offender. That is, when we attempt to make sense of the dynamics which describe the social context of the homicide, we do so by calling attention to common patterns of interaction, or scenarios, which bring together victims and offenders. There are some cases, however, where it is difficult to understand or portray the particular dynamics of the homicide. These are most often cases that are in many ways unique and stand out from the consistencies that are observable across other homicide cases. There were two such cases in the present analysis of child homicides committed by men who were not part of the child's immediate family.

One day upon returning home from playing tennis, the mother of Alice Simpson (age 11) found her daughter lying dead in her bedroom as a result of a combination of head injuries and multiple stab wounds. The killer was a young male neighbour (age 27) who was both intellectually disabled and an epileptic. When asked if he murdered the girl, he replied, 'Yes, I thought it was her mother in the bed.' When his house was searched, some ladies' panties and brassieres were found in his drawer, some of which belonged to Mrs Simpson. When asked why he killed Alice, he said: 'I was bored, I'm a mongrel.' He had apparently first hit Alice over the head with a shovel, and then gone to the kitchen where he obtained a knife and came back and stabbed her several times. He had used gloves so there would be no fingerprints. When pushed further for a motive, he replied: 'Because of the trees, we have been arguing about them and that.' His mother and brother, however, said that the trees had been like that for years, and did not feel that it was an important issue. Alice's mother said that she had had no argument with the offender, and could think of no reason why he would want to harm her or her family. She did note that the young man had previously thrown bottles at the house, and had also cut some branches off trees in her yard. In general, however, she had had little contact with the offender. Witnesses on the day of the murder felt that the offender was behaving unusually, and some noted previous acts of aggression by him. A social worker with the Office of Intellectual Disability said of him that: 'I felt he was unhappy and socially isolated.' [Case No. 88-5122]

A significant feature of the context and circumstances of this event would seem to be the offender's intellectual disability. At the same time, his violence was directed toward a female, and there are indications of an element of sexuality in the development of the event.

A final distinctive case involves the killing of a young boy:

Nelson Apton (age 22) was unemployed and married. His wife at the time was seven months pregnant. He and his wife lived with his parents, who were active participants in a well-regarded religious organisation. Nelson collected knives and watched horror movies.

Nelson awoke one morning, took a shower, and then, according to his later testimony, 'decided thinking that today I would try to kill somebody'. He stated that at that time he did not know whom he would kill. 'So, at, at the time I left … I didn't think I would be killing a little boy or anything like that.' Before leaving the house, he placed a tomahawk, knives, gloves, masking tape and rope into a backpack. He had apparently decided to carry out the killing at a residence in a local suburb where he had done some gardening work with his father. He went up to the door of that house a short time later, saying that he wanted to look at the back yard to see how many plants were going to be needed for some further gardening work. Georgina Bannister, still in her pyjamas because it was relatively early in the day, reluctantly let him in. He went into the rear of the premises, returning a short time later. He began to chat with Georgina, claiming that a friend was coming to collect him in a few minutes. He left after a few minutes, claiming he was going to a local milk bar to call the friend who had not appeared. He returned after a short time, saying that he had been unable to use the telephone. Georgina offered to let him use her telephone, and he pretended to make the call, then telling Georgina that he would be picked up shortly. Georgina then excused herself, saying that she had to shower to get ready for work. After she left the room, Nelson took the tomahawk out of the backpack. He came up behind Georgina's son, Samuel (age 10) who was playing a game quietly on the floor of the lounge room, and struck Sam savagely at the back of his head, following that with several more blows to the neck and back (although the first blow was instantly fatal).

Nelson then went into the kitchen, where he washed the tomahawk and his hands. He then decided to kill Georgina, and returned to his backpack, taking out a knife and masking tape. Nelson accosted Georgina in the shower, forcing her to go into the bedroom and lie down on the bed. He then attempted to fondle her, and raped her digitally. Nelson then attempted to strangle Georgina, but she broke free. At this point Nelson got up out of the bed, saying, 'I can't do this.' After a few more minutes, he released Georgina and told her to call the police. As she ran to a neighbour's house to make the call, Nelson rang his mother and told her what he had done. He said later, 'I sat for a few minutes thinking about whether I should really do it and then, before I realised what I was doing, I was actually doing it.' He said he wanted to kill Georgina because 'I didn't want her to know about her son.' At the end of his police interview he said, 'I do deeply regret what I have done and that I'm glad I've told the truth, and I hope one day people can try to forgive me.' [Case No. 94-1883]

As in the previous case, we know who the killer was, we are able to specify that there was no family relationship between victim and the killer, and we have considerable narrative material regarding what the offender said after he was apprehended. Nonetheless, it is an event that remains difficult to 'understand'. The lesson in this for research on violence, as seen in previous chapters as well, is that our interpretations of homicide will always be limited. Human beings are exceptionally diverse, and the actions of some are so far outside the perimeters of other human actions as we know and understand them within our culture that it is difficult to 'make sense' of them. The consequence is that, no matter how good the data, no matter how sharp the theoretical frame, it is likely that there will remain cases like these two which simply confound the analyst.

## Cases Where the Circumstances Are Unknown

In any set of files such as these, there is another group of killings that involve deaths where little is known about the circumstances. One of the most dramatic cases in these files involved a schoolgirl who was abducted, and her body was found many months later in circumstances where it has not been possible for the police to identify and apprehend the killer (Case No. 92-1041). Similarly, two teenagers (one female, the other male) who had been hitchhiking together from Adelaide to Melbourne were killed along a highway in the remote western part of Victoria, again in circumstances where the authorities are baffled as to motive and circumstances of the death (Case Nos. 90-3945/6). In another case (Case No. 92-4137, described in Chapter 2), the body of a 13-year-old girl was found washed up on a beach, and for some months it was not even clear if this should be considered a homicide (although that is how it is now being treated by the Victoria Police). In a final case, a 16-year-old male was hanging out with his friends during the late evening hours in a suburban shopping mall when another male walked up to him, and according to witnesses said: 'Remember me?', and then stabbed the boy in the chest, resulting in his death (Case No. 95-1298). While there are some important facts known in this case, since the offender has not been apprehended, and since no other information has been uncovered, it is unclear what motivated this encounter.

The events and limited known facts of these events suggest that these are not filicides. All involve victims in their teenage years. Beyond that, however, the conjectures run into the sand. These are all considered to be 'live' cases by the Victoria Police, and perhaps at some point in the future more will be known about the tragedies represented by these five youthful deaths.

## Non-Family Victims of Homicide: Reviewing the Patterns

The present data demonstrate that homicides involving children who are killed by non-family members constitute a distinctly different phenomenon to those in which the offender is a family member. There are especially sharply etched differences in terms of both sex and age. In opening this chapter we pointed out that the offenders in these non-family child homicides were disproportionately male, and the victims were older than filicide victims. Consideration of the narratives has revealed another important element. There are key differences by sex of the victim within the various scenarios. In the scenarios of honour contest, homicide in the course of other crimes, and violence as conflict resolution, twelve of the fourteen victims are male (all of the victims of honour contest and conflict resolution are male). In the narratives involved with violence resulting from either sexual intimacy or sexual predation (including here the victim of serial killing), eight of the nine victims are female (in the one exception, a young female defended herself against a young male unable to accept the break-up of their relationship). In these accounts there is a clear theme of sexual victimisation, which at time shades into what Cameron and Frazer (1987), as noted above, refer to as 'sexual terrorism'. Thus, what initially appeared to be a situation of no difference (the gender distribution appeared equal) on closer investigation is revealed to be a domain of great difference indeed (that is, in general among the non-family killings, boys are victimised in qualitatively different ways than girls). In both, the patterns originate in some aspect of male behaviour on the part of the offender, but the specific content of these varies in important ways according to the gender of the victim. The inclusion in this research of analysis of the killing of children up to the age of 18 years has resulted in the emergence of broader observations of the significance of sex and age to our understandings of child homicide. These observations are considered in more detail in the following chapter.

# CHAPTER 7

## *Observations about Child Homicide*

The many different patterns observed in the preceding chapters demonstrate that there is no one 'thing' that can be called child homicide. There are diverse patterns which require consideration of, we argue, the context of the killing (whether or not the offender is a family member); the gender of the offender; the age of the victim; and then for older victims, the gender of the victim as well. These complex interactions urge caution in attempts to simplify the nature of lethal violence involving children as victims.

At the same time, there are ways of bringing these patterns together so that coherent themes are revealed. Both the literature and the present findings suggest ways in which these events might be ordered and understood. Silverman and Kennedy (1993) attempted such an ordering when they folded a template over their data on child homicide that was derived from 'routine activities' perspectives in criminology. They observed that the pattern of risk shifts as children age: 'Homicide against younger children mainly occurs in the victim's home, as does homicide against older children; however, the probability of becoming a victim of homicide outside of the home is much greater for older than younger children' (p. 187). These writers went on to point out that homicide rates tend to decline after the age of 5, and this may in fact reflect their removal from parents as a source of violence:

> Children over 5 spend large parts of their day in school and out of the house. If they are, indeed, at risk from those with whom they live, then being away from those people alleviates a stress or tension in the home. The new daily activity of school takes children away from those who we like to think are most likely to love and protect them, but in

these instances are the most likely to harm them. [Silverman and Kennedy 1993: 188]

Finkelhor (1997: 29–31), drawing upon a 'developmental perspective', sharpened these observations when he argued that the nature of violent victimisation varies in patterned ways as children pass through the early stages of the life cycle. Finkelhor proposed four principles that in his view captured the available information about development and lethal violence:

*Principle 1:* As children get older, family perpetrators make up a smaller proportion of all perpetrators.
*Principle 2:* As children get older, their victimisation comes to resemble those of adults.
*Principle 3:* As children get older, gender patterns become more specific.
*Principle 4:* As children get older, their risk for victimisation is decreasingly determined by family-centred factors and increasing related to more general social factors.

Each of these principles is consistent with the available data on child homicide. Any number of studies have reported that, when the child victims are very young, the perpetrators are likely to be family members or known child-carers (that is, not 'strangers'). As the analysis shifts to older victims, there is an increasing likelihood that victimisation shifts to non-family perpetrators. The present data are consistent, further, with the observations that many of the older child victims show patterns of violence that resemble those of adults, such as young women becoming the victim of a male partner's violence originating in jealousy and possessiveness, or young males becoming victims of honour contest violence. The third principle is somewhat more contentious; it apparently refers to the gender of victims, which does become more specific with age. On the other hand, it appears to us that gender patterns in relation to offenders are distinguishable throughout the age span: the probability that the offender will be male increases significantly as the age of the victim increases.

Both of these perspectives are useful starting points for the analysis of child homicides, suggesting important links between the age of victimisation and the social context of the violence. Finkelhor further hints at variation in gender patterns with the changing age of the victim. Both call attention to important social facts, such as the context established by the routine activities of children, and the importance that emerging adolescent development plays in altering the forms and content of risk of lethal violence.

### Re-Focusing the Developmental Hypothesis: Observations about Risks of Child Homicide

Although we accept the general thrust of both of these arguments, it is our contention that a somewhat different ordering of the elements contained in these principles will produce a better understanding of child homicide. Let us begin this re-ordering with a restatement of the importance of this pattern of violence within the general data on homicide:

*Observation 1: Children under the age of 18 constitute a major group at risk of homicide, accounting for somewhere between 10 and 20 per cent of all homicide victims in countries such as Australia, Canada, the United Kingdom and the United States.*

The intention of this first observation is to support a general assertion that children constitute a social category within which there is a significant risk of homicide. There are differences in the age categories used in these various countries which make exact comparisons difficult. However, it is clear that children account for a significant proportion ranging from 10 to 19 per cent, of all homicide victims in such countries as Australia (Strang 1994), Canada (Statistics Canada 1992), the United Kingdom (Smith 2000) and the United States (Maguire and Pastore 1994). Any comprehensive analysis of homicide, then, should include consideration of the problems of child victims of lethal violence.

*Observation 2: There is a distinct U-shape distribution to the risk of victimisation by age, with a high level of risk occurring in the first years of life, that risk reducing in the early school years, then rising rapidly with the onset of the teenage years.*

Many observers of homicide have called attention to the fact that the first year of life is a period of exceptional risk for homicide (Rose 1986; de Silva and Oates 1993; Strang 1994). In the United States, for example, the risk of homicide has been found to be greater during the first day of life than at any other equivalent age span (Crittenden and Craig 1990: 202). In Australia between 1989 and 1999 (Mouzos 2000), the rate of homicide for children under one year of age was 2.68 per 100,000, one of the highest risk rates at any age, and exceeded only slightly by the rates observed between 18 and 30 years of age (Table 7.1, Figure 7.1). In the United Kingdom (Smith 2000), the number of homicides in the

**Table 7.1** Homicide victims in Australia, 1 July 1989 – 30 June 1999 (rates per 100,000 relevant population, sex and age group)

| Age (Years) | Male | Female | Persons |
|---|---|---|---|
| Less than 1 | 2.80 | 2.55 | 2.68 |
| 1 to 4 | 1.08 | 1.22 | 1.15 |
| 5 to 9 | 0.58 | 0.53 | 0.56 |
| 10 to 14 | 0.46 | 0.42 | 0.44 |
| 15 to 17 | 1.72 | 1.09 | 1.41 |
| 18 to 20 | 2.95 | 1.90 | 2.67 |
| 21 to 23 | 3.55 | 2.43 | 3.00 |
| 24 to 26 | 4.25 | 2.22 | 3.24 |
| 27 to 29 | 3.66 | 1.86 | 2.76 |
| 30 to 32 | 3.81 | 1.99 | 2.90 |
| 33 to 35 | 3.50 | 1.42 | 2.46 |
| 36 to 38 | 3.32 | 1.75 | 2.54 |
| 39 to 41 | 3.29 | 1.39 | 2.34 |
| 42 to 49 | 2.57 | 1.56 | 2.07 |
| 50 to 64 | 2.32 | 1.08 | 1.71 |
| 65+ | 1.32 | 1.02 | 1.15 |
| Total | 2.35 | 1.36 | 1.86 |
| Median Age | 33 | 31 | 33 |

*Source:* Based on Mouzos 2000.

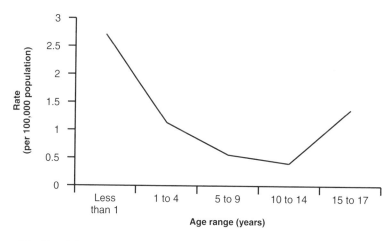

**Figure 7.1** Homicide rates, children, Australia, 1989–1999, by age of victim
*Source:* Based on Mouzos 2000.

under-one age group is actually twice as great as observed at any other age period in the childhood years (Figure 7.2). In all of these countries, the rate of homicide victimisation rapidly drops off after this initial period of high risk in the first year, to a period of low risk of homicide that runs from about age 5 to the onset of the teenage years.

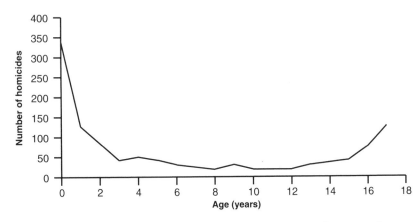

**Figure 7.2** Homicides, children, England and Wales, 1992–1997, by age of victim
*Source:* Smith 2000.

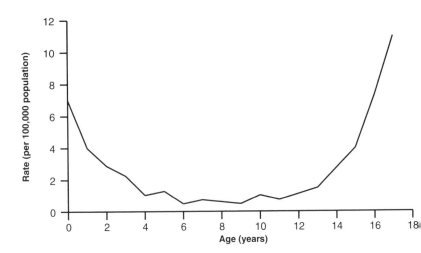

**Figure 7.3** Homicide rates, children, United States, 1998, by age of victim
*Source:* US Bureau of Justice, Statistics.

While these observations are all consistent with the 'routine activities' hypothesis laid out by Silverman and Kennedy, the problem with this formulation is that childhood is a time of not one, but two, periods of high risk of homicide. This is seen most clearly in United States data (Figure 7.3). Initial high rates of victimisation in the first year of life in the United States (7.07 per 100,000) taper down rapidly to a plateau of low rates from age 4 to age 12, at which point the rates go up again, rising steeply in the late teenage years, then continuing to rise to levels of between 17 and 19 per 100,000 in the period of the early twenties; the rates then taper gradually until old age (Table 7.2). In Australia and the United Kingdom, while there is a distinct rise in the later childhood years (15–17), the increase is not as extreme as that observed in American data (Figures 7.1 and 7.2). While something in the 'routine' of daily life may serve to protect children during the middle childhood years, and while this early protection may have something to do with the removal of the child from risks connected to the family, another set of factors kick in during the maturing adolescent years, dramatically altering the level of risk to lethal violence.

*Observation 3: The rate of victimisation in the middle years of childhood is not only low, it is the lowest level found at any point in the age cycle.*

Care must be taken with assertions about homicide risks in the child-hood years. While within the age span of childhood there are two peaks where the risks are quite high, there is, in addition, a striking trough in the middle years of childhood in which the risk is as low as it ever will be anywhere in the individual's age span. The exceptionally low rates of homicide victimisation found in Australia at ages 5–9 (0.56 per 100,000) and 10–14 (0.44 per 100,000) are never again approached at any other time period in the data as they are currently recorded (at age 65 and over, which is the other low point, for example, the rate is 1.15 per 100,000, Table 7.1). It is worth noting that this distribution is also mirrored in the distribution of risks for general injury deaths (from such sources as accidents), where the lowest life risks are in the 5–9 years group. However, the peak for general injury deaths is not as great in the under-school-age group as is the peak for homicide deaths (Bordeaux 1998: 3). In the United States, where the data are somewhat more fine-grained, it can be seen that, while the risk of homicide declines remarkably in the years of old age, the levels of risk in the seventies and eighties (generally varying around 2 per 100,000) still do not dip to the low levels of risk observed in the middle childhood years (Table 7.2). These years from roughly 6 through 12 are remarkable since individuals experience the maximum protections against the threat of lethal violence that will be found at any point in their lifetime.

**Table 7.2** Homicide victimisation by age of victim, United States, 1998 (rates per 100,000 population in age group)

| Age | Rate | Age | Rate | Age | Rate |
|-----|------|-----|------|-----|------|
| 0 | 7.07 | 31 | 9.28 | 61 | 3.04 |
| 1 | 4.03 | 32 | 8.87 | 62 | 2.48 |
| 2 | 2.83 | 33 | 8.55 | 63 | 2.34 |
| 3 | 2.24 | 34 | 8.20 | 64 | 2.30 |
| 4 | 1.13 | 35 | 8.86 | 65 | 2.80 |
| 5 | 1.24 | 36 | 7.92 | 66 | 1.94 |
| 6 | 0.65 | 37 | 7.37 | 67 | 2.03 |
| 7 | 0.79 | 38 | 7.91 | 68 | 2.53 |
| 8 | 0.67 | 39 | 6.49 | 69 | 1.90 |
| 9 | 0.47 | 40 | 6.59 | 70 | 2.06 |
| 10 | 0.81 | 41 | 6.59 | 71 | 2.16 |
| 11 | 0.76 | 42 | 7.01 | 72 | 2.62 |
| 12 | 1.02 | 43 | 5.78 | 73 | 1.89 |
| 13 | 1.32 | 44 | 6.11 | 74 | 2.00 |
| 14 | 2.68 | 45 | 5.52 | 75 | 2.02 |
| 15 | 4.11 | 46 | 4.40 | 76 | 2.45 |
| 16 | 6.71 | 47 | 4.68 | 77 | 2.51 |
| 17 | 11.17 | 48 | 5.14 | 78 | 2.21 |
| 18 | 16.45 | 49 | 4.50 | 79 | 1.67 |
| 19 | 17.21 | 50 | 4.10 | 80 | 2.25 |
| 20 | 17.32 | 51 | 3.63 | 81 | 2.45 |
| 21 | 17.04 | 52 | 4.17 | 82 | 2.45 |
| 22 | 19.11 | 53 | 3.79 | 83 | 2.28 |
| 23 | 16.45 | 54 | 3.18 | 84 | 2.18 |
| 24 | 15.03 | 55 | 3.84 | 85 | 2.25 |
| 25 | 15.84 | 56 | 2.76 | 86 | 3.48 |
| 26 | 14.33 | 57 | 2.53 | 87 | 2.38 |
| 27 | 12.06 | 58 | 3.73 | 88 | 1.15 |
| 28 | 12.34 | 59 | 2.61 | 89 | 1.60 |
| 29 | 10.75 | 60 | 3.09 | 90 | 2.20 |
| 30 | 10.59 | | | | |

*Source:* Bureau of Justice Statistics <www.ojp.usdoj.gov/bjs/homicide>.

*Observation 4: In the pre-school years, the risks of victimisation are almost exclusively within the family and child-caring network.*

A large volume of research supports the assertion that very young children who are victims of homicide are likely to be killed by members of their immediate family, especially their parents. As reported above, in Canada, Silverman and Kennedy (1993) found that in 86 per cent of cases, child victims under the age of 2 were killed by a family member. Similar research in Australia (Strang 1993) and the United States (Crittenden and Craig 1990) has found that young children – infants and toddlers in particular – are rarely the victims of 'stranger' violence (more about that in a moment). In the present research, all victims under the age of 6 were killed by either parents or other family-related child-carers. Young children, emphatically, are rarely the victims of violence from those outside a family or child-caring network.

*Observation 5: There are distinct patterns having to do with the sex of the offender in many of the specific forms of early child homicide.*

In the present research, neonaticides almost exclusively involve female offenders, while if the child is a victim of familicide (where all members of the family are killed), the offender is almost always male. Fatal physical assault may involve either male or female offenders, although close to 80 per cent of offenders in the present case studies are male (Table 7.3). Thus, while it is true to say about filicide that, in contrast to other forms of homicide, women are more likely to be represented as offenders, in fact the level and nature of that involvement varies considerably by the actual form of the filicide.

*Observation 6: With the onset of the teenage years, there is a rapid rise in the risks of homicide victimisation, with the offenders increasingly likely to be from outside of the family network.*

In the countries we are examining, along with the increased risk observed in the teenage years, there is also a change in the source of the violence, which is increasingly found outside the family (Snyder and Sickmund 1995: 29; Finkelhor 1997; Christoffel 1984: 69). Increasing age is accompanied by a significant and rapid increase in victimisation by acquaintances, by strangers, or even by unidentified perpetrators. For example, Jason and Andereck (1983) found a steep rise in homicides accounted for by 'strangers', 'other', or 'unidentified' persons in the teenage years of 15–17. Similarly, a study of child homicide victims in Chicago found that victimisation was related to the developmental characteristics of children, and that older child victims were more likely to display a pattern that could be called 'murder in the community' (Christoffel, Anzinger and Amari 1983: 129).

*Observation 7: The increased risk of homicide in the teenage years is accompanied by a shift in the sex of the offender: almost all of the offenders are male.*

**Table 7.3** Victims and offenders in child homicide, Victoria, 1989–1999, by social context, type of homicide, sex and average age

| Type of homicide | Victims | | | | Offenders | | | |
|---|---|---|---|---|---|---|---|---|
| | No. | Male | Female | Average age | No. | Male | Female | Average age (yrs) |
| **Filicide** | | | | | | | | |
| Neonaticides | 11 | NA | NA | less than 24 hours | 6 | – | 6 | 22 |
| Fatal assaults | 19 | 11 | 8 | 16 mths | 19 | 14 | 5 | 27 |
| Attempt/suicide | 18 | 6 | 12 | 8 yrs | 13 | 7 | 6 | 32 |
| Extreme psychiatric disturbance | 6 | 1 | 5 | 6 yrs | 4 | 1 | 3 | 30 |
| 'Distinctive' | 4 | 2 | 2 | 5 yrs | 4 | 2 | 2 | 34 |
| Total | 58 | 20 | 27 | 4 yrs | 46 | 24 | 22 | 28 |
| **Non-filicide** | | | | | | | | |
| Honour contest homicides | 7 | 7 | – | 17 yrs | 7 | 7 | – | 19 |
| Homicide in the course of other crime | 4 | 2 | 2 | 16 yrs | 4 | 4 | – | 27 |
| Conflict resolution homicides | 3 | 3 | – | 16 yrs | 3 | 3 | – | 21 |
| Jealousy/control homicides | 4 | 1 | 3 | 16 yrs | 4 | 3 | 1 | 21 |
| Predatory sexual homicides | 4 | – | 4 | 11 yrs | 4 | 4 | – | 40 |
| Accidental shootings | 2 | 2 | – | 11 yrs | 2 | 2 | – | 15 |
| 'Distinctive' (inc. 1 serial killing) | 3 | 1 | 2 | 13 yrs | 3 | 3 | – | 24 |
| Unknown | 5 | 2 | 3 | 15 yrs | 5 | NA | NA | NA |
| Total | 32 | 18 | 14 | 15 yrs | 32 | 26 | 1 | 24 |

NA: not available.

While it has been demonstrated repeatedly that child homicide is different from other forms of homicide by virtue of the fact that women appear consistently as offenders, this observation clearly refers to filicides occurring primarily in the early childhood years. As soon as attention is focused on homicides of older children, especially those that occur outside of the family network, we find *virtually no female offenders.* Looking across all of the non-family homicides in our study in Victoria, the offender is overwhelmingly likely to be male, in contrast to filicides. Of the twenty-seven known offenders in non-family child homicides (there were five cases where the gender is unknown), twenty-six were male. The one exception was unusual in that it consists of a young woman who employed lethal violence to protect herself in the course of a violent argument with her male sexual partner who had been unable to accept the fact that the woman wanted to separate from him. While care must be taken when translating small numbers into percentages, this means that over 96 per cent of non-family offenders are male. This proportion is higher than for the proportion of all homicides committed by men, which hovers somewhere between 85 and 90 per cent in most studies.

*Observation 8: While in the early childhood years there are no appreciable differences in risk by sex of the child victim, in the teenage years the rate of increase in levels of victimisation is especially great for boys.*

The upturn in homicide risk with the approaching of early adulthood is distinctly gender-related, in contrast to the early years where there are no discernible differences between the victimisation levels of boys and girls (Figures 7.4, 7.5, and 7.6). The most extreme patterns are found in the United States (Figure 7.6) where the increased risks of boys in the teenage years 15–17 actually surpass the level of risk in the first year. In Australia and the United Kingdom, while there is a distinctive movement upward in risk among teenage males, the risks still remain somewhat lower than observed in the first year of life (Figures 7.4 and 7.5). In Australia and the United States, while there is an increase in the level of risk among girls in the teenage years, the increase is quite moderate when compared to that experienced by boys. In the United Kingdom, in contrast, there is no apparent increase in the level of homicide risk as girls move into the late teenage years (Figure 7.5).

*Observation 9: The form of the homicides involving teenage victims varies with the sex of the victim and reflects the young persons' increasing proximity to the contexts and understandings of adulthood.*

*Observation 9a: For boys, these teenage patterns of risk relate in part to the precocious involvement in more adult activities.*

In order to probe the actual nature of the risks by gender in the teenage years, once again it is necessary to turn away from statisitical data and probe into the patterns of teenage homicide that are revealed by a qualitative analysis of the themes within the scenarios of lethal violence identified in the present investigation. In general, as boys move closer to the early adult years, they can become involved in the same patterns of masculine violence that involve adult victims. These include scenarios such as honour contests between males, homicide that results from the commission of other crimes, and homicide arising from situations in which violence is used as a means of resolving a dispute between former acquaintances, which account for twelve of the eighteen male victims of non-family homicide (Table 7.3). The age of the victim in these scenarios tends to be close to early adulthood (for honour contest victims the average age was 17, and in both other crime and conflict-resolution homicides it was 16). The offenders in these homicides tended to be older than their victim (the average age of offenders in honour contest homicides was 19; it was 27 in homicides in the course of other crime, and 21 in conflict-resolution homicides).

*Observation 9b: Homicides involving teenage girls are more likely to be a consequence of their intimate relationship with a man.*

Girls in their teenage years are increasingly likely to become victims of the distinctive masculine proclivity to use violence as a way of coping with jealousy or the attempt of the female sexual partner to escape from his

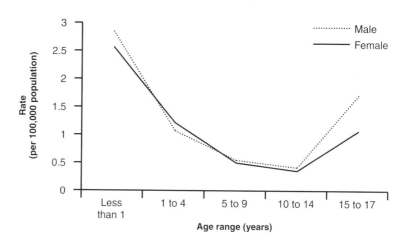

**Figure 7.4** Homicide rates, Australia, 1989–1999, by age and sex of victim
*Source:* Based on Mouzos 2000.

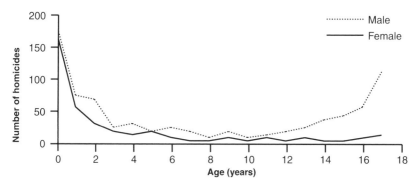

**Figure 7.5** Homicides, England and Wales, 1992–1997, by age and sex of victim
*Source:* Smith 2000.

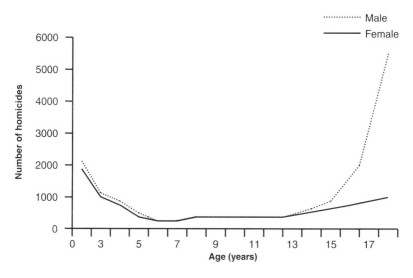

**Figure 7.6** Homicides, United States, 1980–1994, by age and sex of victim
*Source:* Snyder, Sickmund and Poe-Yamagata 1996.

control. The motive frequently given by males for these homicides is 'If I can't have you, no one will.' Most child victims of these violence scenarios are at the outer limits of childhood (the average age was 16), and most of their killers are adults (average age of 21). There were no female victims of honour contest or conflict-resolution violence, although two girls were victims in scenes where another crime had been committed (as might be expected).

*Observation 10: Some children, predominantly female, become victims of homicide as a consequence of predatory sexual attacks.*

There is a final definable theme that is found among the child homicides of this research that involves those individuals who fall victim to one or another form of predatory sexual attack. In the period we were looking at, there were no male victims of such attacks. The female victims tended to range in age, some being in their middle to late teenage years, but there were also two who were quite young (one 6, the other 8). For these young females, their emerging sexuality and the understanding of them as objects of men's sexual desire increasingly place them at risk of male violence. An increase is observed in the level of risk with the onset of the teenage years for boys and girls (although the increase is less for girls), but the sources and the risk are distinctly different for girls and boys.

Before considering the overall meaning of these observations, we turn now to outlining some forms of child homicide that were not found in our research but have been identified elsewhere. In general, the forms of child homicide considered below are relatively unusual events; however, they need to be acknowledged in any comprehensive analysis of child homicide.

### Some Additional Scenarios

*Killings by Non-Familial Child-Carers*

In recent years a number of 'nanny killings' in the United States and the United Kingdom have featured in international media accounts. The following descriptions of cases have been compiled by the authors from across these accounts. For example:

> On 4 February 1997, an 18-year-old British nanny working in the United States, Louise Woodward, dialled the emergency 911 number and reported that an 8-month-old infant in her care, Matthew Eappen, was not breathing. Rescue workers rushed to the scene, and quickly transferred the child to a nearby hospital, where an emergency operation was conducted to alleviate pressure in the infant's skull. The day after, following interviews by the local police, the nanny was charged with assault, but that charge was upgraded to murder when Matthew died on 9 February. The prosecution at the trial argued that Woodward had shaken Matthew violently, tearing the muscles in his neck and back, and causing the retinas in his eyes to haemorrhage. It was also alleged that the child had struck his head against a hard

object with a force equivalent to a drop from a two-storey window, resulting in a fracture of the skull that was ruled as the cause of death. Further, X-rays taken of the infant in the hospital show that he had suffered a fractured right forearm about three weeks before he received his fatal injuries. In a case that provoked international comment, the nanny was convicted of the child's death, but released shortly afterward from her US prison and returned to England, where she was to have a period of non-custodial supervision. [This case narrative is based on information collated from various news sources, such as the Associated Press bulletins of 30 October, 10, 11 and 13 November 1997; the *Boston Globe* of 30 October and 11 November 1997 and 7 October 1998; CNN News of 10 November 1997 and the CBS 'Good Morning' program of 18 June 1998.]

The facts here have much in common with cases where the batterers are members of the family. Notable in this case, as in most of the cases of fatal assault in this book, the autopsy showed that there were severe episodes of violence in the recent past that appeared in the form of broken limbs. Shaking of small children is potentially extremely dangerous, as is illustrated in another US case:

Manuela Etzel, from Germany, was babysitting 18-month-old Katherina Brown at her home in a suburb of Minneapolis–St Paul, on 29 January 1998, almost exactly a year after the death of Matthew Eappen. Katherine, like Matthew, died of head injuries that Etzel initially said were the result of the baby falling out of bed. In subsequent interviews, Etzel admitted that she had shaken Katherina, and that the baby's head had struck the floor two or three times, although in the early interviews she stated that she did not intend to hurt the child. Later Etzel did acknowledge that she was angry with the child at the time of the injuries. In sentencing Etzel to more time than was provided in the sentencing guidelines of Minnesota, the judge argued: 'You were her parent, and as such you had a duty to make sure nothing happened.' The child's mother had asked for the maximum sentence, stating that 'Of all the evil acts, murdering an innocent baby surely must be the worst.' [An extensive summary of the facts of this case can be found in the State of Minnesota Court of Appeals report of 15 April 1998.]

Both of the nannies in these cases pleaded not guilty to the charges laid against them. The severity of the Minnesota sentence is striking when compared to the sentence given to Woodward. But in another recent case in California, involving a 44-year-old child-carer, Manjit Kaur

Basuta, who had been convicted of killing a 13-month-old infant, an even longer sentence of twenty-five years was handed down. (Commentary on this case can be found in the *Detroit News*, 27 November 1998, and a number of Indian sources such as *The Week*, 17 and 31 October 1999, and the *Indian Express*, 25 November 1998.) These lengthy sentences stand in contrast to a recent case in the United Kingdom:

> In January 1999, Louise Sullivan, a 26-year-old Australian nanny, was convicted of involuntary manslaughter of 6-month-old Caroline Jongen. The child had died of head injuries and brain damage while in Sullivan's care in April 1998. The young woman claimed that she had shaken the infant 'a bit'. Sullivan claimed that in school in Australia she had learned a 'shake and shout' technique for dealing with an unconscious person, where the person could be shaken gently by their shoulders to see if they were conscious. Sullivan denied the charge of murder, but entered a plea of guilty to a manslaughter charge and was given a non-custodial sentence. [Descriptions of this case can be found in the Melbourne *Age*, 29 January 1999; *Time Magazine*, 1 February 1999; the UK *Sunday Times*, 31 January 1999; and an extensive account in the *Muswell Hill News*, 20 January 1999.]

While many of the facts of this British case were similar to those in the United States (a nanny being charged with homicide after a death from the shaking of an infant), the guilty plea makes it different from the US cases.

Such events demonstrate that, while children in the early years of life are most at risk from those who are charged with their care, and while these risks are most likely to originate from the family, there are cases where the source of that risk is a designated child-carer such as a nanny. Casual babysitters, as opposed to the long-term, ongoing role of a nanny can also be a source of risk. In the late 1990s in the United Kingdom a 16-month-old Manchester infant, Molly Adams, died from head injuries sustained at the hands of what was described in the newspapers as a 'trusted babysitter' who was aged 12 at the time of the death. An older case from the United Kingdom was described as follows:

> One such killing occurred on an evening in 1958 when a girl of fourteen was sitting with a sixteen-month-old baby. Because the baby cried the girl tied a scarf around the child's neck, hoping to quieten her. The baby was strangled, the girl was found guilty of manslaughter and sent to an approved school. [Lucas 1970: 210]

Similar accounts of homicides at the hands of child-carers can be found in homicide files in the United States. Wilbanks, in his extensive examination of homicide in Miami a few years ago, reported among others the following case:

> Victim, Black Male, 1; … Victim was left with a babysitter by his mother. Baby (V) was hit with blunt object and at first babysitter (a friend of V's mother) blamed a two-year-old playmate. However, police believe now that babysitter did it. Also another child had been injured and died while in her care a few months earlier. Offender, Black female, 28; Identity known but not enough evidence to charge. [Case No. 490, Wilbanks 1984: 300]

Things can go horribly wrong in the early years of life, and at times it is child-carers enlisted and trusted by the family who are responsible for lethal injuries. A note might be added that there is nothing new in this. In his book on the 'rise and fall' of the British nanny, Gathorne-Hardy (1972) devotes a chapter to the 'cruel nanny', and describes several cases in the late nineteenth and early twentieth centuries of child batterings and even murders committed by nannies.

Such cases are quite different from the patterns analysed in earlier chapters, in which all of the women who killed children were the mother of the child. In some ways the cases are similar to the situations in which the child is killed by the male de facto partner of the child's mother. Such, often young, men are likely to be inexperienced in dealing with very young children, whereas the nannies in particular have frequently had some training in child-care. Fortunately, these are exceptionally rare events in light of the number of young women who act as nannies and casual babysitters, but they indicate that in some circumstances women do kill children who are not their own.

### Munchausen Syndrome by Proxy

Another even rarer form of child homicide in which a mother kills her own children is Munchausen syndrome by proxy (Rosen, Frost and Bricker 1987; Rosenberg 1987; McGuire and Feldman 1989; Goss and McDougall 1992, Lowenstein 1997; Gilbert-Barness and Barness 1998). Munchausen syndrome, first described by Asher (1951), refers to medical patients who fabricate illnesses and subject themselves to unpleasant and potentially dangerous procedures in order to become the focus of attention and medical treatment. Munchausen syndrome by proxy refers to cases where the caretaker, nearly always the mother (Goss and McDougall 1991: 814), fabricates or, more dangerously, actually produces illness in a child, which results in numerous hospitalisations, treatments and, in extreme cases, death. The attending physician is often confused by a wide array of symptoms and signs.

The following case is a complicated one which in essence begins with a form of Munchausen syndrome then rapidly shades into Munchausen syndrome by proxy:

> The mother, age 27, during her third pregnancy (her second pregnancy was a boy delivered at 28 weeks' gestation, who died 2 days later because of extreme prematurity), was admitted to hospital for bed rest at 18 weeks' gestation because of recurrent haemorrhages. She had several more episodes of bleeding, and at 26 weeks her membranes ruptured and the child, a boy, was then delivered by caesarean section. The baby was then immediately placed in intensive care and received ventilator therapy for 48 days. He was only able to go home after 5 months. Over the next year it was necessary to return to the hospital on several occasions for such symptoms as apnoeic episodes, febrile convulsions, breathing difficulties, further cyanotic and febrile episodes. Finally at [age] 15 months he was having frequent episodes of breathing difficulty, repeated vomiting and occasional convulsions. In many of these hospital returns, probing of the supposed symptoms would reveal no demonstrable abnormalities. Finally, at one point the father of the child asked to see the hospital notes to determine if the symptoms occurred in the presence of his wife. Further probing of the features of the medical history resulted in the hospital staff diagnosing the case as Munchausen Syndrome by Proxy. While the mother denied the diagnosis, medical staff persisted and were able to obtain the removal from the mother's care for 12 months. In that time, the child made remarkable progress, including extraordinary weight gains, and [had] no further life-threatening episodes. His anticonvulsant, antireflux and persistent asthma treatments were withdrawn. [Goss and McDougall 1991]

This remarkable case displays many of the classic features of the Munchausen syndrome by proxy. The symptoms were often inappropriate and were found only when the mother was present. The mother was constantly with the sick child in hospital and she was happily at ease with staff of the children's ward. The illnesses were unexplained, prolonged, and so extraordinary that medical staff noted that the case was unprecedented in their experience. The treatments were ineffective, the child was under 5 years of age, and there had been a previous death. The real danger in these cases, of course, is that there may be multiple deaths before the real cause of the illness or injuries is recognised. These mothers often engage in frequent smothering attempts (suspected in the breathing difficulties observed here) and poisonings. This case is distinctive in that there are episodes of Munchausen syndrome itself (the woman had induced the premature birth with a knitting needle) as well as the Munchausen syndrome by proxy.

To our knowledge no such case was observed in the narratives found in the present Australian study, but cases of this syndrome as a cause of child homicide have been identified (as in the references listed above) elsewhere in Australia, Canada and the United States. It is hard to gauge the level of this form of lethal violence, but the cases are exceptionally rare. Fortunately, medical authorities have identified some of the specific indicators involved in this pattern of violence to children (Goss and McDougall 1991). Furthermore, once medical practitioners are alerted, there is the possibility that they can intervene while the child is still alive, before there is some extreme episode that results in death.

### Children who Kill Children

While the focus of this book is on children who are victims of homicide, there has been growing concern during the 1990s about situations in which the homicide offender is a child (Ewing 1995; Heide 1996, 1998; McLaughlin 2000). The most notorious example of this is the case of the killing of Jamie Bulger in the United Kingdom:

> On 12 February 1993, Mrs Denise Bulger went to the Strand Shopping Centre in Bootle, near Liverpool, with her sister-in-law, Nicola Bailer, and her child Jamie, 2 years old. They went to several shops, one of them a butcher's, in which both women bought things. Denise Bulger said later that she thought her son was by her side as she was served; however, after she paid for her purchases, she looked around and could not see him. She ran outside the shop but still could not see her son. He was later seen on a video film taken by a security camera in the shopping centre, following two older boys. A search was instigated; two days later, his body was found on a railway line some 3 kilometres from the Strand Shopping Centre. Two 10-year-old boys were charged with his abduction and murder, and with the attempted abduction of another small boy at the same shopping centre that day. They were tried in the Preston Crown Court in November 1993 and found guilty ... They were sentenced to be detained at Her Majesty's pleasure, the equivalent of a life sentence. [Summarised in Young 1996: 113]

This killing became the focus of intense international interest, with the details of the trial and sentence watched closely by the assembled press. What seemed to strike a chord was the obvious youthfulness of both victim and the offenders. Terms such as 'evil' are sprinkled liberally through the coverage, and Young (1996: 113) has commented that the case became viewed in the United Kingdom as 'symptomatic of social decay, the decline of morality, the swelling of parents' fears for the children and a spur to government policy relating to juvenile crime'. The international commentary was provoked, of course, precisely because of the rarity of the event. Children, especially those under the teenage years, infrequently kill, and few child victims of homicide result from the acts of other children. But such cases do occur.

In the United Kingdom in late 1999 there was a revived interest in the case of Mary Bell when details of her present adult existence were revealed. Much of the commentary concerned the difference between the press coverage and public response to that case two decades previously and the more recent Bulger case.

> On 25 May 1968, two boys collecting kindling went into a derelict house in Newcastle, and found the body of a 4-year-old boy in an upstairs room. He had been strangled. A few days later, the body of another boy, this time a 3-year-old, was found in wasteland in the same area. This second victim suffered from cuts to his body as well as being strangled. Two girls, aged 11 and 13, were arrested and charged with the crimes. Mary Bell, the 11-year-old, was found not guilty of murder but guilty of manslaughter, while the other child was acquitted. [See Lucas 1970: 211–13]

As was true in the Bulger case some twenty-five years later, these events sparked considerable controversy and debate. While there were expressions of outrage and various protests regarding the handling of Bell, what is striking in contrast to the Bulger case was the commentary stating concern for the offender, Mary Bell. In a remarkable letter, a convicted felon captured and summarised the feelings of many in the following words: 'One must grieve bitterly for those innocent boys who died, but will our grief be less by destroying the third and surviving child of this tragedy' (cited in Lucas 1970: 221). What may have changed in the years since the Bell case is the gradual evolution of an internationalised media, capable of the instantaneous transfer of 'infotainment' around the globe. While 'ordinary' homicides may receive scarce attention in daily news accounts, these outlets have a special appetite for the bizarre and unusual. The odd contours of homicides committed by children, especially if they are very young, assures a high level of media attention to these cases.

There are smaller-scale versions of these cases, which attract somewhat smaller audiences. In 1998, for example, Australia was transfixed by reports that a 10-year-old was going to face manslaughter charges involving the drowning death of his 6-year-old playmate. The child was the youngest ever to face homicide charges in Australia, and the police brought the charges because of what was described as the 'degree of callousness or recklessness' in the actions of the offender, unusual language to use in relation to so young a child.

### Street Gang Violence

The most frequent scenario in which a child kills another child involves a teenage boy or boys and the death of another teenage boy. The most common cause of such events is the youthful honour contests in which both offender and victim are teenagers. In one of the case studies reviewed in the previous chapter, the killer was a 14-year-old Vietnamese youth who was one of a group which had been confronted by a 16-year-old 'Old Australian' who had clearly been spoiling for a fight.

The dynamics of these cases contain themes of group violence among young males. Further, in some cases the social groupings have a loosely defined collective identity, as in the case where Colin (age 17), a 'Bogan', was killed at a disco by a slightly older youth, Charles (age 19), who was known as a 'Headbanger'. At first, the collective character of such killings would appear to share some characteristics with American street gang homicides. Consider the following case description drawn from an American account of a teenage street gang member, 'Manny':

> Manny was the son of a convict, he was a boy at loose ends described by a staff member as a 'happy follower.' He returned from a juvenile institution with no notion of what he wanted to do, and immediately melted back into the group. We observed him on the street 45 times in the month following his return, and he was alone in only three of those situations. The group was his life and, as it happened, his death:
>
> [8 September] Returned from probation camp. Seen immediately in the company of various core members.
> [22 September] Enrolled in high school with staff help.
> [23 September] With three others, attacked member of a rival gang.
> [4 October] Recommended to a Boys' Club as a youth aid under Neighborhood Youth Corps Program.
> [10 October] Though considered a bad risk, Manny was accepted for the job at the Boys' Club.
> [13 October] Job held up because of [New York City] regulations.
> [15 October] During raid by rival gang, Manny ran up the back stairs of a house only to find the door locked. Trapped there, and with his pals scattering in all directions, he was shot and killed.

Manny was not the particular target of this raid. But his heavy dependence on the group, and staff inabilities to come up with alternative activities soon enough, placed him at that place at that time. [Klein 1971: 84]

This homicide has much in common with other situations in which a young male is killed by another male in the course of a group confrontation. The killing itself is not specifically premeditated, but flows out of a more generalised instance of group violence. The collective identity of the victim is an important feature of his victimisation.

At the same time, there are, some would argue, distinctive features of street gang violence in the American context. Klein (1995), for one, has suggested that there are unique parameters to American street gang violence that should not be confused with patterns of youthful male collective behaviour seen elsewhere:

Despite its considerable variety – over time, across locations, and even in its internal substructures – I see the American street gang as rather different. That it is not totally different is also clear. Although I'll describe counterparts in such contrasting places as Russia, Papua New Guinea, and Berlin, the common varieties of street gang still are essentially an American product. [Klein 1995: 3]

In examining the question of whether the patterns observed in America are unique, Klein (1995: 214) suggests a number of distinctive characteristics. These include: whether the collectives involved are territorial (with gang rivalries); whether they acknowledge themselves as criminally oriented groups; whether they exhibit 'cafeteria-style' crime patterns rather than crime-specific focuses; whether their structures are moderately cohesive (thus neither very tight nor amorphous); and whether they are products of current or growing inner-city areas of poverty, alienation and discrimination. There can be little doubt that such collectives, once they develop, become an important source of violence (Huff 1990; Cervantes 1992; Inciardi, Horowitz and Pottieger 1993; Spergel 1995). In the United States, street gangs have not only been a major part of the homicide picture, they also accounted for a significant component of the increase in homicide observed in the early 1990s. As Block and Christakos observed in Chicago:

The most striking increase in any type of Chicago homicide occurred in street gang-related homicides ... Usually street gang violence (whether fatal or not) has not followed a smooth trend. Instead, it has increased in 'spurts' of violence, often reflecting an escalating series of confrontations between specific gangs fighting over a specific territory of the city. From 1990 to 1993, however, the number of street gang-related murders in Chicago escalated far more than before. [Block and Christakos 1995: 30]

Klein (1995: 230) pointed out that there has been over recent years a significant widening of the distribution of these gangs, so that from a few dozen gang cities in the United States in the 1950s, by the 1990s more than a thousand cities were experiencing gang problems; the 'thousands of gang-related deaths cannot lightly be set aside'. More disturbing, Klein sees initial evidence of the expansion of this problem to other countries (such as Germany and Russia), and there is now a major initiative in Europe to examine the presence of violence relating to street gangs.

Clearly, street gangs pose a specific problem above and beyond the violence that flows out of spontaneous youth collectives found in Australia and the United Kingdom. When the conditions are right to provoke their development (and Klein argues these are basically the creation of an urban underclass of alienated young people), a pattern emerges which can have a major impact on the quality of life of adolescents and young adults, and on the patterns of lethal violence observed in the country involved. The exceptional rise of youth violence observed in the United States in the early 1990s, followed by strong declines toward the end of the decade, are clearly the result of behaviour among young minority males, and presumably much of the rise and fall is related to street gang violence. At this point, while some of the youth violence in Australia is collective, and while at least some of the homicide victimisations of children are related to group violence, a distinctive pattern of street gang violence has not yet appeared. Klein (1995) has argued that in Australia, Canada, and in such cities in the United Kingdom as London and Manchester, there is little evidence yet of the American-style street gang (although in Manchester there are drug-related gangs who are involved in violence). In the present Australian data on child homicide, a major factor of youth risk in the United States, the American-style street gang, is not present.

### Collective Violence Against Girls

While the dynamics of street gang confrontations ending with death involve predominantly male-on-male behaviour, there are other scenarios which involve boys victimising girls. In Australia, one of the more notable of these was the infamous Leigh Leigh case:

On the night of 3 November 1989, Leigh Leigh (age 14) was subjected to a series of violent physical and sexual assaults, and then bashed and bludgeoned to death with a large rock. The cause of death at the autopsy was a fractured skull and brain injury, although as well there was considerable bruising to other parts of her body, and injuries to her genital organs consistent with brutal sexual assault. Several boys were alleged to have been involved, many of them under the age of 18, and three boys were ultimately convicted of the sexual assaults and killing.

This case has been the focus of important scholarly analysis (Carrington and Johnson 1994; Carrington 1998), and was the inspiration for a play and movie (which altered some of the events for dramatic purposes). In her comments on the movie, Carrington (1998: 156) commended the film for its portrayal of the 'disdainful aspects of sexuality and power associated with surfie sub-culture, and their objectification of women as little more than sex objects'. Carrington also expresses the belief that what happened to Leigh Leigh, although it might have been exceptionally brutal, was not all that exceptional (p. 159). The interactional dynamics of this account, like many of the honour contests, illustrate the dark and often tragic side of young Australian masculinity and the demands of 'mateship'. While lethal consequences may be infrequent, there are underlying elements of male behaviour that are all too common, and in this case the events turn on collective violence.

*School Shootings*

One form of lethal violence involving child victims not found in Australia is the high school shootings that have taken place in the United States. One of the most notable of these was the events which took place in 1999 in Littleton, Colorado:

On 20 April 1999, two teenagers, Eric Harris and Dylan Klebold, planned to kill hundreds of their classmates at Columbine High School in Colorado. The two had planted several bombs in the school, which had failed to detonate as planned at 11.17 a.m. Each boy carried two guns into the school, and started shooting. Over the next sixteen minutes, thirteen people were killed, and another twenty-three were wounded. In a videotape made before they began their spree, Klebold promised that 'Seconds will be like hours ... I cannot wait.' Harris added, 'What a rush.' In addition to the guns, the teenagers' arsenal included 48 small carbon dioxide bombs ('crickets'), 27 pipe bombs, 11 propane containers and 7 incendiary devices, but most of the bombs were duds. Had the bombs gone off, hundreds of fellow students might have been killed. The first police arrived at 11.24. The two boys killed their last victim at 11.35, then roamed around the school as hundreds of police officers converged on the scene (including officers from nineteen city police units, five different sheriff's departments, the state police and two federal agencies). After about forty minutes, Harris and Klebold killed themselves. [This case received extensive coverage in the media: for example, *Denver Post*, 20, 21 April, 16, 21 May and 23 July 1999; *Time Magazine*, 21 April, 20 December 1999; *US News and World Report*, 1 November 1999; US ABC News, 20, 21 April 1999; CNN News, 21 April 1999; Fox News, 15 May 2000.]

Unfortunately, however dramatic this case may be, it is not unique. There have been, in fact, eleven of these high school shooting sprees in the United States in the past decade (Hiede, Eyles and Spencer 2000). The Columbine High School story is similar to many of these, in that the offenders were young males, they were obsessed with guns, and they had become isolated from their schoolmates. This event is different in two respects: there were two offenders, and there was extensive planning which resulted in the deaths of so many at the school.

More typical of these kinds of killings are the events that took place a year earlier (21 May 1998) in Springfield, Oregon.

The students of Thurston High School were gathered in the school cafeteria shortly before classes were due to start, when at 8 a.m. Kipland Kinkel entered the cafeteria by a side door, carrying a .22-calibre rifle, a .22-calibre handgun and a 9-mm semiautomatic Glock pistol. Kinkel raised the rifle to hip level, and started firing, swivelling slowly from side to side. He fired off fifty rounds in 90 seconds. As Kinkel started to reload, he was tackled by Jake Ryker, a fellow student; although Ryker was wounded, with the help of his brother he was able to subdue Kinkel before he could fire off any more rounds. In the brief moments of the spree, two students had been killed, and twenty-two others were wounded, some of them critically. Subsequent investigations established that Kinkel had killed his father and mother the evening before.

Kinkel's life had been marred with trouble, and his father had sought out a number of options to help his son, including counselling. Against the desires of the mother, the father had permitted the boy to deepen his interest in guns. Classmates alleged that Kinkel had bragged about torturing animals and building bombs. The day before the spree, Kinkel had been suspended for bringing a gun to school, and faced a hearing that could have resulted in his expulsion. When found with the gun, he was taken by police to the Lane County Juvenile Department, formally charged with possession of a stolen firearm, and then released to the custody of his parents. He apparently had told a fellow student that 'he was probably going to do something stupid today and get back at the people who had expelled him'. [This case was covered extensively by such newspapers in the Pacific Northwest as the *Portland Oregonian* and the *Seattle Times* of 22 and 23 May 1998, and in *Time Magazine*, 1 June 1998, and US ABC and CNN News, 21 May 1998.]

The killer here is a lone, troubled male, and once again we see the theme of gun obsession that tends to run through these accounts. The other school shootings in the United States, like this one, tended to involved single offenders whose isolation is clearly an important feature of the pressures that led to the shootings.

While significantly different in that the offender was much older, there is an example of a school shooting which took place in Scotland:

On 13 March 1996 Thomas Hamilton, age 43, entered the Dunblane Primary School and killed fifteen children (ages 5 and 6) and one adult (a teacher), and wounded a further ten children and three adults before shooting himself. The massacre had been carefully planned, and he had walked his intended route in the preceding days. At the time of the murder, the offender had had at least one failed business, and was heavily in debt. He had only one known close acquaintance, and was regarded by neighbours as 'odd'. In 1973 he was appointed as an assistant scoutmaster, but was asked to resign due to his 'peculiar behaviour'. Hamilton's resentment about these events grew over the years, and at the time of the killings he had come to believe that the police, the scouts and even the Queen were in a conspiracy against him. Hamilton had set up his own boys' clubs and summer camps between 1981 and 1996, but his oddness led to them all eventually failing. Hamilton was fascinated with guns, and had been a member, and then kicked out, of a number of gun clubs. At the time of the killings, Hamilton owned a large number of rifles, pistols, revolvers, and semi-automatic weapons. [See Cantor, Mullins and Alpers 2000]

The Dunblane events differed from the school shootings in the United States in several important factors. First, as indicated, the killer was a mature adult. Second, the child victims were much younger, being a group of 5- and 6-year-olds. There are similarities with the American cases, however since the killer was male, was a loner, had a history of grievances and resentment, and (unusual in the United Kingdom when compared to the United States) was obsessed with guns.

There is something particularly poignant about the killing of children in school. These are places where the community takes on a particular obligation to protect children. Further, in many of these accounts the nature of the resentment of the offender or offenders, and the types of weapons used, ensure that a number of victims are killed and injured in the attack, often in a very short period of time (it only took a minute and a half to produce the deaths and injuries at Thurston High School). This form of violence has only recently emerged, and little systematic information is available. Hopefully, our knowledge and understanding of these events will be aided by further research (e.g., Homa, Menifield and Brewer 1999; Heide et al. 1999; Cantor, Mullins and Alpers 2000; and Heide, Eyles and Spencer 2000).

## Conclusion

The purpose in presenting the several observations about child homicide, and considering the scenarios not contained in our own data, has been to round out analyses of child homicide and to clarify the overall patterning of these events. Without question, Silverman and Kennedy (1993) in their focus on the significance of 'routine activities' are accurate in pointing out that the nature of the life routines of children changes as they move into the school and teenage years, and that these changes are reflected in altered patterns of homicide victimisation. The everyday routines of children below the age of 5 or 6 are likely to be oriented within the family. Therefore, we should not be surprised to find that the child's killer in these years is drawn from the family network, most often either the victim's parents or step-parents.

As correct as this observation is, of course, as a unitary observation it cannot account for the differential patterns of family child killings, in particular their variation in terms of the sex of the offender. Similarly, while it is indisputable that children's life routines change as they enter the school years, a routine activities analysis by itself cannot explain why risks of homicide are so low in the middle years of childhood. Neither does this explanation satisfactorily account for the striking gendered patterns of homicide in terms of both victims and offenders with the onset of the teenage years.

In contrast, the developmental hypothesis advanced by Finkelhor (1997) serves the valuable function of calling attention to the fact that 'gender patterns become more specific' as children age. However, as stated, it is not clear either how this relates to the sharp alteration in the pattern of gender of the offenders in cases of older children (they are virtually all male), or how the gendered risks of victims begin to diverge in the adolescent years. Our analysis, in contrast, emphasises that, in the early years of childhood, there is little apparent difference in rates or patterns of homicide victimisation by sex. However, there are differences in the patterns of *offending* according to sex in these years, this being the period when women are likely to offend. In the later years of childhood, when lethal violence occurs, men are almost exclusively the offenders, and the particular patterns of victimisation risk are also defined by sex (with the sharpest increase in risk being experienced by males).

Child homicide is definitively a matter of social context, gendered offending and, as the child ages, gendered risks. In order of explanatory importance, there is, first, the matter of social context. In the initial years of life, and especially the early months, the social context of the child is almost exclusively contained within the family, and it is therefore within this network that any significant risk of homicide will occur. In these early years, there appears to be no overall difference in the risk by sex of the victim. Both males and females appear in the figures as offenders, but what sets early child homicide apart from almost any other pattern of violence is the significant presence of women among the offenders. However, the nature of the violence in these early years is still shaped by gender, since women (nearly always mothers) tend to kill in different ways from men (most often stepfathers).

The middle years of childhood are distinguished above all else by the exceptionally low risk of homicide. Thus, the first theoretical task is not to explain why homicide occurs in these years, but to explain why it does not. Theoretically, we would suggest that these are the years where two separate phenomena are working. First, in these middle childhood years there is the greatest weight of combined private and public management of socialisation and protection activities. While the family retains considerable responsibility for child-rearing in these years, the school also contributes to children's learning and to managing their protection. In some jurisdictions this is manifested most visibly in mandatory reporting laws that require professionals to report to the child protection authorities any evidence of physical or sexual abuse of children. The entry of the child into the public arena of the school provides an added layer of surveillance over the lives of children that is not present in the earlier childhood years. In a word, the web of social protection becomes particularly dense in these middle years of childhood.

Second, in these years the children are not yet ready, or allowed, to be pulled into the precocious involvement in adult activities that provide the source of so much of the victimisation of teenage children.

Nevertheless, a few of the children in these middle years may become the victims of predatory sexual offenders. Turning this around, what risks there are in these middle childhood years originate from a mix of family and non-family contexts. One source of risk is the family (although at a much lower level than observed in the earliest years). In this middle childhood period in the present study we have found a few examples of natural parents, both fathers and mothers, who take the lives of their children as part of their own suicide plan. (This often involves multiple victims, although mothers rarely kill their spouses, whereas familicide, when found, is most likely to involve the natural father.) A small number of homicides result when the general protective network that surrounds younger children breaks down, and life is taken in such events as sexual predation or perhaps as part of a highly unusual group homicide, as in the course of an armed robbery. There is little differentiation in risk by sex of the victim in this period.

The social context shifts dramatically in the late years of childhood, as the protective web of the family and school begins to break down. In these years, especially those of late adolescence, the context of risk is highly gendered in ways markedly different from the earlier years. The context of offending is definitively gendered, since in virtually all instances involving teenage victims the offenders are male. The victimisation pattern by gender provides a second dimension of difference, but the patterns here are more complicated. While teenagers of both sexes may become victims of homicides, the risks are greater for boys. The earlier protection afforded by both family and school begins to lose its purchase. Boys find their way into risk situations where violence can turn lethal, such as honour contests. Or they engage in crime and thus expose themselves to offender retaliation that is lethal. Or they are killed as a consequence of the offender's inability to find any solution to some dispute other than considered violence. For girls, the risks are more closely aligned to their sexuality. The two major forms of risk for girls in this age group are sexual partners for whom lethal violence is an ultimate device of control, or predatory sexual offenders where lethal violence is part of the sexual attack.

Our analysis underscores the great diversity in the risk patterns of homicide in the childhood years, and the corollary that there can be no simple statement of the role of either age or sex on these patterns of lethal violence victimisation. Great care should be taken in making assertions such as 'childhood is the period of greatest risk of homicide' because such a statement is clearly inaccurate. In statistical terms, the domain of child homicide is highly 'interactive', that is, understanding the level of risk requires the specification of the particular conditions that define risk.

The focus on social context derives from the long-standing tradition in the study of homicide which focuses on the importance of the 'social relationship' between victim and offender. Since the initial argument by Wolfgang (1958) that the dynamics of such relationships are critical to an understanding of homicide, the analysis has remained shackled by some of the terms proposed by Wolfgang which define the content of these bonds. Specifically, the focus has remained fixed upon what has been termed in more recent investigations, 'relational distance' (Silverman and Kennedy 1993): some relationships are seen as 'close' (family relationships); some are in 'middling' ground (friends or acquaintances); others are 'distant', that category being made up of 'strangers'. The analysis typically leads to the conclusion that most homicides occur where relationships are 'close', and that killings involving 'strangers' are relatively less common.

It is lamentable that these terms continue to be used since they tend to confound any proper understanding of the social context of violence. Although we agree that victim–offender relationships are fundamental to understanding homicide, a strong case can be made that the use of such terms as 'friends' and 'strangers' to classify such relationships only confuses the analysis of lethal violence. For one matter, in empirical research such terms are likely to prove hopelessly unreliable. For example, how can one who was not present in the scene when the events happen accurately record whether two people are strangers in a venue such as a pub, or how would one consistently assess the difference between bonds defined as 'friends' or 'acquaintances'? But these pale into insignificance when the examination focuses on the theoretical validity of these terms. A word like 'stranger' deflects attention away from the actual central dynamics of lethal violence. This word 'stranger' is powerful and emotive, and elicits images of strangers lurking in darkened alleys, waiting to pounce on innocent, unsuspecting victims. Very few homicides, including stranger homicides, fit this pattern.

All of the homicides in this investigation, as in the previous study of masculine violence (Polk 1994), can be successfully grouped and analysed without reference to the term 'stranger'. The primary facts where such a classification might arise, we argue, evolve around the dynamics of honour contests, or events occurring within a serious crime that suddenly turns lethal, or the events that lead to sexual predation and a death, or perhaps the tragic trail of a serial killer. Each of these involves relationships where the victim and the offender are not known to each other, but we would argue that this factor is quite secondary to the major elements of the violence which is taking place.

There is a simple fact that must be kept in mind: people do not kill each other *because* they are strangers. They kill for other and more important reasons, and it is these reasons, including the social dynamics of their relationship to their victim, that ought to be significant in the analysis. The events at Dunblane, for example, are best understood as an example of a particular kind of gun-obsessed, lonely, resentful male who explodes at a particular point in his life, and whether he did or did not know the children he killed is not of central relevance to the narrative. Young men, including teenagers, may be provoked into an honour contest that results in the death of another young male, and it is the dynamics of these that should be examined. In fact, in honour contests the interactions appear to be identical whether the parties involved know each other or not.

The intent here is not to deny the centrality of social relationships in the understanding of homicide. Our position is that the analysis of child homicide must proceed initially with the specification of such social dynamics as they define social context. While we have proposed consideration of a 'family/non-family' polarity for social context, we mean something very different than the traditional use of 'relational distance'. Social contexts should not be seen as falling on some continuum that runs from 'family' at one end to 'stranger' at the other. Instead, a variety of emergent social relationships and settings begin to develop as children move into the teenage years, which may lead to violent encounters that will vary by the sex of the offender and sex of the victim. These reflect the varied social patterns that life takes with the onset of early adulthood. Some of these involve 'close' personal relationships, such as the situation of young girls who become attached to males who become jealous and possessive. Some of the distinctive settings and interactional dynamics will take place in venues such as pubs or parties, where young males become involved in mutual challenging of honour, which at some point spills over into lethal violence. In addition, we have identified narratives where either the child is the victim of lethal violence connected with another crime such as armed robbery, or the child is the offender in such a crime, and becomes a 'reverse victim' when violence erupts.

Social context as we have used the term is not to be understood as a continuum of relational distance. Instead, as individuals move into the late teenage and early adult years, their social worlds widen and split outward in a number of directions. With this widening of experience, some adolescents become pulled into social settings where there is a risk of violence. We have taken as our task the attempt to identify the varied content of themes of these potentially dangerous scenes, and as we have done so there has been little need to consider as a distinct issue the role of relational distance.

In summary, in this chapter we have proposed several observations that help refine and define the basic facts of child homicide. Challenging the simple statement that the period of childhood is one of great risk of lethal violence, we have instead proposed that there are two periods of very high risk of homicide during the childhood years, as well as a period where homicide risk is exceptionally low. Further, although overall the actual level of risk may be comparable and high in the first year of life and in the late teenage years, the sources of risk in these two periods are very different. The patterns of violence vary across context, age, and the sex of the offender and the victim. The next task is to examine theoretical perspectives that have been suggested to explain the forms of risk of lethal violence that have been identified here.

CHAPTER 8

# Towards a Theoretical Analysis
# of Child Homicide

The case studies examined in this book are diverse, as are the additional forms of lethal violence involving children considered in the previous chapter. Remarkable differences in patterns result from the different ages at which these children became victims of homicide, and the sex of the person who commits the homicide. In this chapter we review the data presented previously and consider some conceptual frameworks for understanding these events.

## Examining Cinderella Myths

One of the observations in our research was the significance of the relationship between the child and the family member who killed them: there are no stepmothers who killed children; virtually all fatal assaults were committed by the mother's de facto spouse; and only biological fathers committed familicide. One provocative formulation about a major source of childhood violence, including homicide, that has a unique focus on the nature of victim–offender relationship, is the work of Daly and Wilson, especially their recent book, *The Truth about Cinderella* (1998). These writers address the particular risks of violence faced by stepchildren. The book begins with observations that in human folklore the world over, there are myths about the special vulnerability of stepchildren. They argue that Cinderella is not just a character in an old English folk tale, but that 'uncannily similar' tales of the plight of stepchildren are found throughout Europe and Asia, and elsewhere. They argue that these tales could not exist unless there was some resonance with reality; in their words: 'The themes must have something to do with the human condition' (Daly and Wilson 1997: 5). Put simply, the tales exist because stepchildren are, in fact, more at risk of abuse and violence: 'Having a step-parent has turned out to be the most powerful epidemiological risk factor for severe child mistreatment yet discovered' (Daly and Wilson 1998: 7)

Unique in their argument is not just the fact of such risk, but its source. For Daly and Wilson, violence toward stepchildren is a consequence of the workings of Darwinian principles of evolution, which dictate that human parents will love and cherish their genetic children over the claims of children who lack direct biological ties. Daly and Wilson review evidence from various parts of the animal kingdom that shows how dramatic such strategies can be. When a new male lion takes over the pride of a male he has defeated, for example, he systematically searches out and kills all the progeny of the deposed male (or males). This destruction of the genetic material of competitors is not exclusively a male trait, since among jacanas, tropical marsh-dwelling birds, a number of males build nests and compete for the attention of a single, territorial-based female. When a female jacana manages to displace a rival, thereby acquiring a group of dutiful male partners, she goes through the various nests and systematically destroys the eggs of her predecessor (Daly and Wilson 1998: 5–17).

At this point the story becomes complicated: the animal kingdom is diverse, and there are certainly species for whom this genetic strategy is not appropriate. For example, a mother bat who cannot locate her own pup will suckle whatever pup reaches her breast. When the analysis turns to humans, however, the general observation is made that:

Evolutionary reasoning and the evidence were in accord: It seemed clear that assuming step-parental duties must typically be perceived as a cost rather than a benefit in remarriage negotiations, and that the magnitude of the step-parental obligation must be contested and not infrequently resented. [Daly and Wilson 1998: 25]

It is not a matter of mere resentment. One major consequence is a higher risk of various forms of violence. Daly and Wilson (1998: 32) cite data that show in Canada, children of step-parents aged under 2 years were seventy times more like to be killed than were children raised in genetically intact families, and further: 'We now know that the story in Great Britain is much the same as in North America: step-parents are hugely over-represented as perpetrators of registered child abuse and even more hugely as child murderers.'

Considerable work in gathering and reviewing the appropriate statistics is required in order to make the calculations that support these assertions. It is, in fact, difficult to compute accurate comparative rates of forms of violence between children living with genetic parents versus step-parents. It requires not only reliable data on abuse and death properly coded with respect to parental background, but also similarly accurate data for the general population to compute accurate rates showing relative risks by family background. Critical to testing the 'Cinderella hypothesis', for example, is knowledge not simply of the number of children living in stepfamilies, but more specifically, the number of children, by age, living with stepmothers. There are few good sets of such data to draw upon, and one result has been considerable controversy about the comparative risk of violence by genetic parents versus step-parents.

For our purposes, some conclusions seem to be reasonably clear. For one, our data certainly substantiates the observation that young children are at special risk of lethal violence from stepfathers. Among our cases of fatal physical assault, not one involved a genetic father. Further, when other data are examined (Daly and Wilson 1998: 32–6), the weight of the evidence suggests that children living in stepfamilies have elevated risks of exposure to violence.

There is, to be sure, the anomaly in our present data regarding the Cinderella hypothesis, since in that folk tale the child is the victim of the stereotypical 'wicked stepmother'. The problem is that there is not one single case among our ninety homicides where the offender was a stepmother. Our data, however, can in no way provide a test for the hypothesis. As Daly and Wilson point out, only a very small number of children, especially very young children who might be at risk of fatal physical assault or battering, live in a family where there is a stepmother. One would have to have a huge file of homicides to begin to find any number of cases of young children killed by their stepmothers. Lacking the numbers, our present Australian data unfortunately cannot test the hypothesis that children of stepmothers are at greater risk of violence.

However, the present data substantiate the observations of Daly and Wilson in other ways. In our data, consistent with their hypothesis, when genetic fathers kill, they tend to be involved in patterns quite different from the fatal physical assaults where the killers are stepfathers. Further, while not a definitive test, among our child homicides there seems to be evidence of a higher level of psychological distress and illness among genetic parents than we find among the stepfathers who kill, so that we agree with their conclusion that:

> In summary, filicidal genetic parents of both sexes are often deeply depressed, are likely to kill the children while they sleep, and may even construe murder-suicide as a humane act of rescue from a cruel world, whereas homicidal step-parents are seldom suicidal and typically manifest their antipathy to their victims in the relative brutality of their lethal acts. [Daly and Wilson 1998: 35]

If it can be accepted that stepchildren face greater risks of violence, does this necessarily mean that the hypotheses of Daly and Wilson are valid? On this score we are less convinced. We see two basic problems: difficulties in applying animal examples to humans; and complications in the three-way relationship between child, natural parent and step-parent. We will look at them in turn.

First, there are as yet unresolved difficulties in the evolutionary psychological ideas as these apply to humans. It is obvious that there are fundamental differences between humans and other animals that Daly and Wilson describe. The male lions are essentially programmed so that the killing of the cubs of the male they have displaced is an invariable act; it is not 'learned'. In another part of their book, they describe a similar response on the part of one species of birds:

> Guillemots ... are marine birds who lay their eggs on rock ledges only a few centimeters from nesting neighbors. They recognize their newly hatched chicks and even their eggs on the basis of individual markings, and they reject *any* unrelated chicks or eggs that somehow turn up in the nest uninvited. [Daly and Wilson 1998: 41, emphasis added]

The behaviour of the guillemots here is instinctual, not learned, and it occurs every time a suspect egg or chick is introduced into the nest. Such a response is a biological imperative, and its transmission is clearly through genetic inheritance.

The violence of human step-parents clearly lacks this element of an invariable biological imperative. Many thousands of step-parents manage to carry out their parental obligations without being violent toward their stepchildren. This particular line of argument is anticipated, however:

> Human beings are not like langurs or lions. We know that 'sexually selected infanticide' is not a human adaptation because men, unlike male langurs and lions, do not routinely, efficiently dispose of the predecessors' young. ... Many, perhaps most, step-parents derive some pleasure from helping raise their partners' children, and many, perhaps most, stepchildren are better off than if their parents had remained single. [Daly and Wilson 1998: 37–8]

In our view, this creates a problem for their argument. If the behaviour is not a biological imperative that is transmitted genetically as in the case of lions or guillemots, what are the mechanisms for the transmission of these particular traits? A key to understanding their view is the importance they place on the ancestral environment:

we should say that parental psyches are designed to allocate parental efforts in ways that would have promoted parental fitness in the species' ancestral environment of evolutionary adaptiveness (EEA), that is the environment within which the relevant history of natural selection occurred. [Daly and Wilson 1998: 41]

Some hint of the character and workings of these ancestral environments is found in the following:

hypothesizing a complex evolved psychology of parenthood, designed by natural selection to bring about fitness-promoting allocations of parental investment in the EEA, does not necessarily imply that such allocations are goals that the actor is aware of and can pursue with behavioral flexibility in novel situations. [Daly and Wilson 1998: 45]

So, in this view, there are deeply ingrained ways of behaving that humans derive from complex evolutionary process – ways of behaving, such as employing violence toward stepchildren, which are outside adult human awareness. If this view is correct, then some unspecified amount of human behaviour is stamped genetically, and is beyond the reach of learning and rationality.

But Daly and Wilson acknowledge that the vast majority of step-parents are not violent toward their stepchildren. The behaviour of lions and guillemots is *invariable* when presented with the stimulus. In humans, there is obviously enormous variability in the response when confronted with an analogous stimulus. In fact, the overwhelming response of most step-parents is to avoid violence with their stepchildren. The conundrum then becomes, first, precisely what is the nature of the mechanisms of transmission (it has to be genetic if the viewpoint is Darwinian)? And then by what additional mechanisms do the impulses imprinted in the ancestral evolutionary environment become transformed as a result of the organism's contemporary existence? With the nature of this critical mechanism unspecified, we find at this point the hypothesis is not yet proved. It seems especially unpersuasive to argue from animal species where the violence toward non-genetic offspring is a biological imperative, to the human condition where this is clearly not the case.

A second line of argument can be raised against the genetic view of the Cinderella story. The situation of step-parenthood is one where the new parent is introduced into an existing parent–child bond. This existing bond between the genetic parent and her or his child was forged in a situation where the incoming parent was not present. The introduction of the step-parent generates the possibility of tensions and competition among the different parties for affection. As the genetic parent forges the bond with the new step-parent, the relationship with the child undergoes changes that may well be uncomfortable for both child and genetic parent. Young children may not be able to reason clearly about the nature of this emergent competition, but they may feel it very strongly, and then act in the only ways that are available to them. A common response, for example, is to become more overtly demanding of the genetic parent, and at the same time overtly hostile to the incoming step-parent. While it may be that evidence will emerge to show that the resulting conflicts are genetic in origin, it seems reasonable that a simple model of poorly understood and badly negotiated emotional competition explains the same behaviour. It is commonplace to observe that many parents are unprepared for parenthood (and any of us who have been parents will be quick to agree). It also follows that there is little in the way of formal preparation or even sage advice which can be called upon by most soon-to-be step-parents as they move into the role. It seems inevitable in such situations that the emotional insecurities that generate the interactions between child, genetic parent and step-parent can only too easily take the path of competition, hostility, conflict, and then, in extreme cases, violence.

In stating such a view, we are not disputing the observation of Daly and Wilson that there is a greater risk of violence among step-parents, especially stepfathers. Indeed, our own data contain tragic stories of how tensions between child and stepfather produce exceptional levels of conflict and violence. We are persuaded by their analysis of the evidence that supports the idea that physical abuse generally, not just homicide, is greater among families where a step-parent is present. There is, in short, some truth in the Cinderella tale. What we question is whether the present argument of Daly and Wilson, given the absence of critical data regarding the genetic foundations of violent behaviour, provides a compelling account of such violence. Further, we argue that alternative explanations embedded in social and cultural analyses would prove more fruitful.

### A Universal Moment of Attack?

Quite a different approach to the analysis of violence offered by Daly and Wilson is found in explanations that centre analysis on the immediate features of the homicide event, in particular the interaction between the offender and the victim (e.g. Katz 1988; Luckenbill 1977). Before considering some theoretical formulations that might be helpful for understanding the gendered nature of child homicide, we will look at the implications of such interactive analyses for understandings of child homicide.

There is no question that some of the present scenarios of child homicide fit the description of homicides in general as proposed by Katz (1988) or Luckenbill (1977). The dynamic interaction between the victim and the offender is central in their accounts: the lethal violence flows out of, and is to be understood as a result of, such interactions. Among child homicides, fatal assaults provide the classic example that seems to correspond to these forms of explanation. In our accounts of these fatal assaults, the mother's de facto partner, or less frequently the mother, explodes in anger at a disobedient child, in many cases a child who does not stop crying despite the adult's efforts. The child's actions are understood as providing the trigger for the violence: the child would not stop crying, or would not do what it was told, or the child's actions contributed to the offender's frustration and feelings of helplessness. In Katz's terms the continued disobedience develops in the offender a 'righteous' fury and rage that results in the attack on the child. This description fits the ones offered by the offenders for these events: 'I just lost my cool', 'I was just annoyed'. For the offender such explanations allow for some removal of blame: there was something unique to the situation that triggered an irrational action. It removes some element of blame from the offender to the situation. Further, if the event is understood as contingent upon, and emergent from, a unique set of circumstances, then it is something that is not consciously planned and it is not something that is likely to have happened before, or is likely to happen again. The offender, like Katz, is not interested in analysing other contextual issues or precursors to the event.

However, frequently these are not unique actions by the offender, most often the mother's de facto partner. These are cases in which the parent or step-parent has been brutally violent to the child, and often others in the family, on numerous other occasions. The explosions that end in the death of children may not be premeditated, they may be triggered by the action of the child, but these are parents for whom violence is an option of some frequency as a response to issues confronting them. Often in case of fatal assaults, both in our narratives and cases reported elsewhere, the autopsy turns up evidence of prior injuries, sometimes indicating quite exceptional violence. It is not simply a solution that 'emerges' from the contingencies of the specific situation. The analysis of these events in terms of the moment of 'righteous slaughter' leaves us with little understanding of the circumstances in which some parents are violent towards their children over a period of time.

Other child homicides sit even less easily with explanations in terms of the moment of attack. For example, some child homicides are carefully planned in advance: the instrument of death is bought, plans are made for an excursion that ends in death, a suicide note is written, or the setting is carefully arranged in advance for the killing. Even if one's interest is in the immediate interactions leading to the killing, some of these events have a different mood from the fatal assaults. Emotions of extreme despair and hopelessness, or determination and commitment, run through some of these events rather than, or as well as, fury and rage. It is not so much an immediate interaction that provokes the offenders, as a set of circumstances that leaves them feeling that they have few other options.

Explanations in terms of the immediate event assume that the victim is perceived or understood by the offender to pose some form of 'threat' to the offender. However, the 'threat' from children rarely takes the form of direct, physical threat to the personal safety of the offender. In some scenarios the child may represent a threat to the offender's standing or self-definition, for example the continually crying child may be understood as threatening a man's authority, or a woman's standing as a 'good' mother. The threat may be indirect, as in the cases where the perpetrator is concerned that the child is about to reveal criminal activity on his part (e.g. sexual assault). Or a young mother may be concerned that the child's continual crying or disruptive behaviour may frighten off a new lover.

In other scenarios it is not in fact the actions of the ultimate victim that form the basis of the anger or frustration deemed to arise from a 'threat'. Children are sometimes killed by their father when the primary object of his anger is their mother. A previously successful, but now failed, businessman does not kill his family and himself because of anger or frustration engendered by the family. The single young mother on welfare, with little family support and an alcohol problem, may hit out at her child because it is the nearest available target for her despair and frustration that derive from multiple sources. This diversity of scenarios and threats calls for further consideration of the nature of the immediate event, and the adequacy of descriptions of homicide that position rage and anger in response to threats posed by the ultimate victim as central features of these events.

The significance of the sex of the offender is not a 'contour' of the crime specified in the theories proposed by either Katz (1988) or Luckenbill (1977). However, contemporary explanations of female homicide in particular draw upon some similar assumptions. Katz and Luckenbill describe highly emotional events, but there is an assumption that the behaviour is in some sense rational, instrumental and justifiable from the point of view of the offender. Contemporary understandings of homicide by women, on the other hand, represent the homicide as an emotional outburst, a loss of control, in response to a situation of stress.

Ogle, Maier-Katkin and Bernard (1995: 181) argue, as an illustration, that women have 'overcontrolled' personalities and that at 'somewhat random intervals' they erupt 'in a display of uncontrolled aggression that is very extreme and violent'. Silverman and Kennedy (1988) also invoke the notion of loss of control of anger and frustration when postulating explanations for non-infanticide child-killing by mothers.

Campbell (1993) compares women's violence, which is understood as an expressive act, an eruption of fury, with the instrumentality of men's violence. Interestingly in the present research, the form of child homicide that most closely resembles a scenario involving an emotional loss of control is fatal assaults. However, close to 75 per cent of these child homicides were committed by men. Of course the same events may be understood as instrumental in that the immediate intent is to stop the child from crying.

The adequacy of understanding of child homicides as emotional, irrational events when committed by women and rational, instrumental events when committed by men is further challenged by the murder-suicides. Many of the women who kill themselves along with their children carefully plan the deaths, taking care to ensure death with little pain and the ordering of events after the deaths. Their preparations are carried out with the express purpose of saving their children from further harm: it is in some ways a highly instrumental act. We do not argue that these are not highly emotional events: indubitably they are. At the same time, however, they do not necessarily represent a sudden loss of control and are not necessarily irrational. The child homicides committed by men are also emotional events. As with women, a range of emotions is evident, from the loneliness and despair of 'losing' their wife and children, to the anger at the disobedient child. Overall, the analysis of child homicides in this study raises questions about the tendency to talk in terms of binary oppositions of emotions and rationality.

As we strive to understand the phenomenon of child homicide, clearly we would like to have some idea of what happens in the immediate situation of the event. The child homicides examined in this research make clear that there is no single, universal sequencing of events, interactions or emotions that can be identified across the events. On the other hand, it is evident that the offenders all have their own explanation for their actions. Human beings do not engage in totally random acts of violence. In our own minds and in terms of explaining our actions to others, there is usually some rationale for the event: even if this rationale is that the behaviour was irrational. These explanations for our actions are made up of, and draw upon, culturally available and acceptable understandings. Both culturally and legally in our society, violent actions may be legitimated if they are provoked. It is therefore not surprising that most often offenders understand, represent and justify their actions in terms of the actions of others, most often the victim in cases of homicides involving adult victims.

In cases of child homicide these matters become complicated. Children rarely constitute a direct personal threat of the sort that an adult might, and so other understandings also come into play. For example, 'the child's crying provoked me, and "I lost my cool", I was not really responsible for my actions'. Or our cultural understandings of motherhood, fatherhood and childhood inform understandings of the situation. For example, a mother believes that she is ultimately responsible for the care and protection of her children; if they are threatened and she has no other choice, her actions can be couched in terms of fulfilling the responsibilities of motherhood. Here the provocative actions that bring about her actions are not those of the child. Nevertheless the offender can normally be expected to have an account of the immediate circumstances of the event that includes a rationale for why the particular children were victims of their actions. Further, these accounts constitute a significant element of our efforts to understand child homicide.

At the same time, our understanding of child homicide will be limited if we remain at this level of analysis. Homicide is an event that cannot be isolated from the broader context of the lives of the offender and the victim. A man may hit a child because she will not do what she is told and thereby is understood as challenging the man's authority. But the same man will not even assume that he can direct others in the same way: the situation and the expectations of self and other are circumscribed by factors not established in the immediate circumstances. The young mother who hits out at her screaming child may 'lose her cool' with the child, but her anger may be jointly at her spouse who is never there, and the isolation and loneliness of her situation. The teenage male may be angry that his girlfriend is leaving him, but the context of his continued unemployment, painful childhood, and lack of other family contributes to fear of desertion and loneliness that feeds the anger. The unemployed mother whose husband leaves her with three children to support may feel personal despair at not being able to look after her children, but this is in the context of the limited options for finance, housing and emotional support available to a woman in her situation.

Overall a close examination of child homicides challenges the idea that there is a universal scenario based in the interactive dynamics between offender and victim which captures the immediate build-up to lethal violence directed at children. In general, attempts to do so elaborate on an understanding and rationalisation for such events that is essentially an adult male paradigm – the notion of two male antagonists jousting with each other to the end. This can even be found enshrined in the law, especially in terms of the traditional construction of the plea of self-defence. Among these homicides there are some contests of honour in which two males play out the complicated moves of the respect/disrespect game, but most of the present narratives pose very different patterns of interaction and motivation between victim and offender.

We now turn to a discussion of the form of child homicide that most closely approximates the scenario postulated by this perspective on homicide, that is, fatal assaults. We consider the ways in which the sex of the offender and related circumstances have significant ramifications for our understanding of differences within this scenario.

### Fatal Assaults and Sexual Difference

Fatal assaults of children at first appear to have some similar features whether the offender is a man or a woman. Generally they occurred in circumstances of economic and social stress: unemployment and alcohol or drug problems were not uncommon. They are also similar in terms of the immediate circumstances. The adult does not necessarily intend to kill the child; rather, the death is the result of a fatal blow following a build-up of frustration in reaction to continual crying.

Both the men and women who kill children in fatal assaults tend to be people who are willing to use violence regularly. There is often evidence that the child had been assaulted on previous occasions, and that other children in the family had also been physically abused. In the case of the men, there is frequently evidence that they had also physically abused their female partners. These are violent men and women.

These events sometimes have been described as 'child abuse gone awry' and so child abuse research might contribute to an understanding of them. However, most of the child abuse literature has focused on the relationship between the mother and the child (Featherstone 1996: 182), and the situation of abusive fathers has been relatively neglected. Despite similarities between these events, they differ in ways that suggest that those committed by men and those committed by women cannot meaningfully be understood as the same event.

When we look at the fatal assaults committed by women, we note that, although there is some variation in the circumstances of the mothers who commit these crimes, they often have sole, or predominant, responsibility for their children. These women were often living in a de facto situation of short duration, in economically deprived situations that included a number of other highly stressful components. For these women their situation was generally one of ongoing, relentless pressures and demands. Not surprisingly, therefore, their situation is known to social or child welfare organisations: in some situations the mothers themselves have sought assistance.

It might be the continual crying of the child that is the immediate provocation for the assault that results in the child's death, but to understand this as the cause of the event would be naive. The homicide takes place in the context of pressures related to expectations of the woman's mothering responsibilities, and a build-up of frustrations resulting from other factors, including trying to juggle and balance the demands of the child with those of her de facto partner. For some of these women, it is the competing and contradictory demands placed on them that contribute to the stress of the situation. As a 'good mother' she is responsible for the well-being and the control of her children, which when she has a 'demanding' child can be extremely time-consuming and stressful in itself. At the same time, as a 'good wife' she is expected to tend to the needs of her male partner. A woman in a short-term de facto situation may feel that she has to 'win' or 'earn' the commitment of her male partner, and finds herself caught between the demands of her partner and those of her child. When the mother assaults her child, she is hitting out not only at the child, but at the male partner who is absent or offers little assistance, and at her general circumstances from which she feels there is no escape and about which she feels angry. She feels powerless in relation to her general circumstances, and so vents her feelings on the individual over whom she does have some power – her child.

There are significant differences between fatal assaults involving men in contrast to women. One important factor is their frequency. Fatal assaults are three times more likely to involve male than female offenders. Further, in fatal assaults the women were in all cases the natural mother of the child, while for males the offender was most likely to be the de facto spouse of the woman. Given the presumption in the legal and welfare systems that children are best left with their mother in cases of family breakdown, there are likely to be far more de facto male partners in situations where the mother has young children from a previous marriage, than de facto female partners who then assume roles of child-caring. At the same time, the absence of natural fathers in the fatal assaults on young children is striking, and is a topic to which we will return.

We might begin by framing the mothers' actions in fatal assaults in the context of the expectations, responsibilities and pressures of mothering and being a woman. However, it seems unlikely that similar pressures in relation to fathering will be helpful for explaining the actions of most of the de facto spouses in these forms of child homicide. Some of these men were reported by the mothers to 'care' for the child, but they did not carry the ongoing burden of the responsibility for the child's well-being that the biological mothers bore. Most often these incidents occurred in circumstances where the male offender had been looking after the child for a relatively short period of time.

It might be speculated that the child's disobedience in not stopping crying, or otherwise acquiescing to the man's instructions, threatens the man's control of the situation, his authority, his masculinity. The man hits the child as a means of asserting his authority and masculinity. Given the comments by some mothers that her de facto was involved in caring for the child, it is also conceivable that the man was trying to be a 'good father' as he understood it, the disciplinarian, a person to be respected and loved by the child. When his expectations were not being met, but rather, from his perspective, challenged, then he lashed out at the child.

Other narratives, however, suggest male responses of quite a different nature. At least one man indicated that he was jealous of the affection the child gave to the mother but did not give to him despite his efforts. It is conceivable that in these situations the young child (most often in the 12-month to 2-year-old age group) who is feeling insecure about its mother's affection may not be easy to handle for a young, inexperienced man. For other men, it is the competition the child poses to his relationship with the mother that is part of the context of the violence: some men expressed jealousy about the amount of time their partner spent with the child.

Clearly we need to know much more before we can hope to understand these events. While fatal assaults committed by men and those committed by women initially appear similar, as one reads these cases, one gets the sense that some significantly different things are happening. The mothers appear to be frustrated in their efforts to meet the demands of others on them: the child, the de facto, and family and neighbours' expectations in relation to being a 'good mother'. The de facto men appear to be frustrated in their expectation that their needs will be met: their female partner does not give them the time and affection they expect; the child does not show them the same affection as it does the mother; or the child does not affirm their masculine identity by respecting their authority. If for some mothers it is the competing demands of the child and the de facto that contribute to her stress and frustration, for some de facto spouses the frustration that leads to the assault on the child is that their demands on the women are not being met. This analysis suggests that understandings of child homicide require that we consider in further detail the context and circumstances of the event, in particular, the individual's and others' expectations and understandings of them as woman, man, mother, or father.

## 'Doing Gender'

In seeking to understand the relationship between the sex of the offender and the forms of child homicide, we turn to consideration of a recent formulation that purports to explain gender differences in criminal offending. Messerschmidt (1997: 170) describes this 'newly emerging feminist perspective' as focusing on what people in specific social settings do to construct gendered social relations and social structures, and how these structures in turn constrain and channel behaviour in particular ways. A distinguishing component of this perspective is the idea of gender as 'situationally accomplished'. Thus for Messerschmidt (1993: 85), 'crime by men is a form of social practice invoked as a resource, when other resources are unavailable, for accomplishing masculinity'. We are interested in exploring the possibilities of this perspective because it claims to allow us to recognise and understand differences among men and women, as well as similarities between men and women.

The notion of the situational accomplishment of gender seems to fit most straightforwardly with the 'confrontational' scenarios involving teenage males. These are situations in which young men threaten or challenge the 'honour' of other young men, provoking an exchange which leads to violence resulting in an – initially unintended – death. Such scenarios make up the single most prevalent form of non-filicide child murders in our study. In these scenes we see operating the situationally defined 'accountability' that is so central to the accomplishment of gender in the 'doing gender' perspective.

Since gender is 'situationally accomplished', this perspective posits a diversity of masculinities. Most often this is understood as different groups or categories (for example, class or race) of men having different understandings and expectations in relation to what constitutes masculine behaviour. That is, it rejects the idea of a singular 'masculine role'. When we look to fatal assaults, we are presented with an even more complex situation in which we see individual men doing different masculinities in relation to different audiences.

On the one hand, these men present themselves as particularly capable and willing carers of children to their partners and to the public environment in which they participate with the children. These men and their partners frequently vehemently deny violence towards the children and indicate in their statements that they find such behaviour objectionable – it is not 'manly', it is not being a responsible parent, to physically abuse children. That is, when the audience is partner or public, establishing their masculinity for these men entails establishing a caring, non-violent relationship with the children.

On the other hand, the autopsy reports indicate that these men have been violent towards the children on more than one occasion. A persistent and continued high level of physical abuse suggests that the violence, rather than a single 'explosion' that might be rooted in a spontaneous provocation, may be a deeply ingrained and routine method by which these males 'cope' with demanding social situations. In their repertory of psychological and interactional technique, routine violence looms large. Their private actions with the child differ from their public actions – and both may be understood as masculine-affirming, but affirming of different masculinities. In private, the child's actions may have been interpreted as challenging masculine authority, and the violence reaffirms control of the situation. But these same actions cannot be part of a public affirmation of masculinity; in fact, they are actions that if made public might be used to question masculinity. It is not 'manly' to assault children.

These scenarios in particular reveal both the complex and sometimes contradictory understandings of masculinity and the ways in which they are achieved differently in different situations. The 'doing gender' perspective has made a significant contribution to criminological theorising in relation to gender by drawing attention to such complexity and challenging notions of universal notions of masculinity. At the same time we are left with some dilemmas. If we take the notion of the situational accomplishment of gender to an extreme, we would have to argue that there are as many 'masculinities' as there are situations in which men find themselves. If men are always and inevitably 'doing' some form of masculinity, then the usefulness of this concept for understanding particular forms of behaviour, other than in terms of an *ex post facto* description, is questionable.

Maternal filicides seem to present particular difficulties for the 'doing gender' perspective. Messerschmidt has focused most of his discussion of this perspective on men, masculinity and crime. Given the general social construction of crime as masculine, and criminal behaviour as inconsistent with femininity, Kathy Daly (1997) has asked whether the claim that crime is a 'resource for doing femininity' can have any resonance.

More recently Messerschmidt has attempted to utilise 'doing gender' in an analysis of girls' crimes in gangs. He argues that what is usually considered atypical feminine behaviour outside 'the 'hood' is normalised within the context of inter-neighbourhood conflict. 'Girl gang violence in this situation is encouraged, permitted and privileged by both boys and girls as appropriate feminine behaviour. Thus "bad girl" femininity is situationally accomplished and context-bound within the domain of the street' (Messerschmidt 1996: 182). This argument attempts to avoid the position of asserting that gang behaviour is in itself masculine, and that girls who engage in such activities are consequently masculinised. However, the 'doing gender' framework then leaves us in the position of understanding the different actions of men as varieties of masculinity, and those of women as femininities: this verges on the essentialist position that the perspective seeks to challenge.

The killing of a child is so antithetical to notions of femininity and motherhood in our society that it is hard to imagine the social context in which a woman's femininity is situationally accomplished by the killing of her child. It might be possible to make the case that there is some resonance between the idea of 'doing gender' and neonaticides. These are cases in which a woman kills her newborn baby within the first twenty-four hours, usually at birth. Most often these young women have not acknowledged their pregnancy either to themselves or others.

'Doing gender' might speak to the still powerful constraints felt by some young women in regard to single motherhood and its relationship to their sexual, and thereby feminine, status. Neonaticide undoubtedly reflects the significance for some young women of their acceptance by others, their accountability to others, in regard to their feminine status. However, the killing of the newborn infant is not an action that affirms femininity. Perhaps it could be argued that the act can be understood not so much as the woman 'killing a child', but rather as 'the avoidance of negative sanctions in regard to inappropriate feminine behaviour', and therefore it is most clearly evidence of the power of 'doing gender'.

However, 'doing gender' does not allow us to understand why only a very few young women in our society take this action. That is, it does not help us to understand the differences between women in like circumstances, as we would expect of an adequate explanatory framework. It might be reasonably argued that whether or not a young woman feels this threat to her feminine status depends on other aspects of her social situation which have yet to be theorised. This requires an elaboration of the 'doing gender' perspective.

In a second scenario of maternal filicide that might be understood as the mother affirming her role as carer and protector of her children, the mother kills herself and her children, claiming that she believes they are 'better off dead'. The rationale offered by the mother is certainly consistent with pervasive notions of the mother as the person with responsibility for the care and well-being of her children. In this circumstance she claims that killing her children is the only option available to her to meet her responsibilities and protect her children.

Dominant notions of motherhood may form the basis of culturally available and acceptable rationalisations or justifications of her actions for herself and for others, but does this mean that her behaviour is best understood as 'situationally accomplishing' her femininity? In these cases, the mother and her children are in difficult circumstances often related to separation from the children's father. It might be postulated that in these circumstances, where the mother and – she assumes – her children are unhappy, she feels that her status as a good, caring mother is challenged.

However, when attempting to understand these cases, it is questionable how far one can privilege the 'doing of gender', the establishing of her feminine status. Take for example the case of Rosa, the young, unemployed woman, who was in a violent relationship, had a drug problem, had lost the custody of her child and jumped with her child in her arms from the eighteenth floor of a block of public housing flats (Chapter 2). It is not clear from Rosa's perspective how far the accomplishment of her femininity had anything to do with her decision to take this action. Many, but not all of the women who kill their children are in economic and familial circumstances similar to Rosa's. These other features of their lives seem to be more central to their decisions to take their children's lives than simply constituting the context within which they chose to 'do gender', or to do one form of femininity as opposed to another.

Two issues are blended throughout the discussion thus far. One has to do with the extent to which 'doing gender' can be privileged, if you like, in understandings of child homicide. The second has to do with the extent to which, from the mother's perspective, the action is about affirming gender. Can we speak about these events in the same way as Messerschmidt quite convincingly spoke of girls in gangs choosing to commit violent acts as a way of affirming their 'bad girl' femininity? What is the 'femininity' being 'affirmed' when women kill their children?

These concerns relate to the observation in discussions of 'doing gender' that gender is omni-relevant. Lorber (1994: 13) notes, 'Gender, like culture, is a human production that depends on everyone constantly "doing gender"'. West and Zimmerman (1987: 139) claim 'doing gender is unavoidable'. If all human actions are necessarily gendered, then it is not a concept that will help us distinguish why individuals engage in some actions rather than others: all their actions can be understood in terms of 'doing gender'. There is no question that the forms of child murder vary with the sex of the offender and that gender plays a significant part in any explanations for these events. The 'doing gender' perspective might have some part in the development of a descriptive analysis of some of these events. However, as an explanatory theory that will help us understand an individual's decision to take such action, or as a framework for understanding why some people do and others do not take such action, its possibilities seem limited. It might form a necessary part of a theory, but it is not sufficient for understanding human action.

## Motherhood, Fatherhood and Childhood

Child homicides that occur in the family vary not only with the sex of the offender, but with the relationship of the offender to the child victim. For example, in this study similar numbers of fatal assaults were committed by men and women; but the female perpetrators were all biological mothers of the children they killed, while over half of the men were not the biological fathers of the children they killed. This observation, along with the others discussed above, suggests that in thinking further about the gendered nature of child homicide, we need to turn to consideration of parenting, and the structure and understandings of motherhood, fatherhood and childhood in our society.

A consistent observation in research on child homicide is that young children are most likely to be killed by their parents or family carers. A partial explanation for this is no doubt that young children spend most of their time in the family, and so this is where they are most vulnerable. However, time spent in a setting is clearly an insufficient explanation: as children enter school and spend almost as much time with teachers as they do with parents, we do not find a shift to teachers as the most likely perpetrators of child homicide.

In our society, in general young children spend more time with their mothers than with their fathers. This has been offered as an explanation for the relatively high proportion, compared to other violent offences, of women who kill children. It is worth noting at this point the findings of child abuse research: while the number of women who abuse children is higher than the number of men, when the time spent with children is taken into account, the rate of men abusing children is higher than that of women (Featherstone 1996).

As is evident in the cases described in this research, there is far more to why a mother kills her children than the fact that she spends time with them. In our culture and in our time, mothers are generally understood to be particularly bonded with their children, and they carry a stronger burden of responsibility than fathers do for the day-to-day care, control and well-being of their children. To some extent the child is understood as an extension of the mother. The 'good mother' puts the care of her children before all else and spends most, if not all, of her time with her children, especially when the children are young. As evidenced by the expressions of women in this study, this is a powerful ideology. However, it is an ideology that has always been understood differently for women of different classes. Noble and upper-class women have across time had nannies and boarding-schools to send their children to. It is true that even mothers with extensive resources can find motherhood a difficult burden, but for mothers with limited personal, financial and social resources, the burden can become too much to bear.

Sometimes this burden becomes so great that the mother decides to kill herself and her children. The murder-suicides in this research suggest some of the complexities of trying to understand the relationship between being a mother or a father and child homicide. When mothers kill themselves and their children, they tend to do so in situations of 'violence, hopelessness and despair'. They feel that they can no longer cope with the difficult circumstances that they and their children face. These are women, generally with more than one child, who have had a 'family'. However, the family has broken up. In some circumstances the husband has physically departed; in others his affair with another woman and his betrayal has destroyed the marriage as she understood it. These have often been marriages in which the husband has been violent towards the wife; nevertheless she views the breakdown of the marriage as devastating for both her and her children.

While these women are not necessarily as economically vulnerable as the mothers involved in fatal assaults, they are nevertheless concerned about how they will be able to look after the children in changed circumstances. But it is more than changed economic circumstances that concerns these women: the breakdown of the marriage is also personally catastrophic for them. This has to be understood in the context of a society in which for many women the options for establishing self-worth are limited, and their position as women, as a valued person, is established through their status as mother and wife. These statuses are not only essential for self-definition, but carry with them the burden of ensuring the health and well-being of all in the family. In these circumstances, their devastation at the family break-up becomes more understandable.

These mothers kill the children they love, and for whom they feel ultimately responsible. The understanding of motherhood as entailing a special bond between mother and child derives from an assumed 'natural attachment' between mother and child, which was developed in the last quarter of the eighteenth century (Smithey 1997: 256). Nevertheless, it is a concept that is so structurally and institutionally embedded in contemporary Western society that it is understood and experienced as reality by these women. While the significance of an intact nuclear family for children's healthy development is held as foundational in contemporary society, at the same time there is an expectation that it is mothers who are held primarily accountable for their children's well-being. The fulfilment of such expectations places considerable stress on some mothers (Oberman 1996: 64). In the case of some of the mothers in the present study, the concept of mother love and the responsibilities that go with it underpin their actions in taking their children's lives.

Some fathers also express concern about the future well-being of their children when they take the children's lives and attempt to take their own. Noteworthy here is the fact that, unlike the fatal assaults, these child homicides were almost always committed by the biological father. Most often these are also situations of family breakdown. In this research, none of the men who expressed the best interests of their children as a rationale for their actions in fact successfully suicided. This suggests that something different is going on than in the apparently similar circumstances in which mothers kill their children. There appears to be a greater awareness in these men's comments that their actions will also cause their wives pain.

Some biological fathers do take their own lives as well as those of their children; in these cases they generally also killed their wives. Killing the whole family is a distinctly male crime. Women rarely take their husbands' lives along with their own and their children's lives: in the present research there were no such events. Again in these familicides committed by men, it appears that most often the primary object of the man's actions is the wife. These stories involve prior violence towards the wife, and they are consistent with the scenarios of jealousy and possession identified in research on men who kill their wives.

However, the father also kills himself. We can only speculate about the possible rationales and emotions that ended in this action. Is this the ultimate statement of power and control? Are they ultimately not prepared to face the consequences of their actions, or do they think that life would not be worth living without their wife and children? There is probably no one set of understandings for these events. For example, there is also in this research one case in which a father kills himself and family after learning of his business failure. Unlike other familicides, there were no previous reports by friends or family of violence or jealousy towards the wife or children; in fact they were generally considered to be a happy family.

We can only conjecture about circumstances, emotions and rationales that preceded the fathers' actions, but again the overall patterning suggests that there is something about being a father and husband that is a contributing factor. For many of the fathers, as with the women who committed filicide-suicide, the break-up of the family appears to be a significant contextual feature of these events. But it is not clear whether the family break-up meant the same thing to these men and women, or was understood in the same way, or had the same sorts of implications for their self-identity. If one had to characterise these events, there is a sense that the mothers' actions can perhaps be described as expressions of feelings of powerlessness, whereas men's actions seem to be expressing or asserting power. Nevertheless, it would be incorrect to simply describe the mother's actions as those of a powerless person: these women did take control of the situation, they did take action, in a situation in which they had the power to do so. Similarly, it would be oversimplifying to understand the men's actions solely as an assertion of power: while some men seem to be expressing anger and rage, for others the events were surrounded by feelings of 'hopelessness, helplessness and uselessness' and it is conceivable that their actions were a combination of all of these emotions.

The significance of the role of parent in these events is also indicated by the fact that, with very few exceptions, it is only biological fathers who commit familicide. Unfortunately, we know very little about what it means to be a father and a husband, about the personal experiences of fathering or the meanings and definitions attached by men to fatherhood, and particularly how stresses on husbands and fathers come to be acted out with such extreme violence (Clarke and Popay 1998: 203).

It is evident that one has to be wary of assuming a unitary understanding of being a 'father'. As DeKanter 1987, cited in (Clarke and Popay 1998: 203) observes, the contemporary concept of 'the father', like that of 'mother', is far more complex and less unified than the common-sense definition suggests. The conflicting demands and expectations of fatherhood and the ways in which men negotiate their status as a 'good ' or 'bad' father remain somewhat hidden, and thus leave us with unanswerable questions in our efforts to understand familicides.

Understandings of motherhood and fatherhood are constructed in relation not only to understanding of gender, and the sex and sexuality of a person, but also in relation to notions of childhood. The understanding the adult has of the child, and the child's relationship to him or her, underpins child homicides. However, cultural understandings of childhood entail shifts as the child ages. It is therefore to be expected that patterns of child homicide will vary with the age of the child and with the changing contexts in which children find themselves.

In their early years children are deemed to be dependent on parents, and parents are held responsible for the welfare of their children. In some ways children are seen as an extension of the parent; for the parent in particular, the child's identity may very well be closely aligned with their own and others' understandings of them as a 'good parent'. The child can thus be the source of a threat to identity, or indistinguishable from self: both these understandings of children are visible in the child homicides by family members in this research.

As the child enters the school years, independence from the parent begins to become established and their welfare is now shared with teachers and others in a wider social context. During these years the child is at the lowest risk of homicide in the entire life cycle. The child is protected, valued and cared for, but its well-being is entrusted to a broader audience.

In the earliest years the child's sex does not seem to be related to its risk of homicide. However, in our culture as children move towards their teenage years, their ascribed sex and sexuality become increasingly important to their identity and to the ways in which they are understood and treated by others. For some young men, their own assertion of their maleness and the 'testing' of their maleness by others entails a level of risk-taking behaviour and engagement in violent actions that sometimes have tragic consequences.

As young women move into their teenage years, their bodies are increasingly sexualised; they are increasingly understood as the objects for male sexual gratification, which becomes a significant element of their victimisation. Homicides of young women in these years frequently involve the sexual proprietariness of their male partners. Jealousy and possessiveness are not a unique feature of the killing by men of women under the age of 18: it is one of the most common themes of violence directed by men at women across a wide range of ages. Other young women in their pre-teenage and teenage years are killed as the result of the predatory sexual behaviour of a man. These acts by predominantly older men are embedded not only in understandings of what it is to be male, but in cultural understandings of sexuality that value youthfulness and entail notions of male dominance.

## Concluding Comments

Child homicides are so varied that it seems to us that it is unlikely that a single, unitary theory of homicide will provide a meaningful understanding. In our efforts to understand these varied events we suggest that analysis needs to focus on three clusters of features in each event. The first of these relates to the observation that the offenders, in various ways, feel that they are in a situation of stress or tension, that their well-being is under threat. The second cluster relates to the offenders' understandings of self and other, and the relationships between these, that allow them to legitimise their action. The third bundle of issues concerns the alternative options or lack thereof, either perceived or actual, that are available to the offender for resolving the immediate situation. We can begin to understand the differences and similarities in the forms and natures of child homicide committed by men or women as we explore each of these clusters.

Our analysis of the child homicides in this research raises questions about the sufficiency of explanations for homicide which focus on the immediate interaction and the threat perceived by the offender in the scene. Nevertheless, in each of the cases there is no question that the offender perceived that their well-being was under threat. This threat, however, was not necessarily direct, immediate, or presented by the ultimate victim. Five different forms of threat were evident in the cases of this research. One is the classic understanding of the direct, immediate threat that the ultimate victim poses to the physical integrity of the offender (e.g. fights between teenage males, or young men who are killed in the course of committing another crime). This is a common pattern of male-on-male violence for individuals aged both above and below the technical definition of childhood, but it is not common when the focus shifts to violence involving younger children. In a second understanding of threat, the offender perceives that the ultimate victim poses an indirect danger to their physical well-being (e.g. sexual assault cases, conflict resolution). In other cases the victim is understood by the offender to pose a hazard to their personal standing (neonaticides, fatal assaults, and honour contests). Other offenders feel that their emotional well-being is jeopardised (e.g. familicides following a wife's departure, or loss of custody of children). However, in these latter cases of child homicide, it is not the ultimate victim who is always the cause of the pain, but the child's mother. That is, in some child homicides the ultimate victim may not in fact be the source of the perceived threat to the offender's well-being (murder-suicides).

This is not meant to be an inclusive list of 'threats'; nor are the forms of perceived danger necessarily mutually exclusive. Further, the situation in which the homicide occurs is not in itself necessarily threatening. How – or indeed, whether – a person experiences a situation as threatening is not something that can be determined by a description or an analysis of the immediate circumstances alone. A person's experience of a situation as threatening depends on their understanding of themselves and others, and their resources and possibilities for resolving the situation. Each of these can be expected to vary depending on whether the person is a man or a woman.

When we consider the second cluster of factors, which relates to the offender's understandings of self in relation to others which underpin the decision to commit homicide, we begin with the simple observation that child homicides are not random events. The perpetrator somehow comes to the belief that they can, and may, kill their intended victim. Whether or not they 'can' kill a person is in part determined by understandings of power in relation to the intended victim. The offender's actions are also founded in assumptions which allow him or her to understand them as justifiable or, at some level, permissible. People know that in general they should not kill and certainly that they should not kill children. Something has to occur whereby the offender comes to accept the fact that they not only can, but that they may, kill. At this point, while this observation emerges from our data analysis, we would suggest that this aspect of child homicides requires further research in order to be fully elaborated. Nevertheless, it seems clear that such rationales, explicit or implicit, are embedded in, or draw upon, social and cultural understandings of acceptable behaviour. For example, it would be overly simplistic to equate all forms of masculinity with violence; nevertheless, for men there are available more social and cultural understandings of acceptable or expected behaviours for engaging in violent actions than there are for women. Or, in our society there are available understandings that support the use of violence to discipline a child. Again these are not universal beliefs that operate in all settings and contexts, but they are socially and culturally available understandings which legitimate violence when specific contextual contingencies arise, and provide a set of rules or guides within which some people may be able to frame their actions. These ideas have been elaborated most extensively with respect to the interactional dynamics that characterise the male-on-male honour contests (Polk 1999), but are surely not unique to this one form of violence.

In child homicide this legitimation process draws upon understandings of family (including motherhood and fatherhood), childhood, gender, and sexuality. These understandings are multifarious and variable, for example, with context, race and class. Nevertheless a person's understanding of who they are, and their standing in relation to the other, which allows them to commit the homicide, is constituted within assumptions embedded in sets of cultural practices and understandings, and the structural arrangements within which they are constructed. These understandings are almost inevitably gendered. It would seem that further explication along these lines will enable us to more fully understand the different forms of child homicide as they vary between and within the sexes. For example, why it is that mothers may kill themselves and their children, whereas fathers will kill not only themselves and their children, but also their wives? Why it is that approximately equal numbers of men and women kill children in the family context, whereas only men kill children outside the family?

The third cluster of features of an event that needs to be explicated in understandings of child homicides relates to the alternative options that are, or are not, available to the perpetrator. A factor operating in many of these scenes is economic stress. Among the general conditions that cry out for attention, one of the most important is the economic plight confronted by many of the young families that appear in these narratives. Despite the general trend of economic improvement observed in such indicators as unemployment with the onset of the twenty-first century, in countries such as Australia, the situation of dependent children and their families has demonstrably worsened. Despite the general gains, and the apparent health of large business enterprises, there has been an increase in children living in poverty and dependency in recent years, with currently more than one child in four relying on some form of government support (Gray 2000: 1). A persistent theme both in our account and in those of other investigators of child homicide in young families is that of economic abandonment. These are families, and individuals, where the adults are not simply unemployed, they face a lifetime of exclusion from full-time work. Lacking a living wage, they are constantly buffeted by economic and social stresses, forced to make do with too little. Pressures begin to build on individuals and families that lead to the frequently observed pattern of hopelessness, despair, alcoholism, drug use, and with these, violence (which might be directed at a small child, or perhaps flare up between males). One of the most important steps in addressing the problem of violence toward children consists of social policies directed toward ensuring access of all in our society to a living wage.

In terms of the everyday experiences of the men and women in this study, their economic circumstances contributed in many cases to the feeling that they had no other options to reduce the threat, the tension, the frustrations that confronted them. For many, their economic situation was related to their access to other personal and social resources: many of the offenders described themselves or were described by others as 'lonely' or isolated.

We began this research struck by the distinctive sex distribution of those who commit child homicide. As we investigated these cases we were able to elaborate both the differences and the similarities in child homicides committed by men and by women, and also the different forms committed by each. A detailed analysis of child homicide cases reveals that differences in the situation of men and women, and differences in their understandings of themselves and of themselves in relation to others (in this case particularly children and family), play out in ways that are reflected in the nature of the child homicides they commit. In these pages we have tried to document the content of the various forms of violence. In so doing, it appears to us that there are complex sets of interactions between the context, the sex of the offender, and the structures, understandings, and expectations related to the offenders' sex and the victim's sex and age. Clearly, much more work at both theoretical and empirical levels is needed which focuses on these interactions, and it is our hope that we have made a contribution to this task.

# References

Adelson, L. 1959, 'Some medico-legal observations on infanticide', *Journal of Forensic Sciences* 4: 60–72.

Alder, C. M. 1986, 'Unemployed women have got it heaps worse: exploring the implications of female youth unemployment', *Australian and New Zealand Journal of Criminology* 19: 210–24.

—— and Baker, J. 1997, 'Maternal filicide: More than one story to be told', *Women and Criminal Justice* 9: 15–41.

—— and Polk, K. 1996, 'Masculinity and child homicide', *British Journal of Criminology* 36: 396–411.

Allen, H. 1987, *Justice Unbalanced: Gender, Psychiatry and Judicial Decisions*, Milton Keynes: Open University Press.

Allen, J. 1988, 'The "masculinity" of criminality and criminology: Interrogating some impasses', in M. Findlay and R. Hogg (eds), *Understanding Crime and Criminal Justice*, North Ryde, NSW: Law Book Company, pp. 1–24.

—— 1990, *Sex and Secrets: Crime Involving Australian Women since 1880*, Melbourne: Oxford University Press.

American Academy of Pediatrics 1999, 'Investigation and review of unexpected infant and child deaths', *Pediatrics* 104: 1158–60.

Andrews, B. 1994, 'Family violence in social context: Factors relating to male abuse of children', in J. Archer (ed.), *Male Violence*, London: Routledge, pp. 195–210.

Archer, J. 1994, 'Introduction: Male violence in perspective', in J. Archer (ed.), *Male Violence*, London: Routledge, pp. 1–20.

Armstrong, K. L., and Wood, D. 1991, 'Can infant death from child abuse be prevented?', *Medical Journal of Australia* 155: 593–6.

Asher, R. 1951, 'Munchausen syndrome', *Lancet* 305: 339–40.

Athens, L. 1980, *Violent Criminal Acts and Actors*, London: Routledge & Kegan Paul.

Backhouse, C. B. 1985, 'Desperate women and compassionate courts: Infanticide in nineteenth-century Canada', *University of Toronto Law Journal* 34: 447–78.

Baker, J. 1991, 'You can't let your children cry: Filicide in Victoria, 1978–1988', Master's thesis, Department of Criminology, University of Melbourne.

Baron, L. 1993, 'Gender inequality and child homicide: A state-level analysis', in A. V. Wilson (ed.), Homicide: *The Victim/Offender Connection*, Cincinnati, Ohio: Anderson Publishing Company, pp. 207–27.

Bartholomew, A. A., and Milte, K. L. 1978, 'Child murder: Some problems', *Criminal Law Journal* 2: 2–17.

Behlmer, G. E. 1979, 'Deadly motherhood: Infanticide and medical opinion in mid-Victorian England', *Journal of the History of Medicine* 34: 404–27.

Bergman, A. B. 1997, 'Wrong turns in sudden infant death syndrome research', *Pediatrics* 99: 119–21.

Block, C. R., and Christakos, A. 1995, 'Chicago homicide from the sixties to the nineties: Major trends in lethal violence', in C. Block and R. Block (eds), *Trends, Risks, and Interventions in Lethal Violence: Proceedings of the Third Annual Spring Symposium of the Homicide Research Working Group*, Washington, DC: United States Department of Justice, pp. 17–50.

Bordeaux, S. 1998, *Injury Mortality Australia: 1996*, Adelaide: Australian Institute of Health and Welfare National Injury Surveillance Unit.

Briggs, C. M., and Cutright, P. 1994, 'Structural and cultural determinants of child homicide: A cross-cultural analysis', *Violence and Victims* 9: 3–16.

Broadhurst, R. 2000, personal communication regarding homicides in Hong Kong (4 September)

Browne, A. 1987, *When Battered Women Kill*, New York: Free Press.

Brownstein, H. H., Spunt, B. J., Crimmins, S., Goldstein, P., and Langley, S. 1994, 'Changing patterns of lethal violence by women: A research note', *Women and Criminal Justice* 5: 99–118.

Brozovsky, M., and Falit, H. 1971, 'Neonaticide: Clinical and psychodynamic considerations', *American Academy of Child Psychiatry* 10: 673–83.

Cameron, D., and Frazer, E. 1987, *The Lust to Kill: A Feminist Investigation of Sexual Murder*, New York: New York University Press.

Campbell, A. 1993, *Men, Women, and Aggression*, New York: Basic Books.

Campion, J. F., McCrafen, J. M., and Covan, F. 1988, 'A study of filicidal men', *American Journal of Psychiatry* 145: 1141–4.

Cantor, C. H., Mullen, P. E., and Alpers, P. A. 2000 'Mass homicide: The civil massacre', *Journal of the American Academy of Psychiatry and the Law* 28: 55–63.

Carlen, P. 1988, *Women, Crime and Poverty*, Milton Keynes: Open University Press.

Carrington, K. 1993, *Offending Girls: Sex, Youth and Justice*, St Leonards, NSW: Allen and Unwin.

—— 1998, *Who Killed Leigh Leigh: A Story of Shame and Mateship in an Australian Town*, Milsons Point, NSW: Random House.

—— and Johnson, A. 1994, 'Representations of crime, guilt and sexuality in the Leigh Leigh rape/murder case', *Australian Feminist Law Journal* 3: 49–60.

Cervantes, R. C. 1992, *Substance Abuse and Gang Violence*, London: Sage.

Chesler, P. 1974, *Women and Madness*, London: Allen Lane.

Cheung, P. K. T., 1986, 'Maternal filicide in Hong Kong, 1971–1985', *Medicine, Science and the Law* 26: 185–92.

Christoffel, K. K. 1984, 'Homicide in childhood: A public health problem in need of attention', *American Journal of Public Health* 74: 68–70.

—— and Liu, K. 1983, 'Homicide death rates in childhood in 23 developed countries: U.S. rates atypically high', *Child Abuse and Neglect* 7: 339–45.

—— Anzinger, N. K., and Amari, M. 1983, 'Homicide in childhood: Distinguishable patterns of risk related to developmental levels of victims', *American Journal of Forensic Medicine and Pathology* 4: 129–37.

—— Zieserl, E. J., and Chiaramonte, J. 1985, 'Should child abuse and neglect be considered when a child dies unexpectedly?', *American Journal of Diseases of Children* 139: 876–9.

Clarke, S., and Popay, J. 1988, '"I'm just a bloke who's had kids". Men and women on parenthood', in J. Popay, J. Hearn and J. Evans (eds), *Men, Gender Divisions and Welfare*, London: Routledge, pp. 196–230.

Collier, R. 1998, *Masculinities, Crime and Criminology*. London: Sage.

Copeland, A. R. 1985, 'Homicide in childhood: The Metro-Dade county experience from 1956–1982', *American Journal of Forensic Medicine and Pathology* 6: 21–4.

Cornwall, A., and Lindisfarne, N. 1994, 'Introduction', in A. Cornwall and N. Lindisfarne (eds), *Dislocating Masculinity: Comparative Ethnographies*, London: Routledge, pp. 1–10.

Crittenden, P. M., and Craig, S. E. 1990, 'Developmental trends in the nature of child homicide', *Journal of Interpersonal Violence* 5: 202–16.

Daly, K. 1994, *Gender, Crime and Punishment*, New Haven: Yale University Press.

—— 1997, 'Different ways of conceptualizing sex/gender in feminist theory and the implications for criminology', *Theoretical Criminology* 1: 25–51.

Daly, M., and Wilson M. 1988, *Homicide*, New York: Aldine de Gruyter.

—— and —— 1989, 'Parent–offspring conflict and violence in evolutionary perspective', in R. W. Bell and N. J. Bell (eds), *Sociobiology and the Social Sciences*, Dallas: Texas Tech University Press, pp. 25–43.

—— and —— 1990, 'Is parental–offspring conflict sex-linked? Freudian and Darwinian models', *Journal of Personality* 58: 163–89.

—— and —— 1998, *The Truth about Cinderella: A Darwinian View of Parental Love*, New Haven: Yale University Press.

de Silva, S., and Oates, R. K. 1993, 'Child homicide: The extreme of child abuse', *Medical Journal of Australia* 158: 300–1.

Dobash R. E., and Dobash, R. P. 1992, *Women, Violence and Social Change*, London: Routledge.

d'Orban, P. T. 1979, 'Women who kill their children', *British Journal of Psychiatry* 134: 560–71.

Dowdy, E. R., and Unnithan, N. P. 1997, 'Child homicide and the economic stress hypothesis', *Homicide Studies* 1: 281–90.

Dougherty, J. 1993, 'Women's violence against their children: A feminist perspective', *Women and Criminal Justice* 4: 91–114.

Egger, D. A. 1998, *The Killers Among Us*, Upper Saddle River, NJ: Prentice Hall.

Emery, J. L. 1978, 'The deprived and starved child', *Medicine, Science and the Law* 18: 138–42.

—— 1993, 'Child abuse, sudden infant death syndrome, and unexpected infant death', *American Journal of Diseases of Children* 147: 1097–100.

Ewing, C. P. 1995, *Kids Who Kill*, New York: Avon Books.

—— 1997, *Fatal Families: The Dynamics of Intra-familial Homicide*, Thousand Oaks, Calif.: Sage.

Falk, G. 1990, *Murder: An Analysis of Its Form, Conditions and Causes*, London: McFarland & Company.

Featherstone, B. 1996, 'Victims or villains? Women who physically abuse their children', in B. Fawcett, B. Featherstone, J. Hearn and C. Toft (eds), *Violence and Gender Relations*, London: Sage, pp. 178–87.

Finkelhor, D. 1997, 'The victimization of children and youth', in R. Davis, A. Lurigio and W. Skogan (eds), *Victims of Crime*, Beverly Hills, Calif.: Sage, pp. 17–34.

Gathorne-Hardy, J. 1972, *The Rise and Fall of the British Nanny*, London: Hodder and Stoughton.

Geberth, V. J., and Turco, R. N. 1997, 'Antisocial personality disorder, sexual sadism, malignant narcissism, and serial murder', *Journal of Forensic Science* 42: 49–60.

Gelles, R. J. 1996, *The Book of David: How Preserving Families Can Cost Children's Lives*, New York: Basic Books.

—— and Cornell, C. P. 1985, *Intimate Violence in Families*, Beverly Hills, Calif.: Sage.

Gilbert-Barness, E., and Barness, L. 1998, 'What we've learned about SIDS', *Patient Care* 30: 98–111.

Goetting, A., 1988, 'When parents kill their young children: Detroit, 1982–1986', *Journal of Family Violence* 3: 339–46.

—— 1989, 'Patterns of homicide among children', *Criminal Justice and Behaviour* 16: 63–80.

—— 1994, 'Violence as a consequence of parenting', in C. Block and R. Block (eds), *Trends, Risks and Interventions in Lethal Violence: Proceedings of the Third Annual Spring Symposium of the Homicide Research Working Group*, Washington, DC: United States Department of Justice, pp. 183–191.

Gordon, L. 1988, *Heroes of Their Own Lives: The Politics and History of Family Violence*, New York: Viking.

Goss, P. W., and McDougall, P. N. 1992, 'Munchausen syndrome by proxy: a cause of preterm delivery', *Medical Journal of Australia* 157: 814–17.

Gray, D. 2000, 'Welfare net supports one in four children', *Age*, 28 August, pp. 1, 6.

Greenfeld, L. A. 1996, *Child Victimizers: Violent Offenders and Their Victims* Washington, DC: United States Department of Justice.

Hargrave, D. R., and Warner D. P. 1992, 'A study of child homicide over two decades', *Medical Science and Law* 32: 247–50.

Hearn, J. 1990, '"Child abuse" and men's violence', in The Violence Against Children Study Group (ed.), *Taking Child Abuse Seriously*, London: Unwin Hyman, pp. 63–86.

Hearn, J. 1996, 'Is masculinity dead? A critique of the concept of masculinity/masculinities', in M. Mac an Ghaill (ed.), *Understanding Masculinities: Social Relations and Cultural Arenas*, Buckingham: Open University Press, pp. 202–18.

Heide, K. M. 1996, 'Juvenile homicide in the United States', in M. Riedel and J. Boulahanis (eds), *Lethal Violence: Proceedings of the 1995 Meeting of the Homicide Research Working Group*, Washington, DC: United States Department of Justice, pp. 129–34.

—— 1998, *Young Killers: The Challenge of Juvenile Homicide*, London: Sage.

—— Eyles, C. H., and Spencer, E. 2000, 'School shootings in the United States: A typology of lethal and nonlethal injury', in P. H. Blackman, V. L. Leggett, B. L. Olson and J. P. Jarvis (eds), *The Varieties of Homicide and Its Research: Proceedings of the 1999 Meeting of the Homicide Research Working Group*, Washington, DC: United States Department of Justice, pp. 183–8.

Hickey, E. W. 1990, 'The etiology of victimization in serial murder: An historical and demographic analysis', in S. A. Egger (ed.), *Serial Murder: An Elusive Phenomenon*, London: Praeger, pp. 53–72.

—— 1997, *Serial Murderers and Their Victims* (2nd edn), Belmont, Calif.: Wadsworth Publishing Co.

Hobbs, M., and Rule, A. R. 1997, *The Evil: Inside the Mind of a Child Killer*, Kew, Vic.: Reed International Books Australia.

Hodgins, S., and Dube, M. 1996, 'Parents who kill their children: A cohort study', in M. Riedel and J. Boulahanis (eds), *Lethal Violence: Proceedings of the 1995 Meeting of the Homicide Research Working Group*, Washington, DC: United States Department of Justice, pp. 141–4.

Hoffer, P. C., and Hull, N. E. H. 1981, *Murdering Mothers: Infanticide in England and New England, 1558–1803*, New York: New York University Press.

Holmes, R. M., and De Burgher, J. 1988, *Serial Murder*, London: Sage.

Holmes, R. M., and Holmes, S. T. 1996, *Profiling Violent Crimes: An Investigative Tool* (2nd edn), Thousand Oaks, Calif.: Sage.

Homa, J., Menifield, C. E., and Brewer, A. K. 1999, 'Urban vs. rural school violence: Media coverage of the Mississippi, Kentucky and Arkansas school shootings', paper delivered at the annual meeting of the Academy of Criminal Justice Sciences, Orlando, Florida.

Home Office 1993, *Criminal Statistics England and Wales 1991*, London: HMSO.

Hotaling, G. T., and Finkelhor, D. 1990, 'Estimating the number of stranger-abduction homicides of children: A review of available evidence', *Journal of Criminal Justice* 18: 385–99.

Huff, C. R. 1990, *Gangs in America*, London: Sage.

Husain, A., and Daniel, A. 1984, 'A comparative study of filicidal and abusive mothers', *Canadian Journal of Psychiatry* 29: 596–8.

Inciardi, J. A., Horowitz, R., and Pottieger, A. E. 1993, S*treet Kids, Street Drugs, Street Crime: An Examination of Drug Use and Serious Delinquency in Miami*, Belmont, Calif.: Wadsworth Publishing Co.

James, J., and Carcach, C. 1998, *Homicide in Australia, 1989–1996*, Canberra: Australian Institute of Criminology.

Jason, J., and Andereck, N. D. 1983, 'Fatal child abuse in Georgia: The epidemiology of severe physical child abuse', *Child Abuse and Neglect* 7: 1–9.

Jason, J. M., Carpenter, M. M., and Tyler, C. W. Jr 1983, 'Underrecording of infant homicide in the United States', *American Journal of Public Health* 73: 195–7.

Jefferson, T. 1994, 'Theorising masculine subjectivity', in T. Newburn and E. A. Stanko (eds), *Just Boys Doing Business*, London: Routledge, pp. 10–32.

Jones, A. 1980, *Women Who Kill*, New York: Holt, Rinehart and Winston.

Jurik, N. 1983, 'The economics of female recidivism: A study of TARP women ex-offenders', *Criminology* 21: 602–22.

Jurik, N. C., and Winn, R. 1990, 'Gender and homicide: A comparison of men and women who kill', *Violence and Victims* 5: 227–42.

Kaplun, D., and Reich, R. 1976, 'The murdered child and his killers', *American Journal of Psychiatry* 133: 809–13.

Kashani, J. H., Darby, P. J., Allan, W. D., Hartke, K. L., and Reid, J. S. 1997, 'Intrafamilial homicide committed by juveniles: Examination of a sample with recommendations for prevention', *Journal of Forensic Sciences* 42: 873–8.

Katz, J. 1988, *The Seductions of Crime: Moral and Sensual Attractions of Doing Evil*, New York: Basic Books.

Keppel, R. D., and Walter, R. 1999, 'Profiling killers: A revised classification model for understanding sexual murder', *International Journal of Offender Therapy and Comparative Criminology*, 43: 417–37.

Kirsta, A. 1994, *Deadlier than the Male: Violence and Aggression in Women*, London: Harper Collins.

Klein, M. W. 1971, *Street Gangs and Street Workers*, Englewood Cliffs, NJ: Prentice-Hall.

Klein, M. W. 1995, *The American Street Gang: Its Nature, Prevalence, and Control*, New York: Oxford University Press.

Korbin, J. E. 1986, 'Childhood histories of women imprisoned for fatal child maltreatment', *Child Abuse and Neglect* 10: 331–8.

Langer, W. L. 1974, 'Infanticide: A historical survey', *History of Childhood Quarterly* 1: 353–65.

Laster, K. 1989, 'Infanticide: A litmus test for feminist criminological theory', *Australian and New Zealand Journal of Criminology* 22: 151–66.

Lloyd, A. 1995, *Double Deviant, Double Damned: Society's Treatment of Dangerous Women*, Harmondsworth: Penguin.

Lomis, M. J. 1986, 'Maternal filicide: A preliminary examination of culture and victim sex', *International Journal of Law and Psychiatry* 9: 503–6.

Lorber, J. 1994, *Paradoxes of Gender*, New Haven: Yale University Press.

Lowenstein, L. F. 1997, 'Infanticide: A crime of desperation', *The Criminologist* 21: 81–92.

Lucas, N. 1970, *The Child Killers*, London: Arthur Barker.

Luckenbill, D. 1977, 'Criminal homicide as a situated transaction', *Social Problems* 25: 176–86.

Lupton, D., and Barclay, L. 1997, *Constructing Fatherhood: Discourses and Experiences*, London: Sage.

Maguire, K., and Pastore, A. L. 1994, *Sourcebook of Criminal Justice Statistics, 1993*. Washington, DC: United States Department of Justice, Bureau of Justice Statistics.

Mann, C. R. 1993, 'Maternal filicide of preschoolers', in A. V. Wilson (ed.), *Homicide: The Victim/Offender Connection*, Cincinnati, Ohio: Anderson Publishing Co., pp. 227–49.

—— 1996, *When Women Kill*, New York: SUNY Press.

Marks, M. N., and Kumar, R. 1993, 'Infanticide in England and Wales', *Medical Science and Law* 33: 329–39.

Marsiglio, W. 1995, *Fatherhood: Contemporary Theory, Research and Social Policy*, Thousand Oaks, Calif.: Sage.

McClain, P. W., Sacks, J. J., Froehlke, R. G., and Ewigman, B. B. 1993, 'Estimates of fate child abuse and neglect, United States, 1979 through 1988', *Pediatrics* 91: 338–48.

McGuire, T. L., and Feldman, K. W. 1989, 'Psychological morbidity of children subjected to Munchausen syndrome by proxy', *Pediatrics* 87: 289–92.

McKee, G. R., and Shea, S. J. 1998, 'Maternal filicide: A cross-national comparison', *Journal of Clinical Psychology* 54: 679–87.

McLaughlin, V. 2000, 'Juvenile homicide offenders in Savannah, 1896–1903 and 1986 to 1993', paper presented at the annual meeting of the Homicide Working Group, Center for the Advancement of Research, Training and Education, Loyola University, Chicago.

Meadow, R. 1999, 'Unexplained deaths in infancy', *Archives of Diseases of Childhood* 80: 7–14.

Mendlowicz, M. O., Rapaport, M. H., Mecler, K., Golsham, S., and Moreas, T. M. 1998, 'A case-control study on the socio-demographic characteristics of 53 neonaticidal mothers', *International Journal of Law and Psychiatry*, 21: 209–19.

Messerschmidt, J. 1993, *Masculinities and Crime: Critique and Reconceptualization of Theory*, Lanham, Maryland: Rowman & Littlefield.

—— 1995, 'From patriarchy to gender: feminist theory, criminology and the challenge of diversity', in N. Rafter and F. Heidensohn (eds), *International Feminist Perspectives in Criminology*, Buckingham: Open University Press, pp. 167–89.

—— 1997, *Crime as Structured Action: Gender, Race, Class, and Crime in the Making*, Thousand Oaks, Calif.: Sage.

Miedzian, M. 1991, *Boys Will Be Boys: Breaking the Link Between Masculinity and Violence*, New York: Doubleday.

Miller, E. 1986, *Street Woman*, Philadelphia: Temple University Press.

Mokhiber, R. 1989, *Corporate Crime and Violence: Big Business Power and the Abuse of Public Trust*, San Francisco: Sierra Club Books.

Monahan, J., and Steadman, H. J. 1982, *Mentally Disordered Offenders: Perspectives from Law and Social Sciences*, New York: Plenum Press.

Montag, B. A., and Montag, T. W. 1979, 'Infanticide: A historical perspective', *Minnesota Medicine*, May: 368–72.

Morgan, D. H. J. 1987, 'Masculinity and violence', in J. Hanmer and M. Maynard (eds), *Women, Violence and Social Control*, London: Macmillan, pp. 180–209.

Mouzos, J. 1999, *Mental Disorder and Homicide in Australia*, Trends and Issues Monograph Series No. 133, Canberra: Australian Institute of Criminology.

—— 2000, *Homicide Encounters: A Study of Homicide in Australia, 1989–1999*, Canberra: Australian Institute of Criminology.

Myers, S. A. 1967, 'The child slayer', *Archives of General Psychiatry* 17: 211–13.

National Committee on Violence 1990, *Violence: Directions for Australia*, Canberra: Australian Institute of Criminology.

National Committee on Violence Against Women 1993, *National Strategy on Violence Against Women*, Canberra.

New South Wales Child Protection Council 1995, *Preventing Child Homicide*, Sydney.

Newburn, T., and Stanko, E. A. 1994, *Just Boys Doing Business: Men, Masculinities and Crime*, London: Routledge.

Nixon, J., Pearn, J., Wilkey, I., and Petrie, G. 1981, 'Social class and violent child death: An analysis of fatal non-accidental injury, murder and fatal child neglect', *Child Abuse and Neglect* 5: 111–16.

Oberman, M. 1996, 'Mothers who kill: Coming to terms with modern American infanticide', *American Criminal Law Review* 34: 1–110.

O'Donnell, C., and J. Craney, 1982, 'The social construction of child abuse', in C. O'Donnell and J. Craney (eds), *Family Violence in Australia*, Melbourne: Longman Cheshire.

Office of Juvenile Justice and Delinquency Prevention 1995, *Juvenile Offenders and Victims: A Focus on Violence*, Washington, DC: United States Department of Justice.

Ogle, R. S., Maier-Katkin, D., and Bernard, T. J. 1995, 'A theory of homicidal behavior among women', *Criminology* 33: 173–95.

Ollis, D., and Tomaszewski, I. 1993, *Gender and Violence: Position Paper*, Department of Employment, Education and Training, Canberra: Australian Government Publishing Service.

Overpeck, M. O., Brenner, R. A., Trumble, A. C., Trifiletti, L. B., and Berendes, H. W. 1998, 'Risk factors for infant homicide in the United States', *New England Journal of Medicine* 339: 1211–16.

Parton, C. 1990, 'Women, gender oppression and child abuse', in The Violence Against Children Study Group (ed.), *Taking Child Abuse Seriously*, London: Unwin Hyman, pp. 41–63.

Pearson, P. 1998, *When She Was Bad: How Women Get Away with Murder*, London: Virago Press.

Piers, M. W. 1978, *Infanticide*. New York: W. W. Norton.

Pinholster, G. 1994, 'SIDS paper triggers a murder charge', *Science* 264: 197–8.

Polk, K. *When Men Kill: Scenarios of Masculine Violence*, Melbourne: Cambridge University Press, 1994.

——— 1995, 'Lethal violence as a technique of conflict resolution', *Australian and New Zealand Journal of Criminology* 28: 93–115.

——— 1999, 'Males and honor contest violence' *Journal of Homicide Studies* 3: 6–29.

——— and Ranson, D. 1991, 'The role of gender in intimate homicide', *Australian and New Zealand Journal of Criminology* 24: 15–24.

——— and Weitekamp, E. 1999, 'Emerging patterns of youth violence,' paper presented at the annual meeting of the American Society of Criminology, Toronto, November.

Reese, R. M. 1993, 'Fatal child abuse and sudden infant death syndrome: A critical diagnostic decision', *Pediatrics* 91: 423–9.

Resnick, P. J. 1969, 'Child murder by parents: A psychiatric review of filicide', *American Journal of Psychiatry* 126: 73–82.

——— 1970, 'Murder of the newborn: A psychiatric review of neonaticide', *American Journal of Psychiatry* 126: 1414–20.

Rodriguez, S. F., and Smithey, M. 1999, 'Infant and adult homicide', *Journal of Homicide Studies* 3: 170–84.

Rose, L. 1986, *Massacre of the Innocents: Infanticide in Great Britain, 1800–1939*, London: Routledge and Kegan Paul.

Rosen, C. L., Frost, J. D., and Bricker, T. 1983, 'Two siblings with recurrent cardiorespiratory arrest: Munchausen syndrome by proxy', *Pediatrics* 71: 715–20.

Rosenberg, D. A. 1987, 'Web of deceit: A literature review of Munchausen syndrome by proxy', *Child Abuse and Neglect* 2: 547–63.

Sauer, R. 1978, 'Infanticide and abortion in nineteenth-century Britain', *Population Studies* 32: 81–93.

Scott, P. D. 1973a, 'Fatal battered baby cases', *Medicine, Science and the Law* 13: 197–206.

——— 1973b, 'Parents who kill their children', *Medicine, Science and the Law* 13: 120–6.

Siegal, L. 1990, *Slow Motion: Changing Masculinities, Changing Men*, London: Virgo.

Silva, J. A., Leong, G. B., Dassori, A., Ferrari, M. M., Weinstock, R., and Yamamoto, L. 1998, 'A comprehensive typology for the biopsychosociocultural evaluation of child-killing behavior', *Journal of Forensic Sciences* 42: 112–18.

Silverman, R. A., and Kennedy, L. W. 1988, 'Women who kill their children', *Violence and Victims* 3: 113–27.

——— and ——— 1993, *Deadly Deeds: Murder in Canada*, Scarborough, Ontario: Nelson Canada.

Silverman, R. A., Reidel, M., and Kennedy, L. W. 1990, 'Murdered children: A comparison of racial differences across two jurisdictions', *Journal of Criminal Justice* 18: 401–16.

Smith, J. 2000, 'Homicide in England and Wales', PhD thesis, London: Brunel University.

Smithey, M. 1997, 'Infant homicide', *Deviant Behaviour* 18: 255–72.

Snyder, H. N., and Sickmund, M. 1995, *Juvenile Offenders and Victims: A National Report*, Washington, DC: Office of Juvenile Justice and Delinquency Prevention.

Snyder, H. N., Sickmund, M., and Poe-Yamagata, W. 1996, *Juvenile Offenders and Victims: 1996 Update on Violence*, Washington, DC: Office of Juvenile Justice and Delinquency Prevention.

Sorenson, S. B., Peterson, J. G., and Richardson, B. A. 1997, 'Child homicide in the City of Los Angeles: An epidemiological examination of a decade of deaths', *Journal of Aggression, Maltreatment and Trauma* 1: 189–205.

Spergel, I. A. 1995, *The Youth Gang Problem: A Community Approach*, New York: Oxford University Press.

Stanko, E. A. 1985, *Intimate Intrusions*, London: Unwin Hyman.

Statistics Canada 1992, *Homicide in Canada, 1991*, Ottawa: Statistics Canada.

Steinschneider, A. 1972, 'Prolonged apnea and the sudden infant death syndrome', *Pediatrics* 50: 646–54.

Stone, E., and Johnson H. 1987, *Forensic Medicine*, London: Waterlow.

Strang, H. 1992, *Homicides in Australia, 1990–91*, Canberra: Australian Institute of Criminology.

—— 1993, 'Child abuse homicides in Australia: Incidence, circumstances, prevention and control', paper presented at the Second World Conference on Injury Control, Atlanta, Georgia, May.

—— 1994, 'Homicide in Australia', Master's thesis, Department of Criminology, University of Melbourne.

Stubbs, J. 1994, *Women, Male Violence and the Law*, Sydney: Institute of Criminology Monograph Series No. 6.

Totman, J. 1978, *The Murderess: A Psychological Study of Criminal Homicide*, San Francisco: R. and E. Research Associates.

Tuteur, W., and Glotzer, M. A. 1959–60, 'Murdering mothers', *American Journal of Psychiatry* 116: 447–52.

Unnithan, N. P. 1991a, 'Children as victims of homicide: Part I, Historical and anthropological research', *Criminal Justice Abstracts* 23: 46–60.

—— 1991b, 'Children as victims of homicide: Part II, Research on child homicide in contemporary societies', *Criminal Justice Abstracts* 23: 315–330.

—— 1996, 'Child homicide in developed countries', *International Review of Victimology* 4: 313–26.

Walker, L. E. 1989, *Terrifying Love: Why Battered Women Kill and How Society Responds*, New York: Harper and Row.

Walker, N. 1968, *Crime and Insanity in England*, vol. 1, Edinburgh: Edinburgh University Press.

Wallace, A. 1986, *Homicide: The Social Reality*, Sydney: New South Wales Bureau of Crime Statistics and Research.

Weisheit, R. A. 1986, 'When mothers kill their children', *Social Science Journal* 23: 439–48.

West, C., and Zimmerman, D. H., 1987, 'Doing gender', *Gender and Society* 1: 125–51.

West, D. J. 1966 *Murder Followed by Suicide*, London: Heinemann.

White, C. 1999, 'Some "cot deaths" are child abuse', *British Medical Journal* 318: 147–8.

Wilbanks, W. 1982, 'Murdered women and women who murder: A critique of the literature', in N. H. Rafter and E. A. Stanko (eds), *Judge, Lawyer, Victim, Thief: Women, Gender Roles and Criminal Justice*, Boston: Northeastern University Press, pp. 151–80.

—— 1984, *Murder in Miami: An Analysis of Homicide Patterns and Trends in Dade County (Miami) Florida, 1917–1983*, Boston: University Press of America.

Wilczynski, A. 1991, 'Images of women who kill their infants: The mad and the bad', *Women and Criminal Justice* 2: 71–88.

—— 1997, *Child Homicide*, London: Greenwich Medical Media.

—— and Morris, A. 1993, 'Parents who kill their children', *Criminal Law Review* 793: 31–6.

Wilkey, I., Pearn, J., Petrie, G., and Nixon, J. 1982, 'Neonaticide, infanticide and child homicide', *Medical Science and Law* 22: 31–4.

Wilson, M., and Daly, M. 1985, 'Competitiveness, risk taking and violence: The young male syndrome', *Ethology and Sociobiology*, 6: 59–73.

Wilson, P. R. 1985, *Murder of the Innocents: Child-killers and Their Victims*, Melbourne: Rigby Publishers.

Wissow, L. S. 1998, 'Infanticide', *New England Journal of Medicine* 339: 1239–41.

Wolfgang, M. 1958, *Patterns of Criminal Homicide*, Philadelphia: University of Pennsylvania Press.

Wolfgang, M., and Ferracuti, F. 1967, *The Subculture of Violence: Towards an Integrated Theory in Criminology*, London: Tavistock Publications.

Worrall, A. 1990, *Offending Women: Female Lawbreakers and the Criminal Justice System*, Andover: Routledge.

Young, A. 1996, *Imaging Crime*, London: Sage.

# Index